IMAGES
of America

THE GEORGIA STATE CAPITOL BUILDING

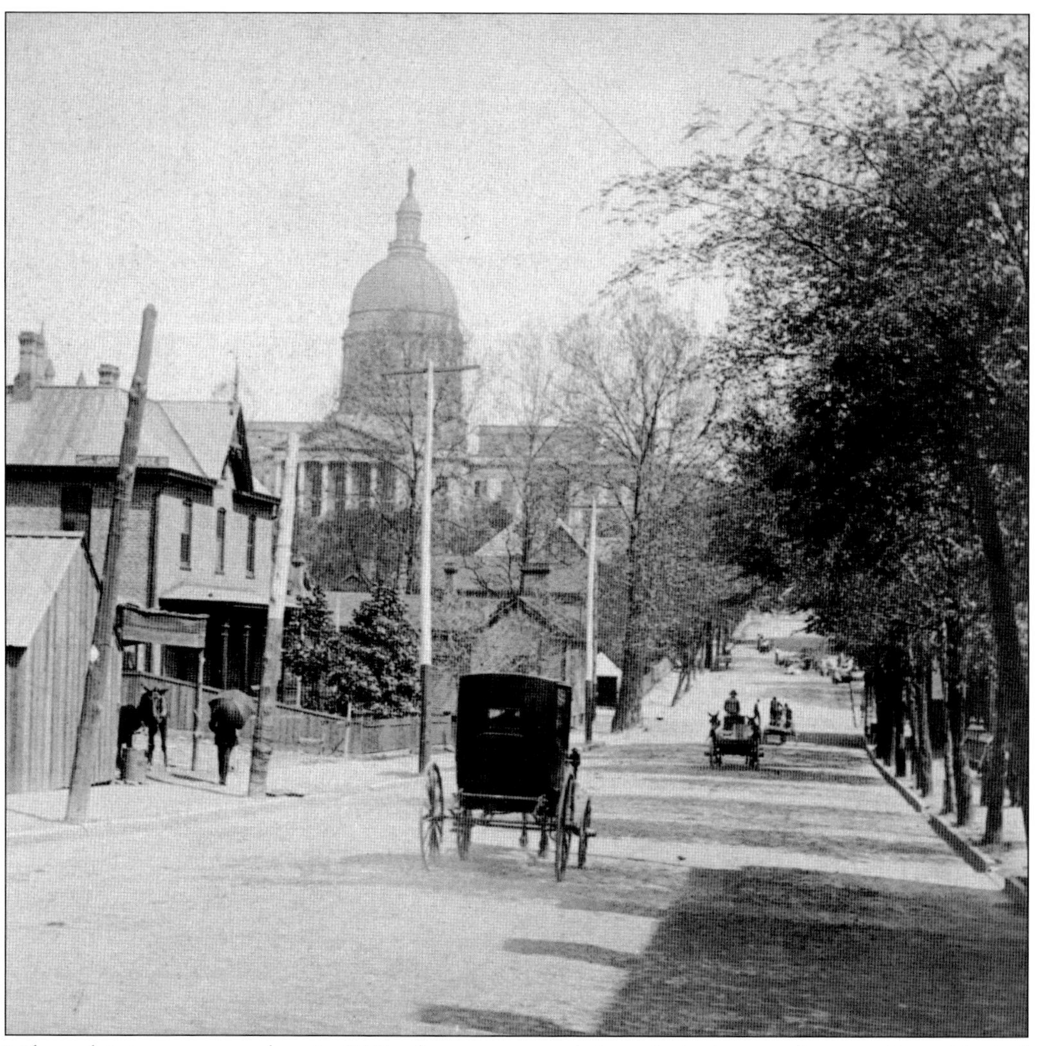

When this image was taken in 1891, the area around the relatively new Georgia State Capitol building was still largely residential with numerous churches. Looking east along Mitchell Street toward what is considered the main entrance of the capitol, a boardinghouse called Capital House can be seen on the left. Records show it was operated by a Mrs. T.W. Tucker. (Library of Congress.)

On the Cover: This 1916 image of the Georgia State Capitol was taken from the roof of a building at the corner of Alabama and Pryor Streets looking east. Mansions still lined Hunter Street (now Martin Luther King Jr. Drive). Directly across the street from the capitol is the Central Presbyterian Church on Washington Street, and the Catholic Shrine of the Immaculate Conception is in the foreground on Hunter Street. (Georgia State Archives.)

IMAGES
of America

THE GEORGIA STATE CAPITOL BUILDING

Janice McDonald

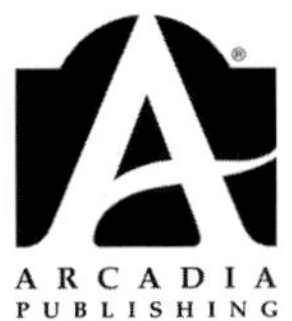

ARCADIA
PUBLISHING

ISBN 978-1-4671-0951-2

Published by Arcadia Publishing
Charleston, South Carolina

Printed in the United States of America

Library of Congress Control Number: 2022949425

For all general information, please contact Arcadia Publishing:
Telephone 843-853-2070
Fax 843-853-0044
E-mail sales@arcadiapublishing.com
For customer service and orders:
Toll-Free 1-888-313-2665

Visit us on the Internet at www.arcadiapublishing.com

This book is dedicated to Willoughby J. Edbrooke and Franklin Burnham, whose architectural vision influenced not just Georgia but buildings and cities across the United States.

Contents

ACKNOWLEDGMENTS

This book has been a treasure hunt for images and information about the Georgia State Capitol. That gold domed building and its history strikes a chord with many, and everyone I approached did not hesitate to enthusiastically get behind the project. Strangers took my random cold calls to answer questions or offer suggestions, and I cannot thank them enough.

My dear friend Barbara Lynn Howell introduced me to Paul Melvin, who was first on board, welcoming me into the governor's mansion and offering resources. There were untold hours in the Atlanta History Center, where Serena McCracken patiently guided me, with Jena Jones coming to the rescue in accessing the center's many photographs. Last minute panics were quelled with information and photographs from Karen Gravel and Susan Turner of Lord Aeck Sargent, Robert Marshall of R. Alden Marshall & Associates, and Frank Welsh.

Capitol expert Dr. Tim Crimmins offered great advice, as did Karin Johnson Dalton of the Georgia Capitol Museum. Even Gov. Henry McDaniel descendent Jonathan Glaefke got involved, and once again, Judith Anderson Vanderver delved into the family archives of her great-great-grandfather Gov. Joseph E. Brown.

Among those who took time to counsel me and provide images and/or research materials were Monroe historian Steve Brown, Atlanta Masonic Hall Masonic Library curator Danny Wofford, Donnie Richardson of the Georgia Department of Transportation, Michelle Asci of Georgia State University's Digital Archives, Allison Hudgins of the Georgia State Archives, Dan Murphy of the Cathedral of St. Philip, Marc Jamieson of Heather & Little, Tim Little of the Kenilworth Historical Society, photographer Kelly Holtz, John Stallard of the Carriage Museum of America, Sherrie Crow, and Alan Perry of the Georgia Building Authority.

Finally, I would like to thank my editor at Arcadia Publishing Caroline (Anderson) Vickerson, who reached out to me about writing this book. She had incredible patience in answering questions about images and tolerating me when work threatened deadlines.

Because many of the images in this book have the same sources, I have used the following abbreviations: Atlanta History Center (AHC), Georgia State Archives (GSA), Georgia State University (GSU), Library of Congress (LOC), and the New York Public Library (NYPL).

Introduction

The history of the Georgia State Capitol long predates the building itself and speaks to the birth of the state of Georgia as well as the city of Atlanta. Atlanta was never supposed to be a city. It was just a crossroads for railroads in the early to mid-1800s as the United States began its western expansion. And yet now it is considered the Capital of the New South.

There was nothing but wilderness in the region that became Georgia when British soldier and parliamentarian general James Oglethorpe first created a colony here in 1732. The thriving port city of Savannah became the first seat of government. As the colony grew, the capital moved. First to Augusta, then briefly to Louisville, and ultimately to Milledgeville, where the capital remained for almost 65 years until the seat of Georgia's government transferred to Atlanta after the Civil War.

When Gen. William Tecumseh Sherman departed Atlanta, he burned or destroyed much of what had been built, and with Reconstruction, the real evolution of the city began.

The hustle, bustle, and boomtown growth prompted a call for Atlanta to be named the capital, and city officials lobbied hard to make it happen. They promised buildings and concessions, and Atlanta won approval.

But it was not a done deal. At first, the state leased buildings for its needs, including Atlanta's city hall and then the grand, recently completed Kimball Opera House. When the opera house burned after five years, some called for the capital to be moved back to Milledgeville.

It was readily apparent that Georgia needed a building dedicated to and worthy of the state's business. To sweeten the deal to keep the capital in Atlanta, the city offered the five-acre spot where city hall was located. Surrounded by churches, mansions, and grand hotels, it sat on a hill in the heart of the growing city and promised to be the perfect location.

In 1883, the new governor, Henry D. McDaniel, began leading the call for building a new capitol that would be "worthy of the dignity of the state" and that could adequately "protect public records, documents and archives of priceless value." Not all were on board, and it was hotly contested in newspaper editorials across the state. The *Sparta Ishmaelite* argued, "Now is not the time for the erection of such a building. The present capitol will do." In Atlanta, however, the *Atlanta Constitution* countered, saying not only was now the time, "there would certainly never be a better time."

Within four months of becoming governor, McDaniel signed the Capitol Act, which had been carefully written with so many limitations and restrictions that even the opponents of the measure ultimately admitted that it would be virtually impossible for the building to result in anything like extravagance or waste of public money. The state legislature authorized a budget of $1 million for construction, and the Capitol Commission, led by the governor, began soliciting architects for plans as well as samples of materials to be used.

The task of designing it went to a Chicago architectural firm called Edbrooke and Burnham, which had already made a name for itself. Principals Willoughby J. Edbrooke and Franklin Burnham gained recognition by designing buildings for the University of Notre Dame in Indiana and the World's Columbian Exposition in Chicago. Individually, the two designed hundreds of buildings across the United States that hold landmark status today.

It took six months for the firm to design a Neoclassic Renaissance Revival–style building that met all the specifications desired by the Capitol Commission. But when bids were offered for the construction, the only two companies to provide estimates came in well over the $1 million cap put forth by the legislature. A second round was needed, and the Toledo, Ohio, construction firm of Miles and Horn, led by William Burtis Miles and Charles Horn, won the contract by coming in at $862,756.75.

From there, the matter again became complicated as a debate raged over what materials should be used in constructing the building. Georgia marble and granite companies argued that only state stones should be considered. The cost to do so would have raised the price of materials by more than $175,000. The *Athens Banner* editorialized that "all the talk about state pride was the merest sham to raid upon the state purse."

Ultimately, oolitic limestone was chosen for much of the structure, although the foundation was laid with granite, and marble was used for all interior floors and steps, some walls, and the cornerstone. In addition, the structure contains about half a million bricks that were repurposed from the old Atlanta City Hall that was torn down to make room for the new capitol.

The project broke ground on November 13, 1884. It was estimated that between 6,000 and 10,000 people crowded the construction site on September 2, 1885, to watch the setting of the marble cornerstone. More than 250 workmen took almost four and a half years to complete the building, which was finished on March 20, 1889. Atop the tin-covered terra-cotta dome was a 26-foot-tall copper statue named the *Goddess of Liberty* (now called "Miss Freedom") helping to make the building an impressive 272 feet tall, the tallest in Atlanta at the time.

On July 4, 1889, the new Georgia State Capitol building was officially dedicated. In addition to housing all branches of the state government and its various offices, it also had a library and state laboratories and was still only half occupied. By 1910, it was overcrowded. Capitol Square today includes several buildings housing legislative offices, courts, and a variety of government entities that more than a century and a half ago could be housed under one roof.

Major renovations have taken place to the building, which now holds national historic landmark status. The first major undertaking was in 1929 when it was modernized with more elevators and new wiring. The most obvious change occurred in 1959 when the entire dome was rebuilt at a cost of over $1 million. Some private funding was used to help gild it with gold from Dahlonega so that it now stands out easily on the horizon among the towering buildings of the Atlanta skyline.

One

The Capitals

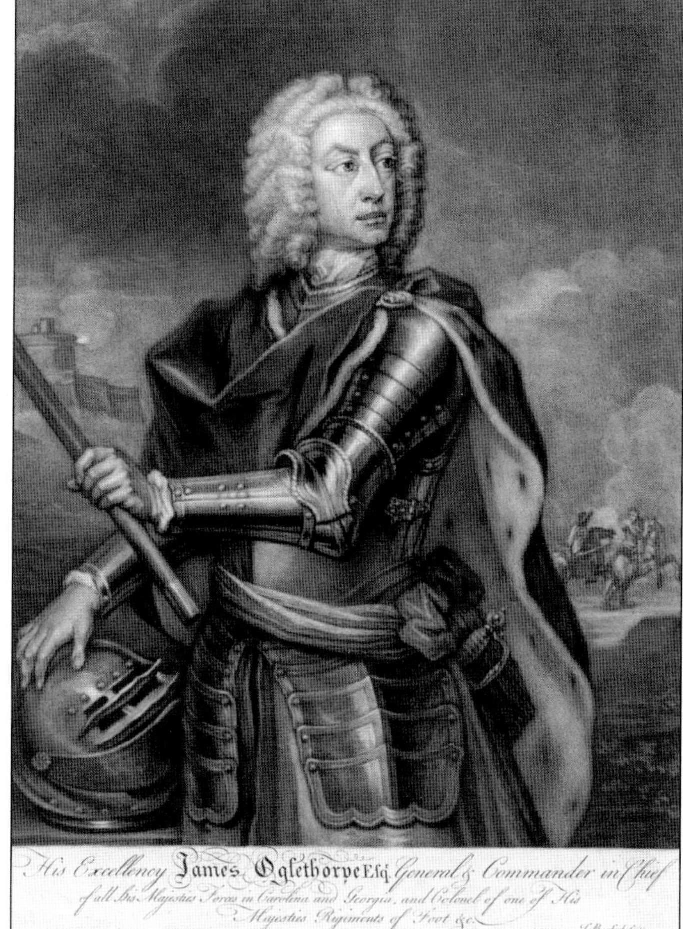

Philanthropist and general James Oglethorpe first landed in what is now Savannah, Georgia, on February 1, 1733, with 130 debtors and unemployed workers to establish what he called a charity colony. A proponent of prison reform, Oglethorpe had petitioned King George II for land in the New World and was granted land between the Savannah and Altamaha Rivers. (National Portrait Gallery.)

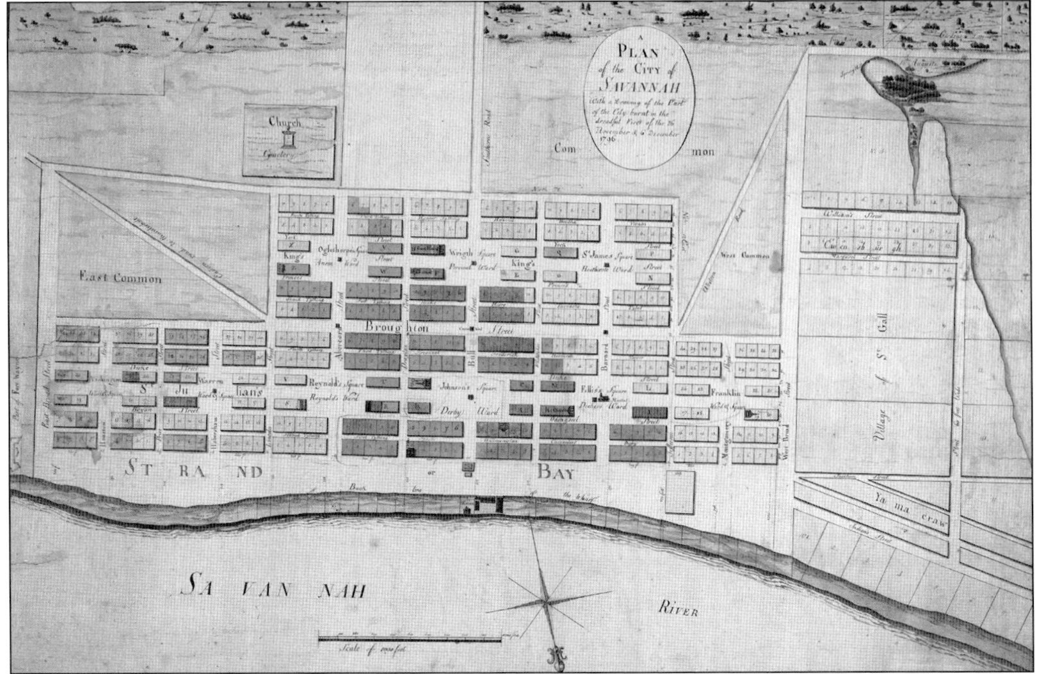

Savannah grew and was the largest city in Georgia when the colony officially became a state in 1776 amid the American Revolution. Given its position as a seat of commerce, the state constitution of 1777 directed the state legislature meet in Savannah, making it the unofficial first capital. (LOC.)

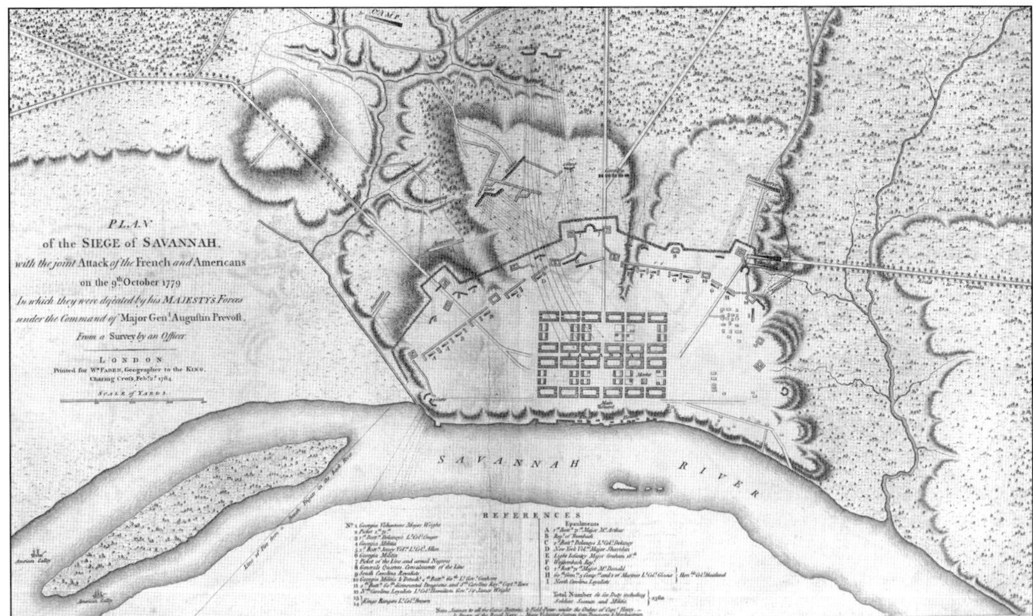

Savannah fell to forces led by British lieutenant colonel Archibald Campbell on December 29, 1778. Georgia's government escaped to Augusta to reorganize. In January 1780, the assembly began meeting in Heard's Fort, northeast of Augusta. Eventually, the capital rotated between the two cities. In 1785, the legislature resolved that "all future meetings of the Legislature shall be and continue at that place (Augusta) until otherwise ordered by the General Assembly." (LOC.)

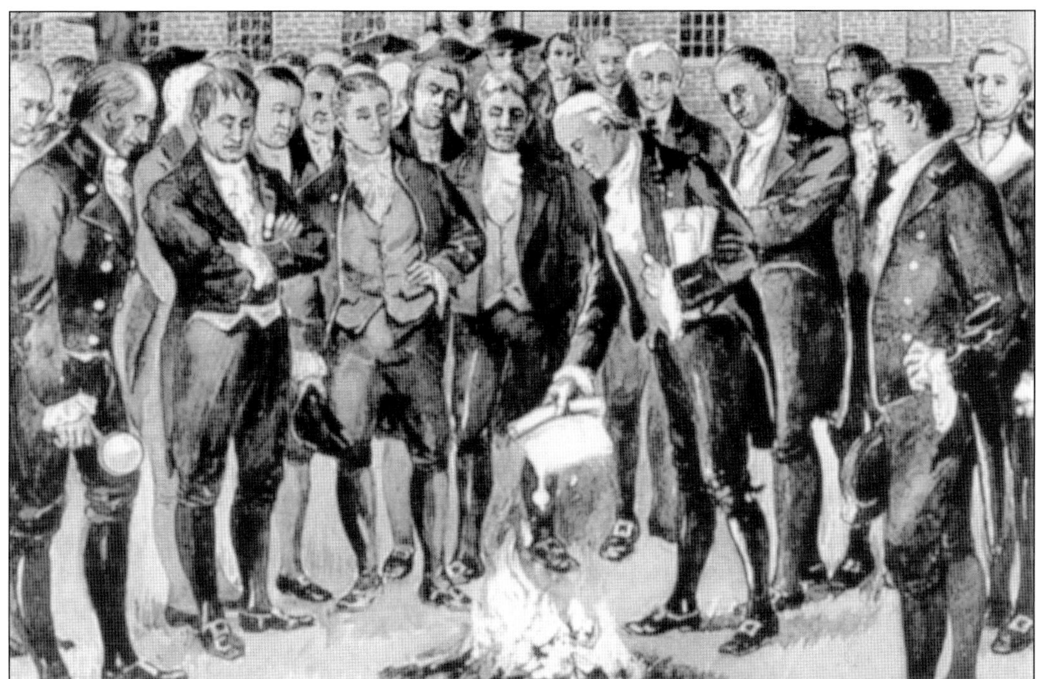

Within a year, the capital moved again to an old Indian trading post on the Ogeechee River in what is now Jefferson County. The site would be renamed Louisville. A redbrick Georgian structure was completed in March 1796. The only known depiction of the building is in this image showing the burning of the Yazoo Act in 1796 on capitol grounds. The act was a massive land fraud scandal during the 1780s involving legislators. (Georgia Historical Society.)

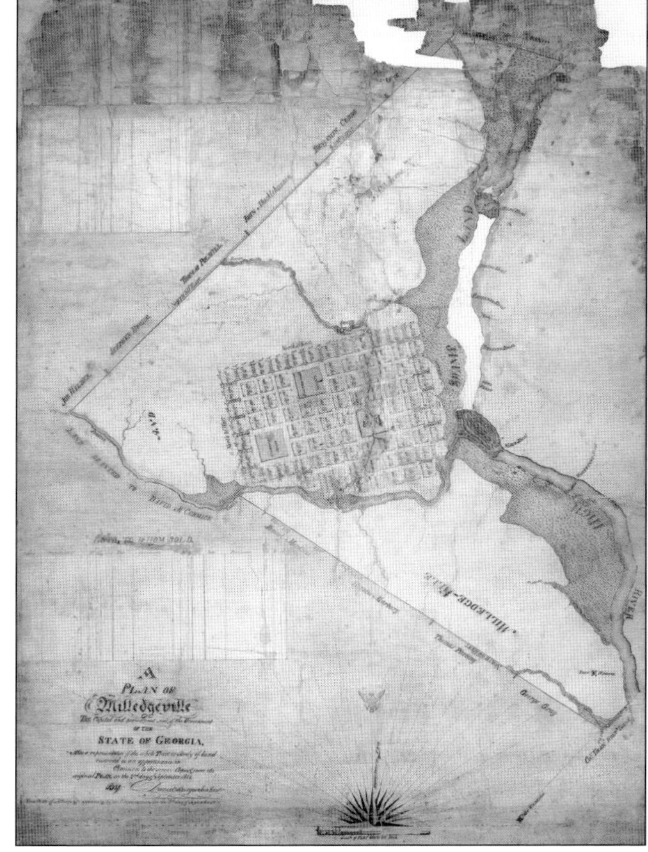

Concern over malaria in Louisville and a push for Georgia development to expand westward as Indian lands were claimed again prompted the call for a new capitol. Milledgeville was established on the Oconee River, honoring then governor John Milledge. This Baldwin County city served as the state capitol from 1806 until the end of the Civil War in 1865. (GSA.)

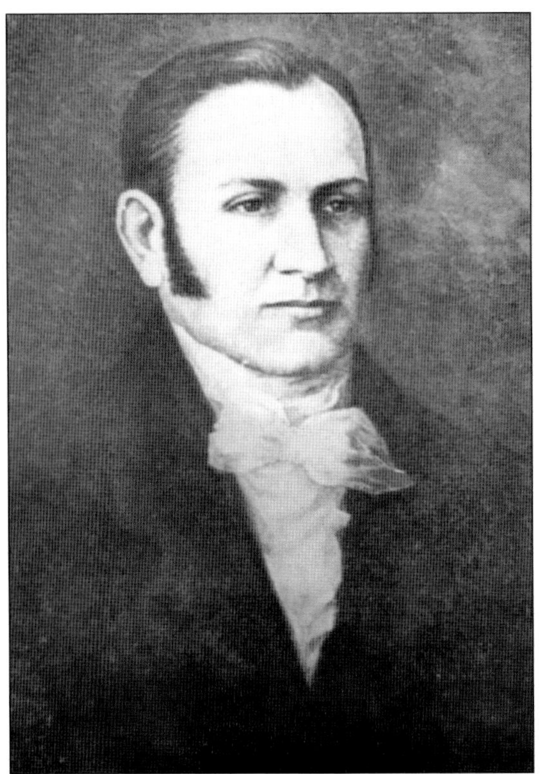

Not everyone approved of Governor Milledge giving his name to the new capital city. In a 16-page argument before the legislature in 1804, an unnamed opponent passionately argued that Milledge was not worthy of the honor, citing some of the governor's shortcomings. "Call it anything but Milledgeville, that the faces of its inhabitants may not flush with the glow of shame, and their brows curl with indignation in naming the place of their residence." (GSU.)

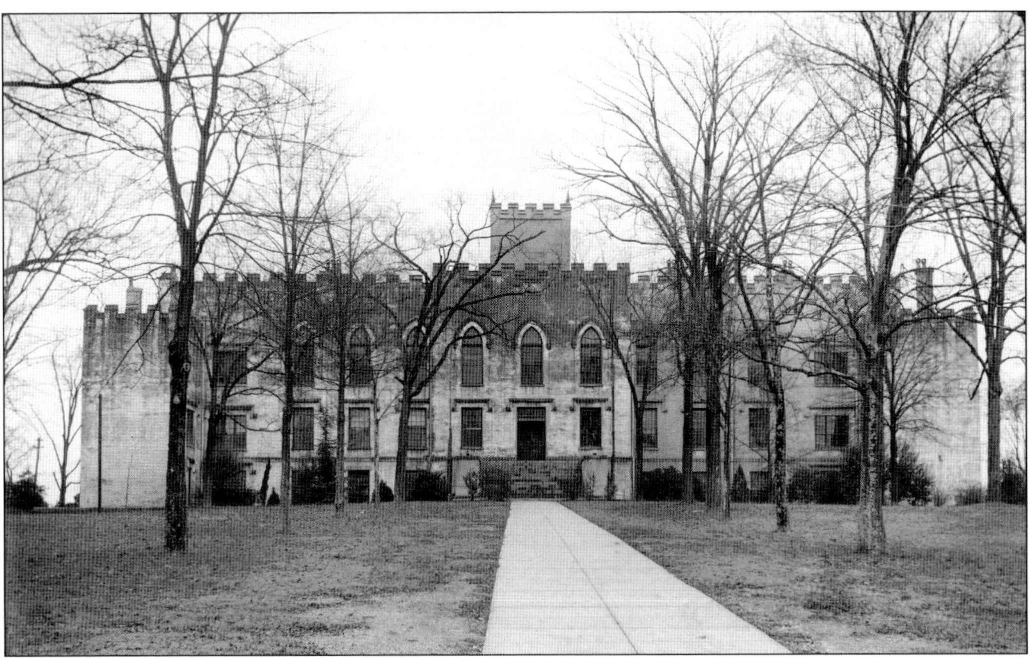

Roughly 3,240 acres were appropriated for the city of Milledgeville, with 20 acres to be used for Government Square. Proceeds from the sale of lots in the new city were used to help pay for the new statehouse. Resembling a fortress, the structure took two years to build and had walls four feet thick. (LOC.)

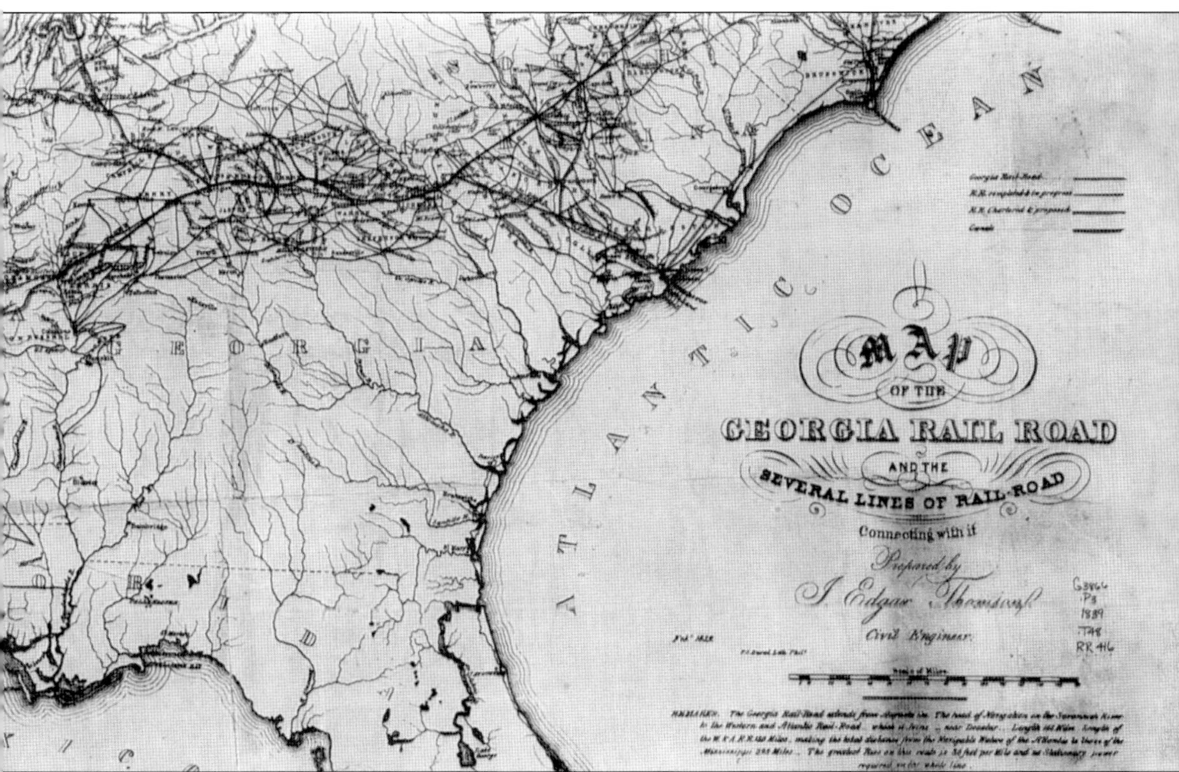

As the fever for western expansion caught hold in the United States, Georgia was not to be left behind. Between 1827 and 1831, Georgia stripped the Cherokee Indians of their rights and forcefully removed them from their lands to clear the way for settlers and railroads to move into their territory. This 1839 Georgia Railroad map shows the growing number of railroad lines throughout the southeastern United States, including the Western & Atlantic Railroad efforts to connect the Chattahoochee and Tennessee Rivers. When several lines came together in North Georgia not far from the town of Decatur to the northwest of Milledgeville, businesses began popping up to support the rail traffic, and the new community was given the name Terminus. (LOC.)

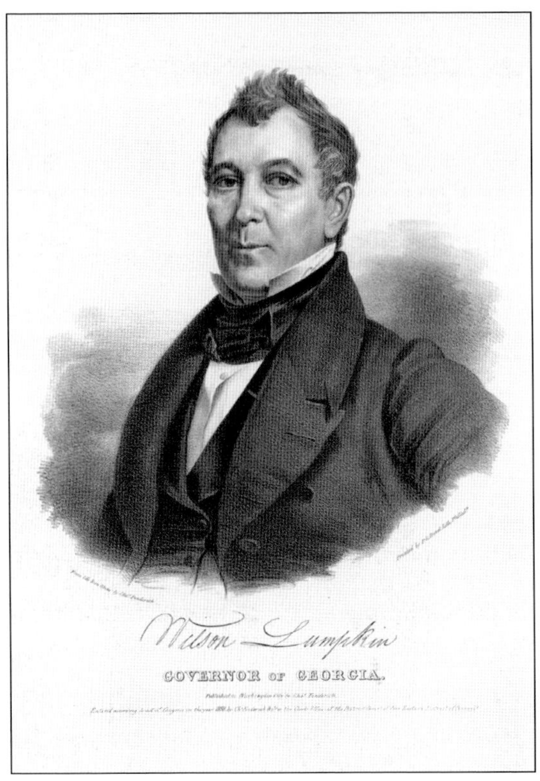

Terminus became a boomtown with the growth of the railroads in North Georgia. When the city was incorporated on December 23, 1843, former governor Wilson Lumpkin (left) was chairman of the Western & Atlantic Railroad. He suggested the new city be named Marthasville after his youngest daughter Martha (below), who was just 16. When the Georgia Railroad moved to the new town, chief engineer J. Edgar Thompson suggested changing the name to honor the Western & Atlantic line, coining the name Atlanta. The town was renamed in 1845 and incorporated in 1847. Interestingly, Martha Lumpkin's middle name was Atalanta, after the Greek goddess of running. (Left, LOC; below, AHC.)

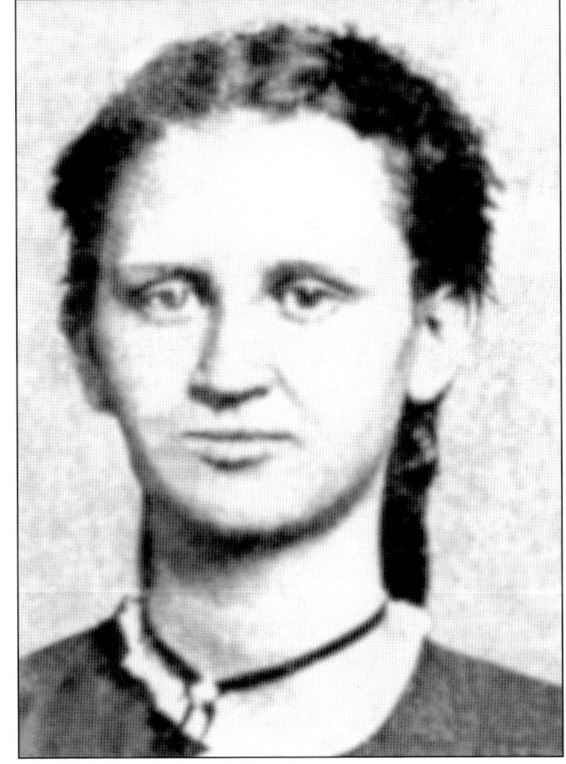

A push began in 1853 to move Georgia's capital yet again, this time to Atlanta. Ira O. McDaniel and five others were appointed by Atlanta's first mayor, Moses Formwalt, as a commission to go before the legislature at Milledgeville and exert their influence. Their efforts failed, but their determination continued. (Monroe History Museum.)

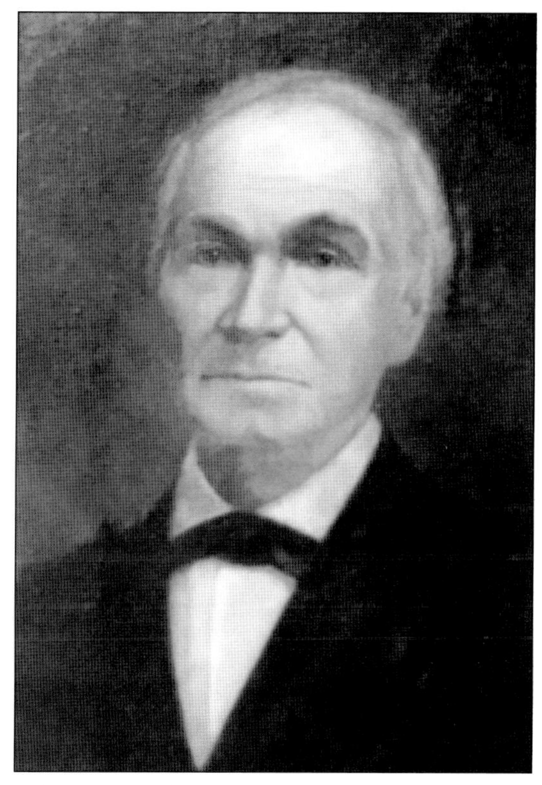

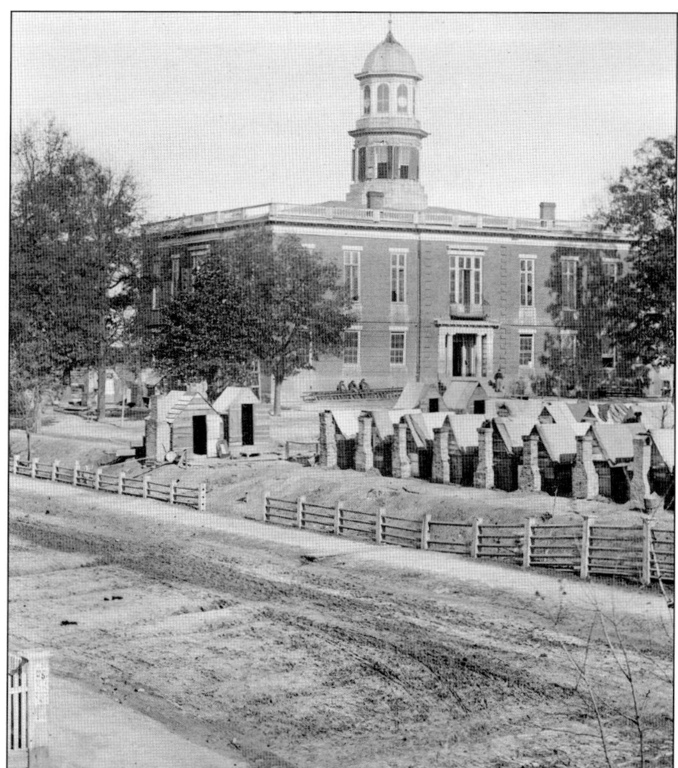

The Civil War made discussions of moving the capital a low priority as much of Georgia experienced front-line involvement. While Union troops occupied Atlanta, the area around city hall was used as an encampment. These structures were used by the 2nd Massachusetts Infantry just prior to Sherman's fiery departure. (LOC.)

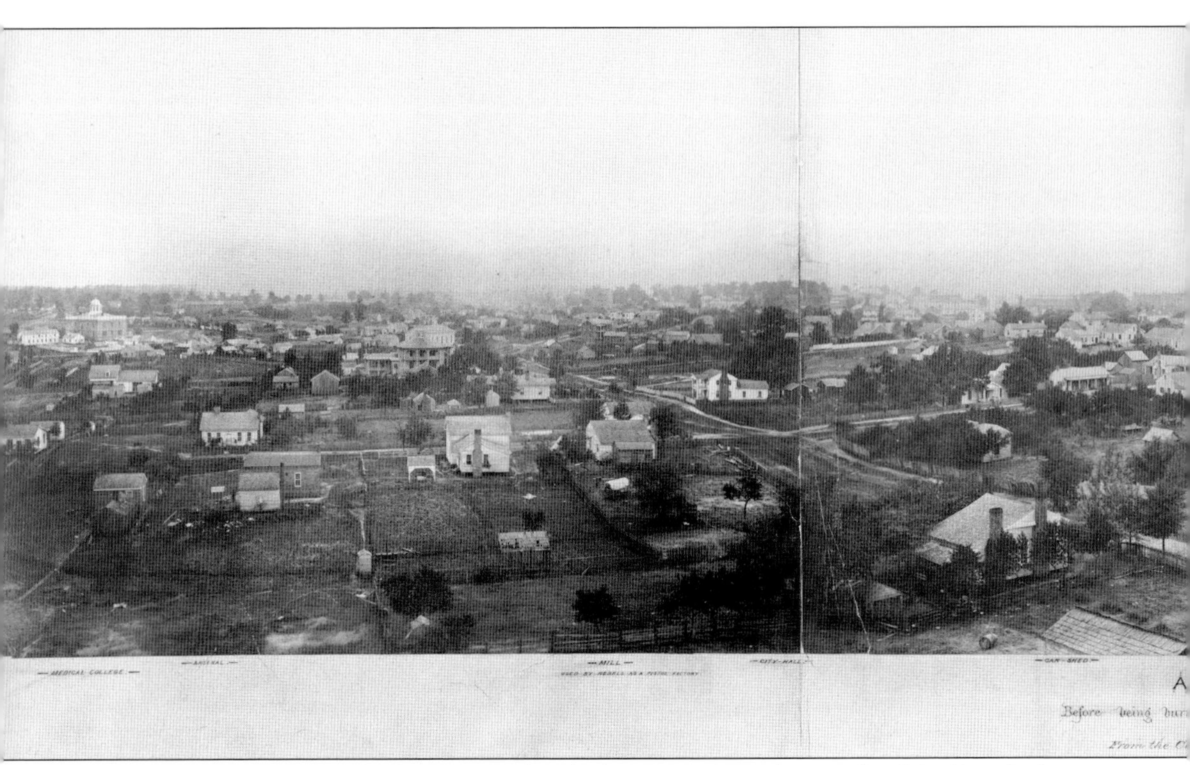

This panoramic view of Atlanta was taken looking west from the cupola of the Female Seminary in October 1864, a month before General Sherman's troops were ordered to burn the city. The distinctive building with the cupola at far left, near the horizon, is the Medical College, at the time the southeastern edge of downtown. The tall brick building to its right is a mill that was used

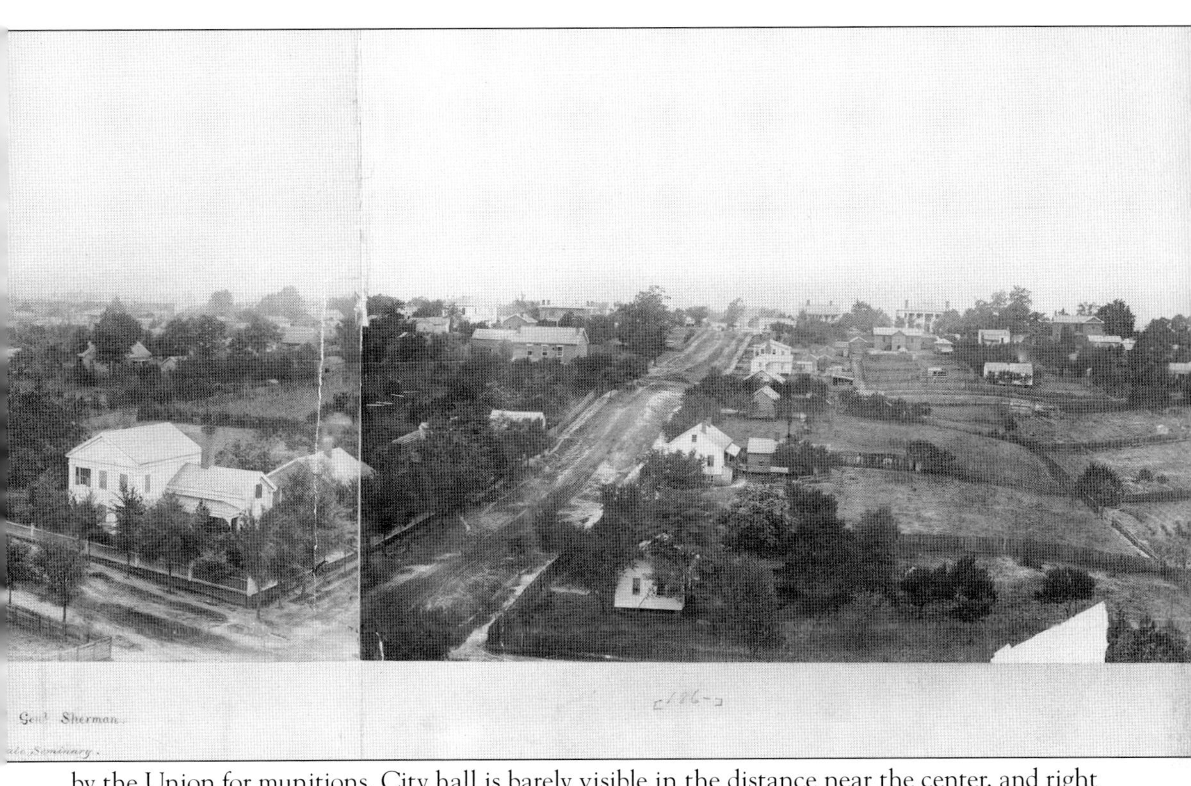

by the Union for munitions. City hall is barely visible in the distance near the center, and right of center is a railcar shed where Sherman's troops accumulated supplies before their evacuation of Atlanta. The image continues west along Peachtree Street. (LOC.)

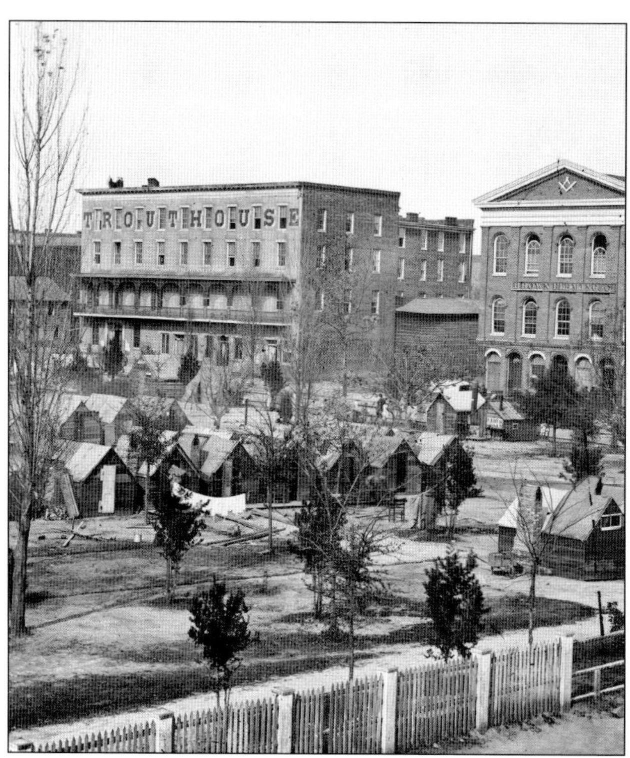

Another encampment stretches in front of the Trout House Hotel and the Masonic lodge on Decatur Street, just a few blocks from Atlanta City Hall. On November 15, Union engineers began burning designated sites. Among those targeted and destroyed was the Trout. The Masonic lodge and all downtown churches were spared. (LOC.)

As Atlanta began to rebuild, city officials again lobbied the constitutional convention to transfer Georgia's capital. They promised to furnish a suitable location for a permanent capitol building and guaranteed a temporary building for the legislature for a period of 10 years without cost to the state. They offered the site where city hall stood as the potential location. (LOC.)

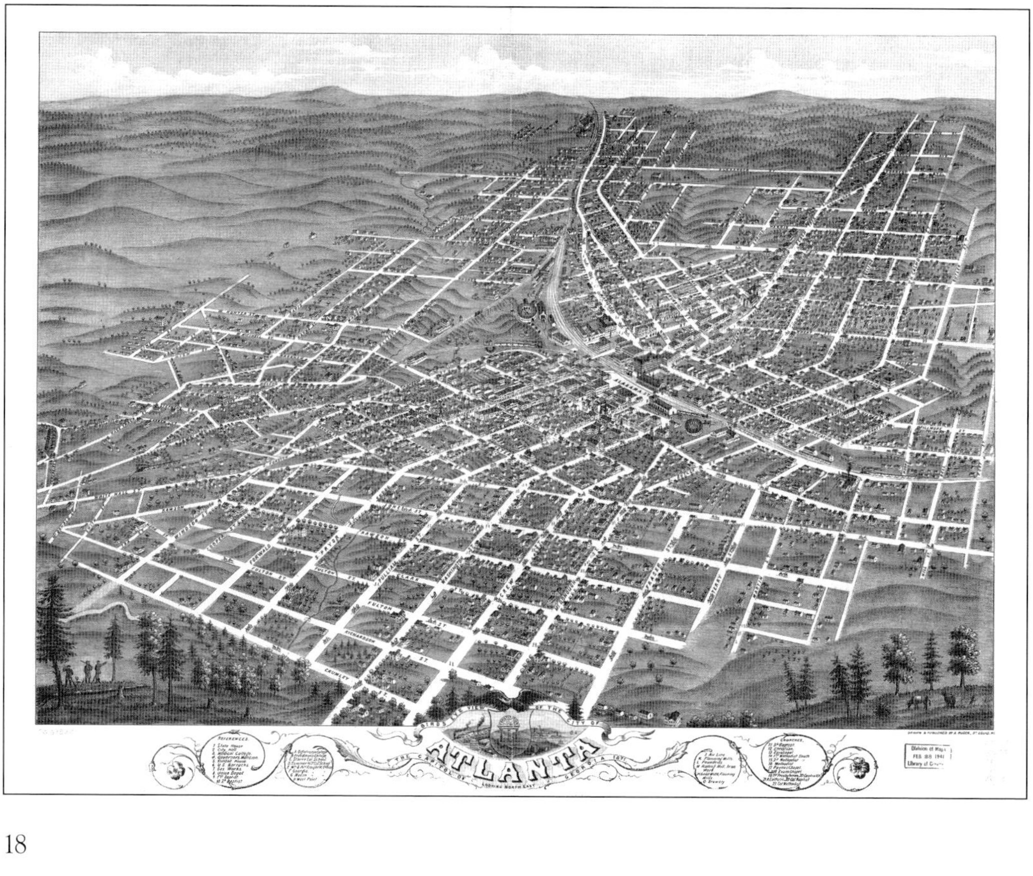

Atlanta City Hall was a well-known landmark in the city. It had been completed in 1854 and stood on a five-acre square in the heart of Atlanta, not far from the railroad lines that had precipitated the city's birth. The two-story redbrick edifice faced Hunter Street (now Martin Luther King Jr. Boulevard) and measured 50 by 70 feet. On its roof was a distinctive two-staged wooden tower capped by a cupola and bronze eagle. (GSA.)

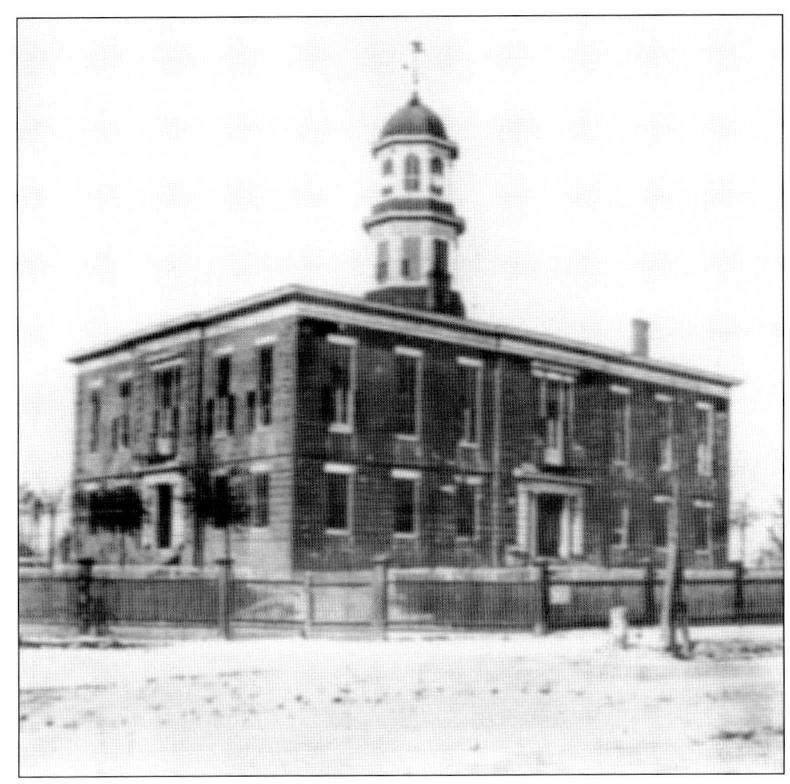

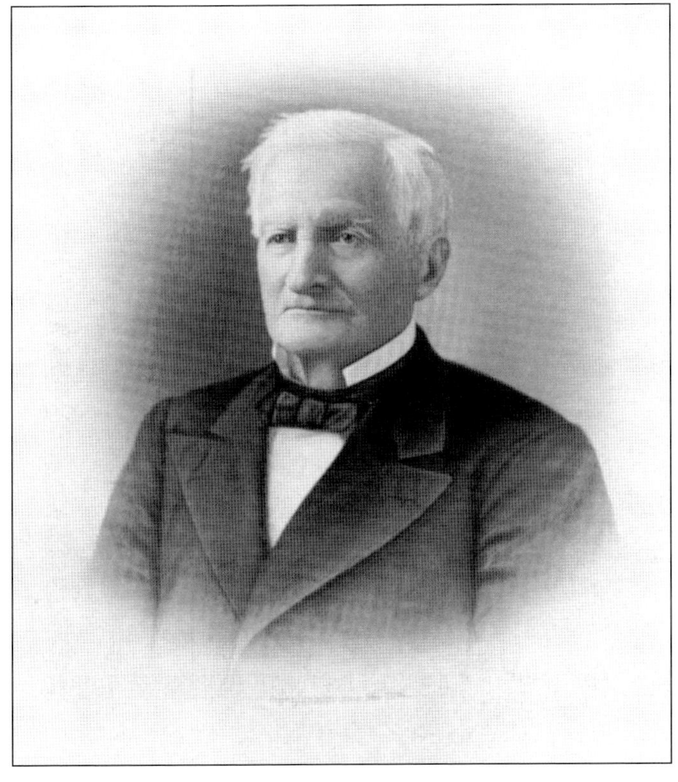

City hall sat on land that had been previously owned by Richard Peters. A railroad man from Pennsylvania, Peters was instrumental in Atlanta's founding and at one time owned 405 acres of land that is now Atlanta's Midtown. He was chairman of the city's Committee on Capitol Removal and is credited with drafting the proposal put before the delegates of the constitutional convention to entice them to vote to make Atlanta the new capital. (AHC.)

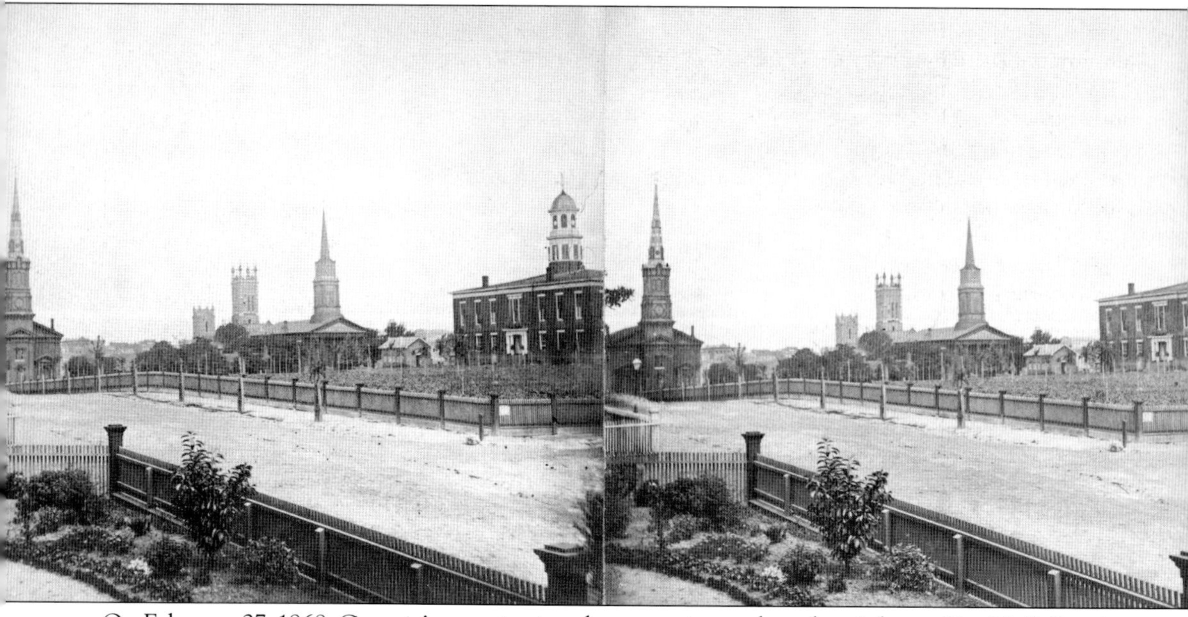

On February 27, 1868, Georgia's constitutional convention gathered at Atlanta City Hall. For the first time, it included black delegates, most of whom were freed slaves. Atlanta's railroads and its geographical location were strong selling points for making it the capital. City hall was offered as a five-year option to house the state government if the move was made. Peters took it a step further, promising the state meeting space for 10 years at no cost as well as a choice of locations to erect a new dedicated statehouse. The convention accepted and voted to relocate Georgia's capital to Atlanta, adding an article directing the Georgia General Assembly to provide funds for construction of a new capitol building. (AHC.)

At the time Atlanta was designated the capital of Georgia, the population was just shy of 22,000, but those numbers had more than doubled over the previous decade as more people moved to the region. The early structures of Central Presbyterian Church and Second Baptist Church are on the right in this view looking south on Washington Street. The churches bordered the western side of what is now Capitol Square. (NYPL.)

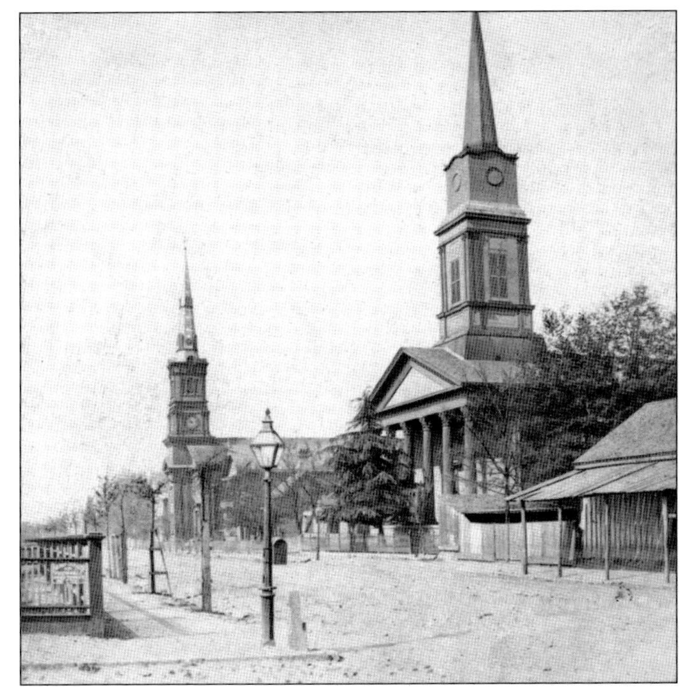

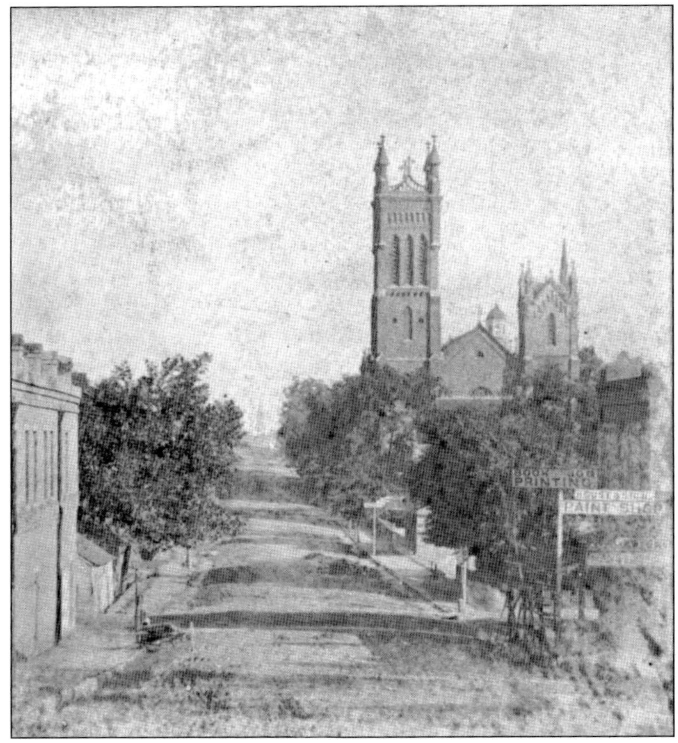

The top of Atlanta City Hall is visible to the right of the bell tower of the Catholic Shrine of the Immaculate Conception in this view looking east on Hunter Street (now Martin Luther King Jr. Boulevard). Bergstrom's Printing House was at 21 East Hunter Street and occupied part of the site where the Fulton County government building is now. (NYPL.)

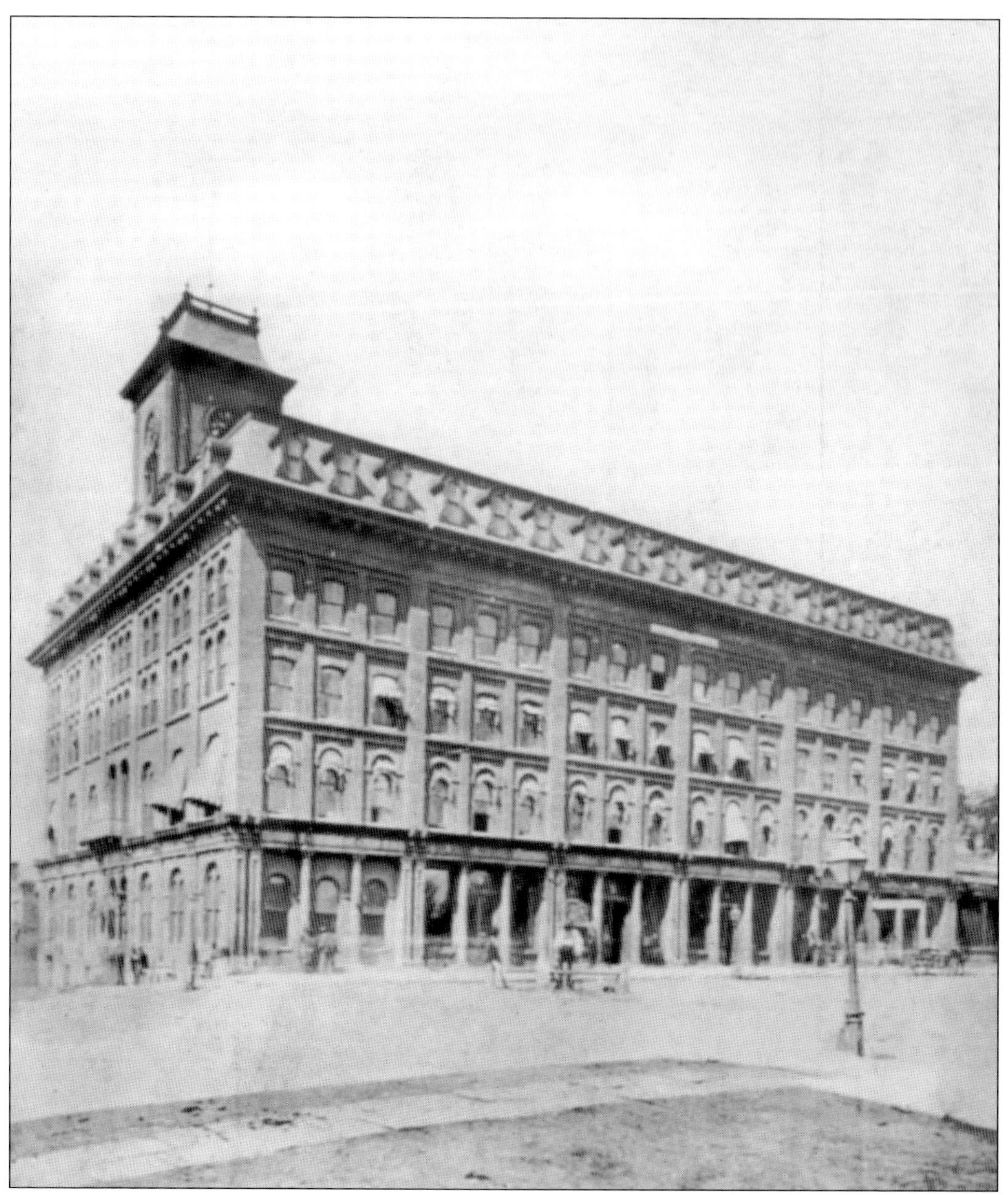

It was proposed that the unfinished opera house at the corner of Marietta and Forsyth Streets could serve as the interim capitol. The Atlanta Opera House and Building Association had begun constructing the structure in April 1867, hoping to establish a space for performances and civic gatherings. The project proved to be too expensive for the fledgling opera organization, and its funds ran out in less than a year. The five-story brick shell sat empty and roofless until it was purchased in June 1868 for $31,750 by Edwin N. Kimball. At that point, even unfinished, it was the largest building in Atlanta. (NYPL.)

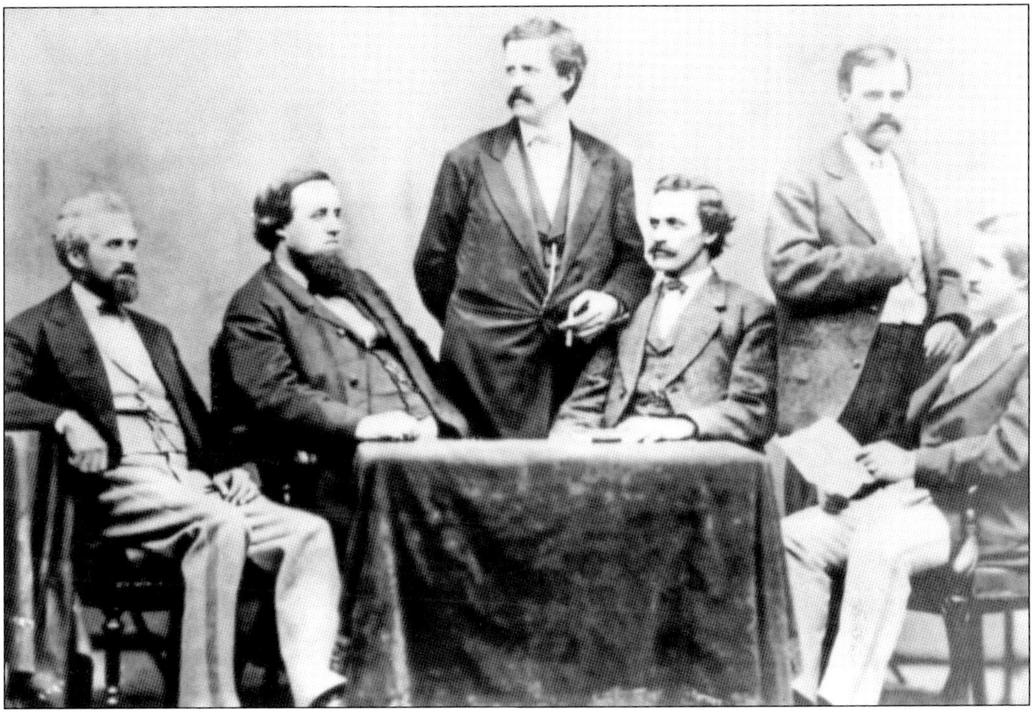

Edwin Kimball was the youngest in a family of 10 children, including six brothers, raised in Bethel, Maine. Their father, Peter Kimball, was a well-known carriage maker who was a sixth-generation wheelwright. The four oldest sons carried on their family tradition while Edwin and his brother Hannibal both moved to Atlanta to become wealthy entrepreneurs. In this photograph are, from left to right, James, Charles, Hannibal, George, John, and Edwin Kimball. (Carriage Museum of America.)

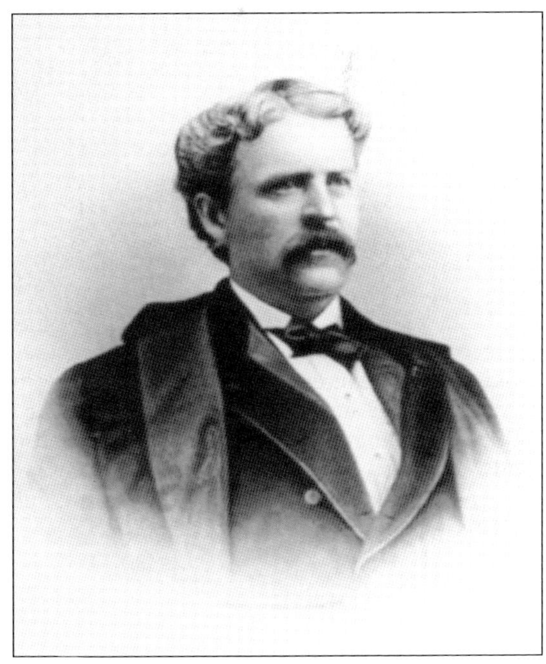

Edwin Kimball appointed his brother Hannibal as the opera house's manager. Hannibal I. Kimball was new to Atlanta and was becoming involved in numerous ventures, including railroad construction projects throughout Georgia. Hannibal orchestrated a deal with Atlanta City Council to use the opera house as the capitol. On August 17, 1868, the council accepted the proposal. Hannibal later helped establish the Atlanta Canal & Water Company, which built Atlanta's first sewer system. (AHC.)

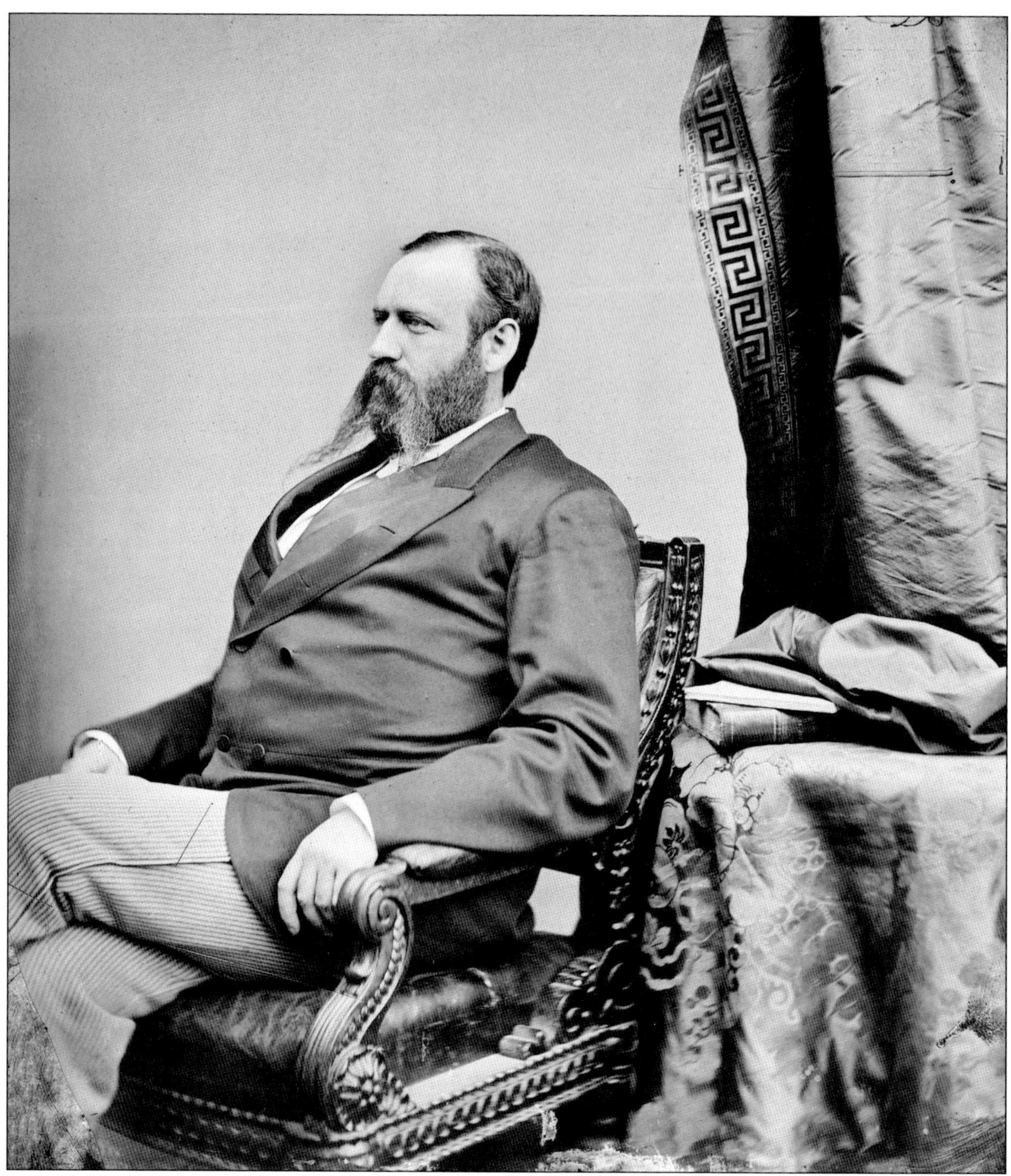

On August 24, 1868, the city officially leased the top four floors of the Kimball property for five years at $6,000 a year. Once plans were set in motion to move the state offices, Hannibal Kimball announced that the city needed to pay extra for heat, light, and furniture. The city refused. The newly elected governor, Rufus Bullock, intervened and advanced Kimball $54,500 in emergency state funds. The allocation was made without consulting the Georgia General Assembly or state treasurer Needom L. Angier. Angier accused Bullock of misuse of state funds, and the legislature refused to approve the advance. While Angier and Bullock were trading barbs, Georgia was being placed under military rule after the General Assembly expelled 28 black members and prevented blacks from voting in the 1868 presidential election. (LOC.)

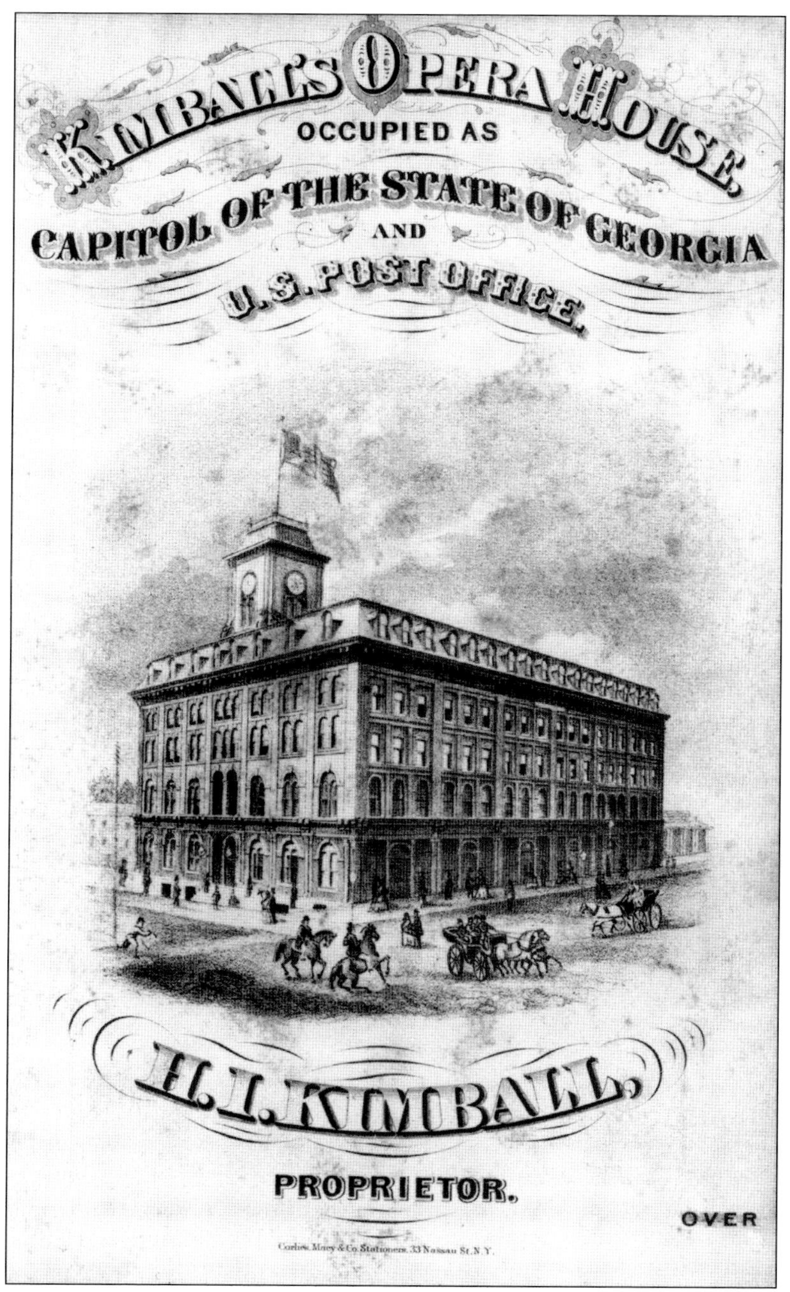

Amid the controversy over the capitol real estate deal, the grand opening of the Kimball Opera House took place on January 12, 1869. It was reported in the *Atlanta Constitution* that "the house is brilliantly lighted by a circular of gas jets some thirty feet from the floor, and at least fifteen feet in its diameter. All around these jets was placed a fluted glass mirror, that threw the bright rays of light completely over the room, rendering all side lights completely unnecessary. The fresco work on the ceiling, and indeed all over the room, was really magnificent, and elicited loud marks of approval from all who visited the building. The Senate Chamber is very beautiful, though not so imposing as the House of Representatives. Over the seat of the President of the Senate is a full-length portrait of George Washington." (AHC.)

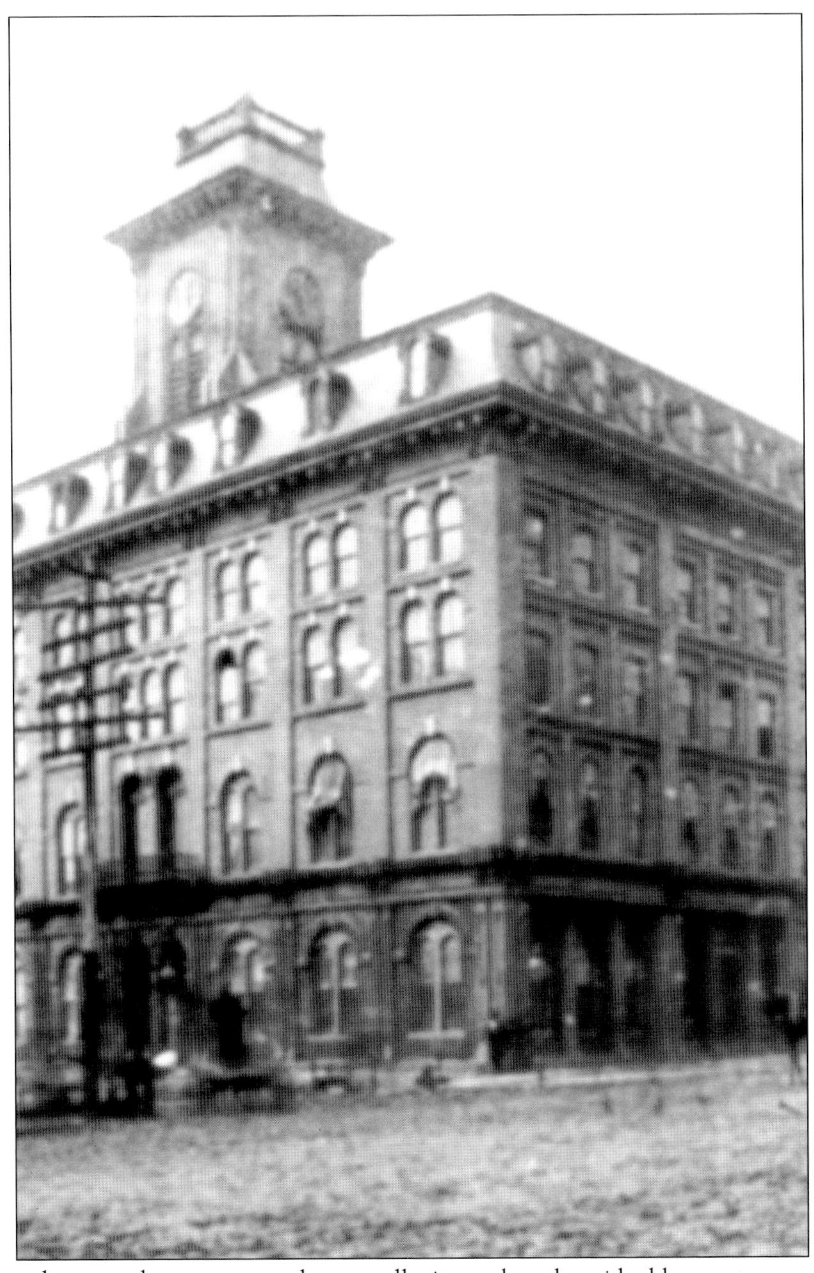

As grand as the opera house appeared outwardly, it was less than ideal by most accounts. There were numerous complaints about how poorly the building had been constructed. Walls bowed in areas, and the acoustics of the halls of the House of Representatives and Senate were said to be so bad that a network of wires had to be stretched over the heads of the legislators to deaden echoes so speeches could be heard. Records from the board of the Capitol Commission show that the House Committee appointed to confer with the City of Atlanta did not approve of the utilization of the opera house. It reports that the contract with the city "has not been carried out in good faith." Again, citing the building's construction, the report labeled it "insecure and unsafe from the contingencies of fire." The building ultimately burned down after it was sold by the state. (AHC.)

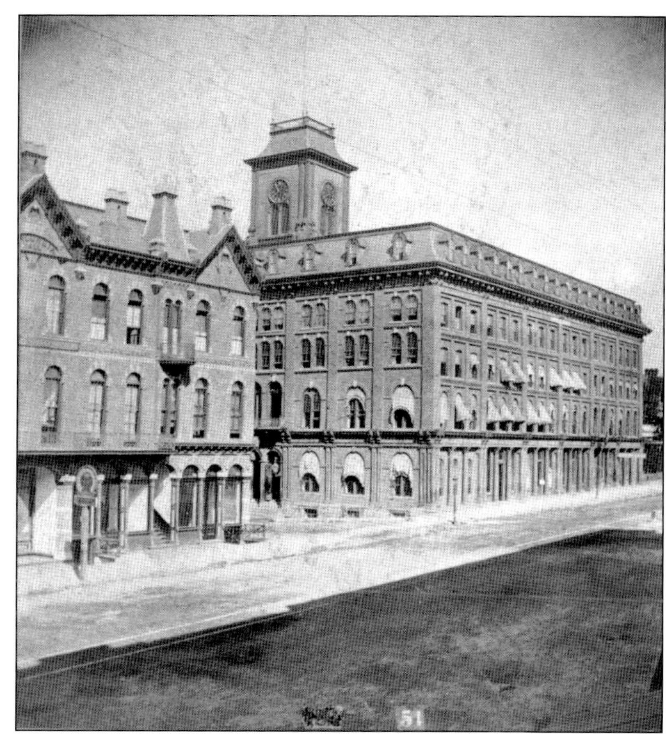

In 1870, yearly rental of the Kimball Opera House was estimated to be about $10,500, which was $4,500 more than original projections. A deal was negotiated to pay off the five-year lease. The General Assembly approved the building's purchase in October for $380,000. A joint legislative committee recommended that the costs be covered by $130,000 in Atlanta city bonds and $250,000 in bonds by the state. (AHC.)

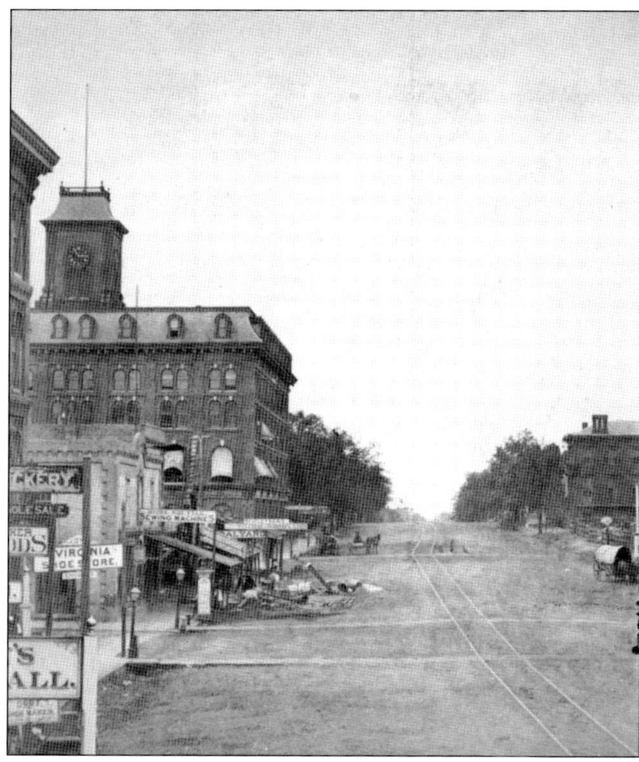

Despite its shortcomings, the opera house served as the state capitol for 20 years. In 1889, the state sold the building for $132,241.56. An additional $2,051 was raised through the sale of the furniture. This image was taken from the roof of the Kimball Opera House/statehouse looking southwest along Forsyth Street. (NYPL.)

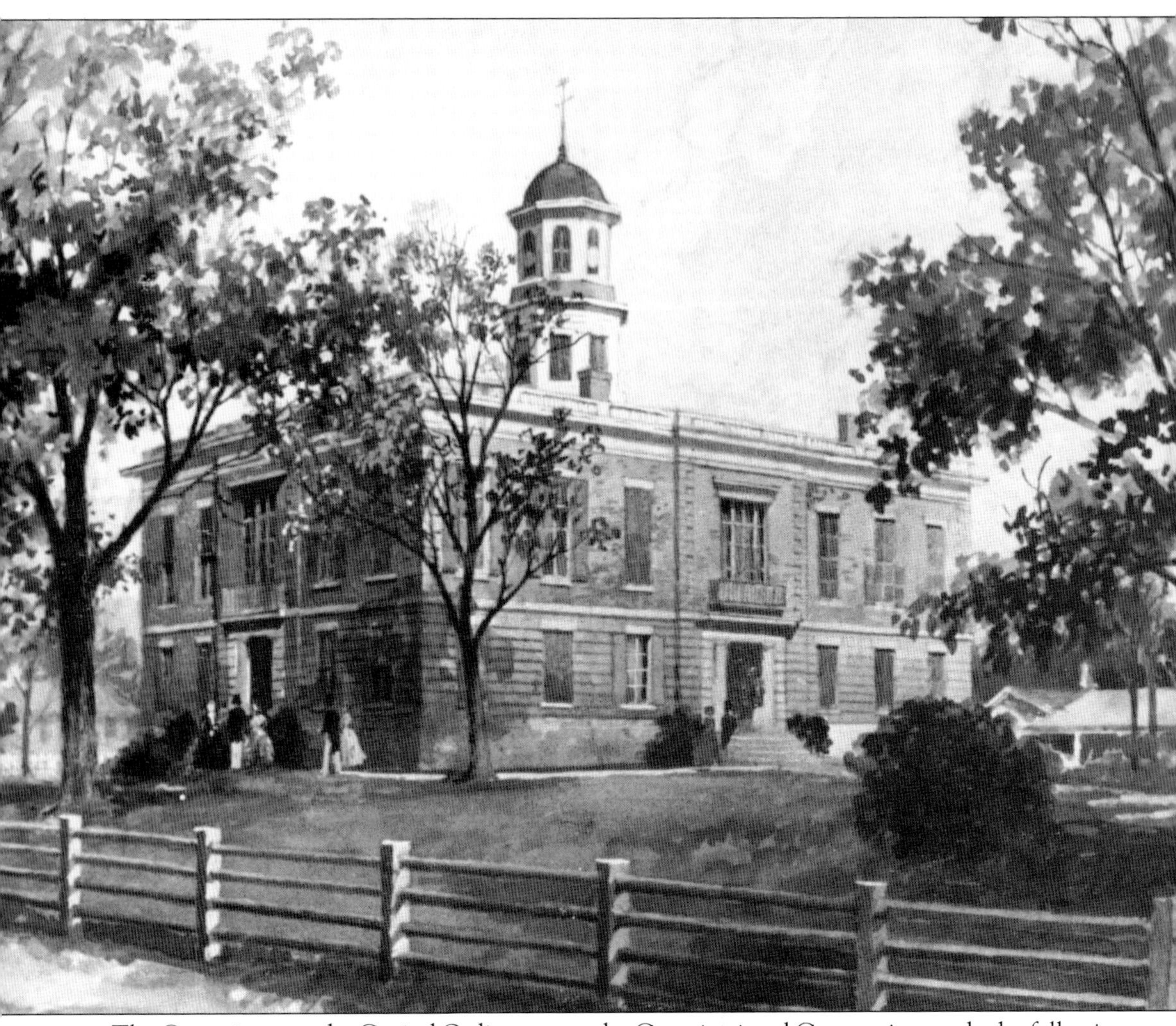

The Committee on the Capitol Ordinance on the Constitutional Convention made the following proclamation on July 19, 1877: "If Atlanta is selected by the Convention as the permanent Capital of the State, and if such selection is submitted to and the same is ratified by the people, the City of Atlanta will convey to the State of Georgia any ten acres of land in or near the City of Atlanta, now unoccupied, or the square in the heart of the City, known as the City Hall Lot, containing five acres of land, and bounded by a street on every side, on which to locate and build a Capitol for the State. Second: The City of Atlanta will build for the State of Georgia on the location selected a Capitol Building as good as the old Capitol building in Milledgeville." (AHC.)

Two

Building the New Capitol

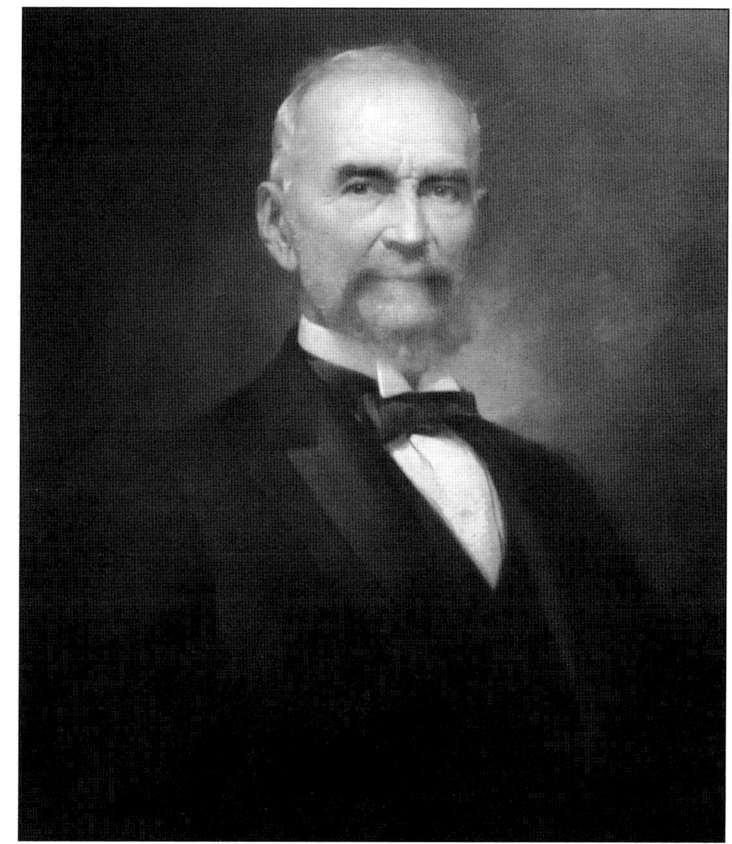

When Henry D. McDaniel became governor of Georgia in 1883, the legislature made a firm move to build a new capitol. Having witnessed his father, Ira's, dedication to the project 30 years earlier, McDaniel committed to building a structure "worthy of the dignity of the state," which could adequately "protect public records, documents and archives of priceless value." (Janice McDonald.)

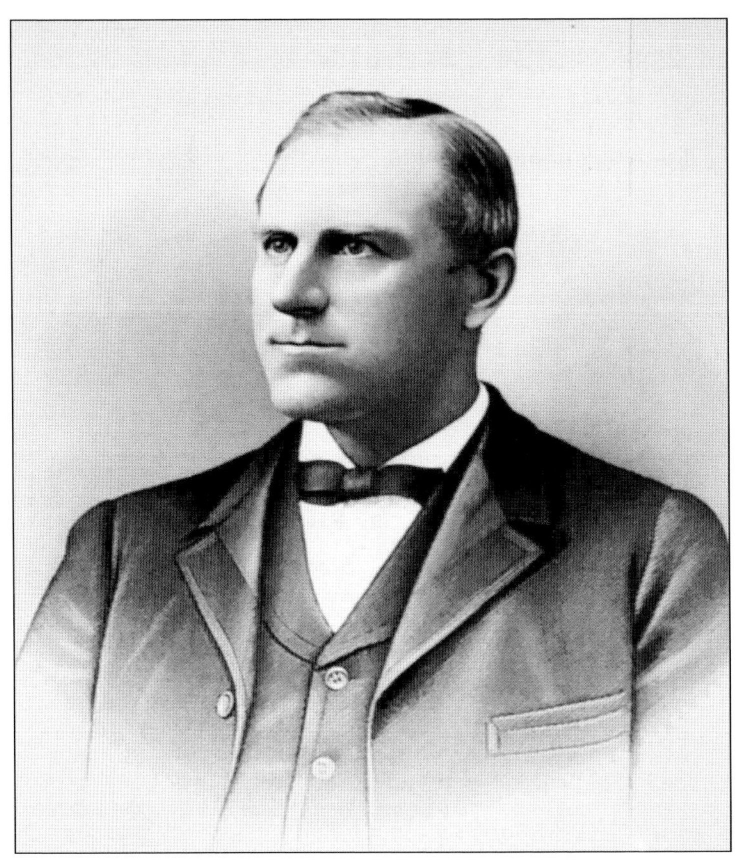

Fulton County's legislative representative, Frank P. Rice, was also a former Atlanta city councilman. He began structuring an appropriations bill to fund the new capitol so that it could be presented to the House Finance Committee in August. The bill was hotly debated in the full house. The Act to Provide for the Erection of the State Capitol Building ultimately passed with a 93-58 majority on August 16, 1883. (AHC.)

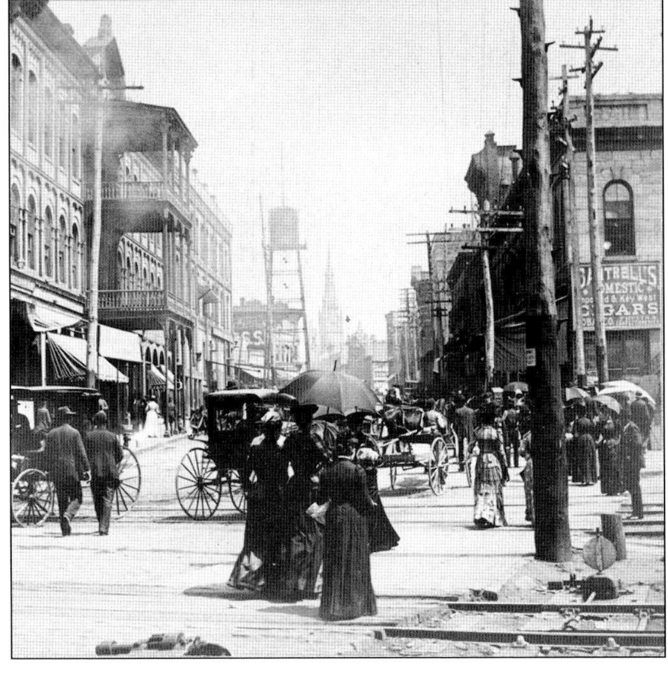

Atlanta's population had doubled to almost 20,000. As ex officio chairman of the Capitol Commission, Governor McDaniel was anxious for the building to become a reality. The act required the building plan to include accommodations for all branches of government and state house officers and had to be completed by January 1, 1889. The act further stipulated that costs of labor, material, and other expenses could not exceed $1 million. (AHC.)

SEALED PROPOSALS

—FOR THE—

FURNISHING OF MATERIALS

AND CONSTRUCTION

—OF THE—

GEORGIA STATE CAPITOL BUILDING

AT ATLANTA.

UNDER THE ACT OF THE GENERAL Assembly, approved September 5, 1883, are invited by the Board of Capitol Commissioners, until July 15 1884, at noon.

Plans, Specifications and "Instructions to Bidders" may be seen after May 10, 1884, at the office of the commission in Atlanta, Ga., and at the office of Messrs. Edbrooke & Burnham, Supervising Architects, No. 154 Deerborn street, Chicago, Ill.

Proposals may be submitted for the entire work, or for any classified portion, and the Commissioners reserve the right to accept any bid or any part of any bid, or to reject the whole.

No proposal will be considered unless made out on the schedule blanks, and accompanied by a copy of the Instructions to Builders, both of which, together with copies of the Act aforesaid, will be furnished to intending bidders upon application to the Commission at Atlanta or the Architects at Chicago.

All bidders will be required to furnish bond and security or a certified check, payable to the order of the Commissioners, equal in amount to 5 per cent of the bid submitted, which bond or check will be forfeited to the Board in the event of the failure or refusal of the bidder to enter into contract with the Board, should his bid be accepted.

"For the materials used in the construction of said building preference will be given to those found and procured in the state of Georgia. Provided, the same can be procured in said state as cheaply as other materials of like quality in other localities."

All bids must be sealed and endorsed "Proposals for State Capitol Building," and addressed to the Board of Capitol Commissioners, Atlanta, Ga.

For further information apply to the office of the Commissioners or to the Supervising Architects as above.

HENRY D. McDANIEL,
Governor, and Ex Officio Chairman Capitol Commission

The call for bids began on October 16, 1883. In addition to architects, commissioners were also consulting engineers about what building materials should be used to best "hold up the walls." By the time architectural drawings began being considered on January 16, 1884, specimens of limestone, sandstone, granite, and marble, including 23 types of Georgia stone, had been examined by the commissioners. Chosen by Governor McDaniel, the commissioners included E.P. Alexander of Richmond County, Benjamin E. Crowe of Fulton County, A.L. Miller of Houston County, Phillip Cook of Sumter County, and W.W. Thomas of Clarke County. (AHC.)

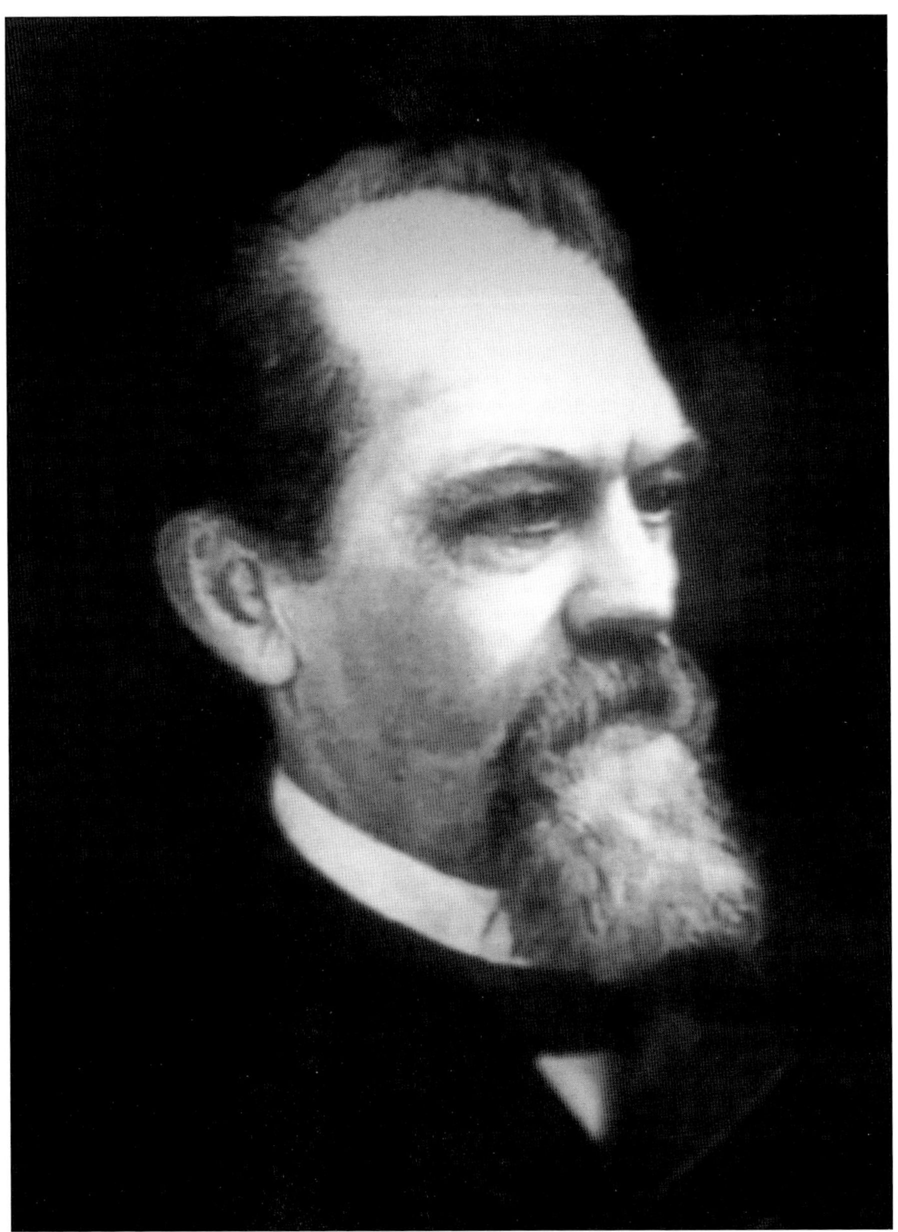

The Chicago architectural firm of Edbrooke & Burnham was awarded the contract for the capitol design. Willoughby J. Edbrooke and Franklin P. Burnham formed their partnership in 1879 after working together on the chamber of commerce building and designing several structures for the University of Notre Dame. Their firm had been commissioned to design the YMCA building in Atlanta before they submitted proposals for the Georgia capitol. Edbrooke was born into a family of builders and architects, training under his father and other master architects. He took a hands-on approach to the capitol project, visiting Atlanta several times during the design to confer with the Capitol Commission. In 1891, after the capitol was completed, Edbrooke became supervising architect of the US Treasury Department and moved to Washington, DC. He is credited with designing more than 40 structures across the United States, including numerous federal buildings. (Georgia Capitol Museum.)

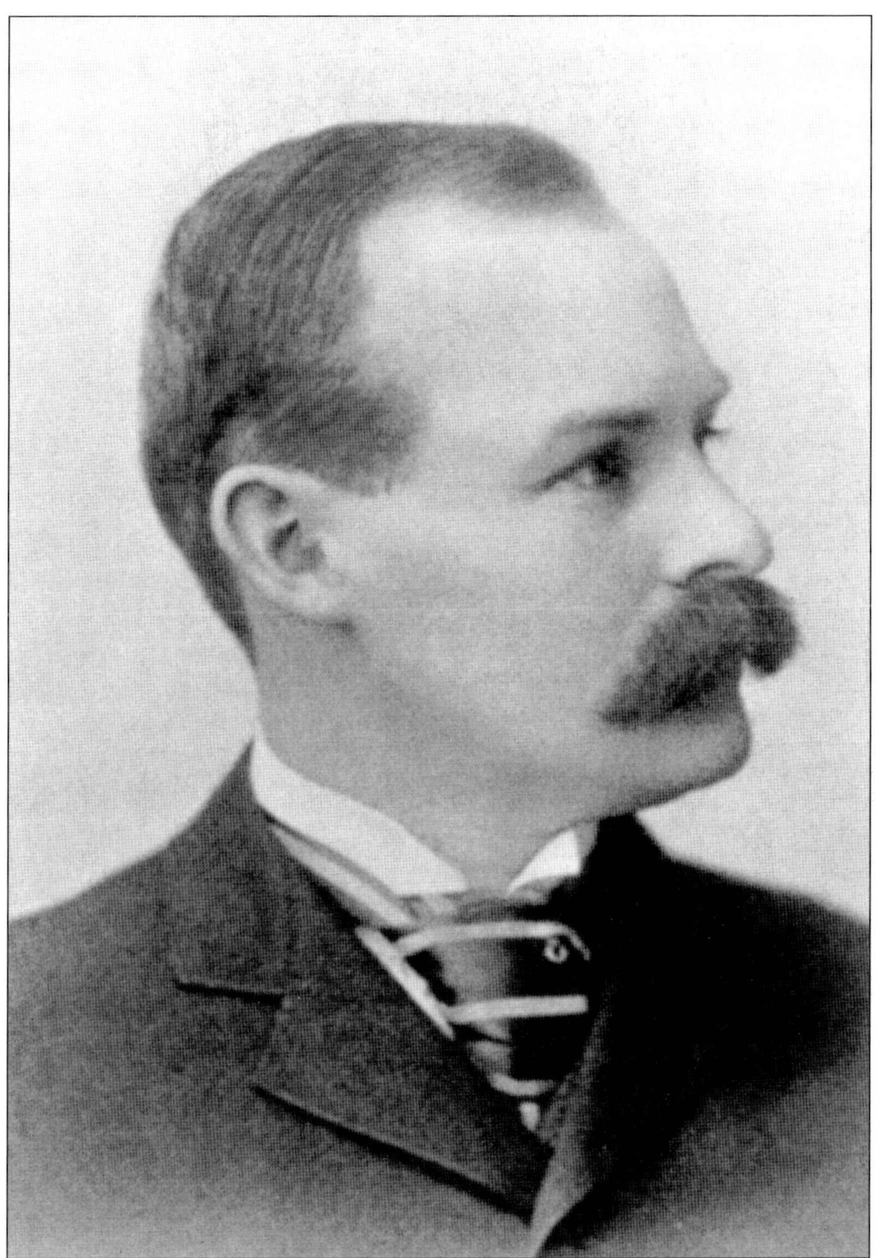

Franklin Burnham was the son of a carpenter and learned his craft through working at an architectural firm starting at the age of 14. Even though he was partnered with Edbrooke, who was 12 years his senior, he worked independently as the Kenilworth Company architect, designing numerous residences and city buildings in the Chicago suburb of Kenilworth. After Edbrooke received his treasury appointment, the two men dissolved their partnership in 1892, and Burnham moved to Los Angeles. He went on to design numerous buildings, including 12 Carnegie libraries, three of which remain standing. At least five Burnham-designed buildings are now listed in the National Register of Historic Places, including the Georgia State Capitol building. Edbrooke & Burnham received $5,000 initially for their capitol design and were also paid $4,000 a year to help oversee construction. (Kenilworth Historical Society.)

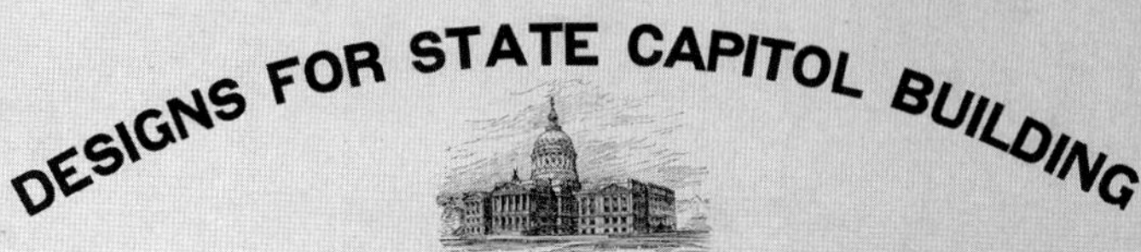
DESIGNS FOR STATE CAPITOL BUILDING

TO BE ERECTED AT ATLANTA, GEORGIA

EDBROOKE & BURNHAM, ARCHITECTS,

CHICAGO, ILL.

THESE PLANS TO BE HANDLED WITH CARE. NOT ALLOWED TO GO FROM THIS OFFICE.

No. 16.

The governor signed a contract with Edbrooke & Burnham on February 15, 1884, and the architects posted the required bond of $25,000. Edbrooke made several trips to Atlanta to work with Governor McDaniel to create designs for the structure. The detailed plans took a year to complete. Six months into the planning, an invitation for construction bids for the capitol was released, with September 23 as the date set for awarding the contract. While fires have destroyed many records and photographs from the construction of the Georgia State Capitol building, copies of Edbrooke & Burnham's original drawings, as approved by the Capitol Commission, still exist today. The set includes 12 drawings and one partial sheet, floor plans of all four stories, the roof and foundation plans, two transverse sections, and a longitudinal section. (GSA.)

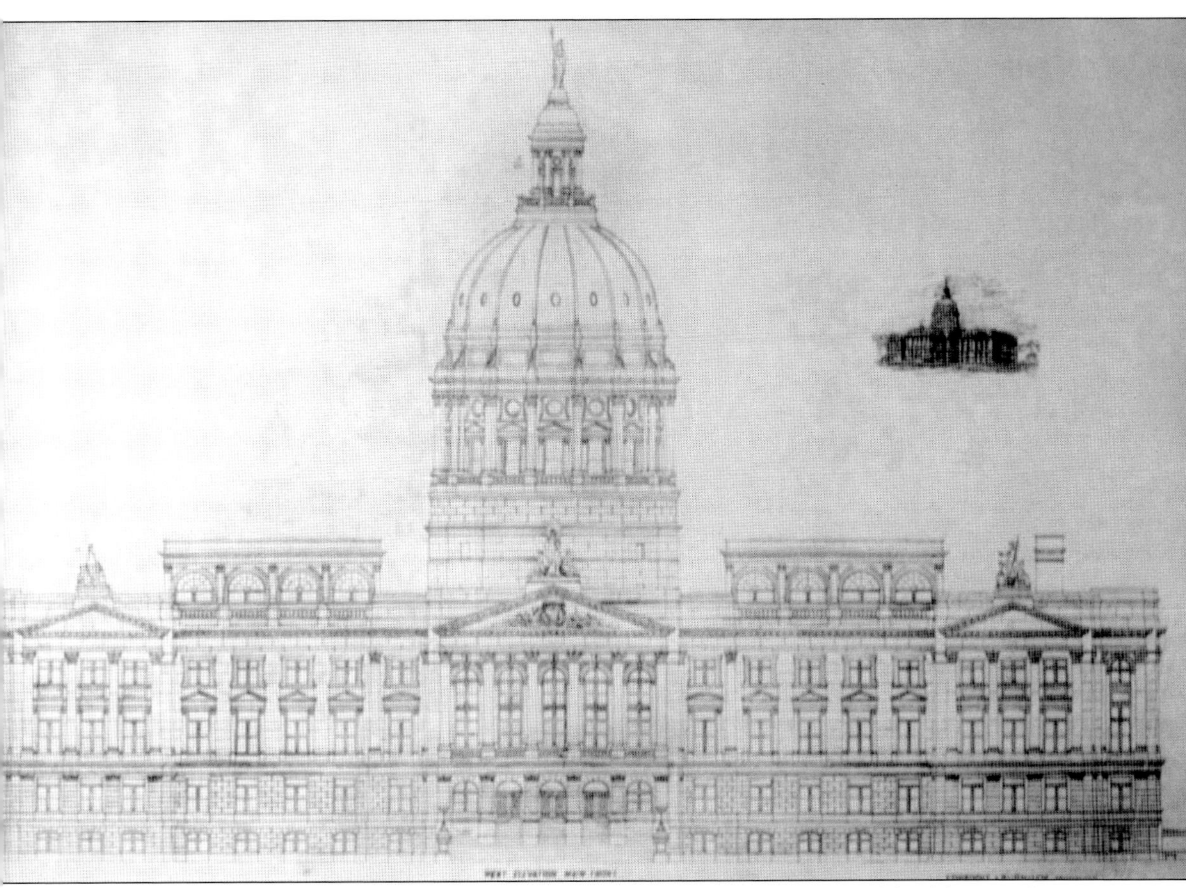

Edbrooke & Burnham's vision was for a Neoclassical Renaissance Revival building with an imposing dome, strongly resembling the structure of the US Capitol. While the western entrance was considered the main point of entry, the Georgia State Capitol building was designed to be entered from all four sides. The entrances had varied looks, but the western entrance features a plaza in front and a relief, including the 1777 Georgia state seal flanked by a woman holding a caduceus, a man welding a hammer, and another man in a helmet with sword in hand, above its hexagon-shaped facade. The state constitution had stipulated that "the great seal of this State shall have the following device: on one side of a scroll, whereon shall be engraved 'The Constitution of the State of Georgia;' and the motto 'Pro bono publico,' " Latin for "for the public good." (GSA.)

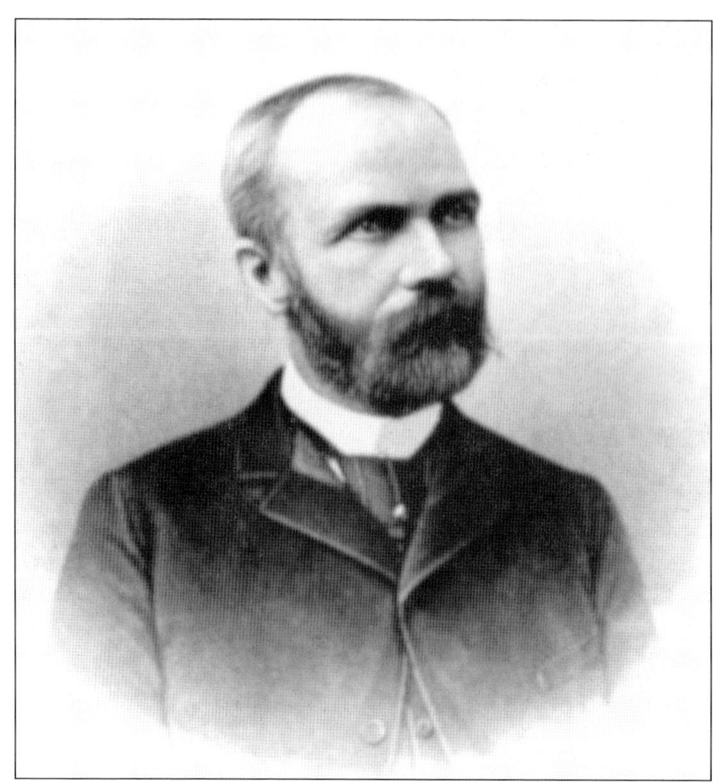

In the initial round of bidding, all submissions were rejected because they exceeded the $1 million cap set by the Capitol Act. The firm of Miles and Horn from Toledo, Ohio, was awarded the contract on September 24, 1884, with a low bid of $862,756.75. William B. Miles (left) and partner Charles D. Horn (below) moved to Atlanta to personally be on hand to oversee construction. The firm was a new collaboration for the men, who had previously partnered with Israel K. Cramer in Ohio at Miles, Cramer & Horn. Excavation for the building began on November 13, 1884. (Both, AHC.)

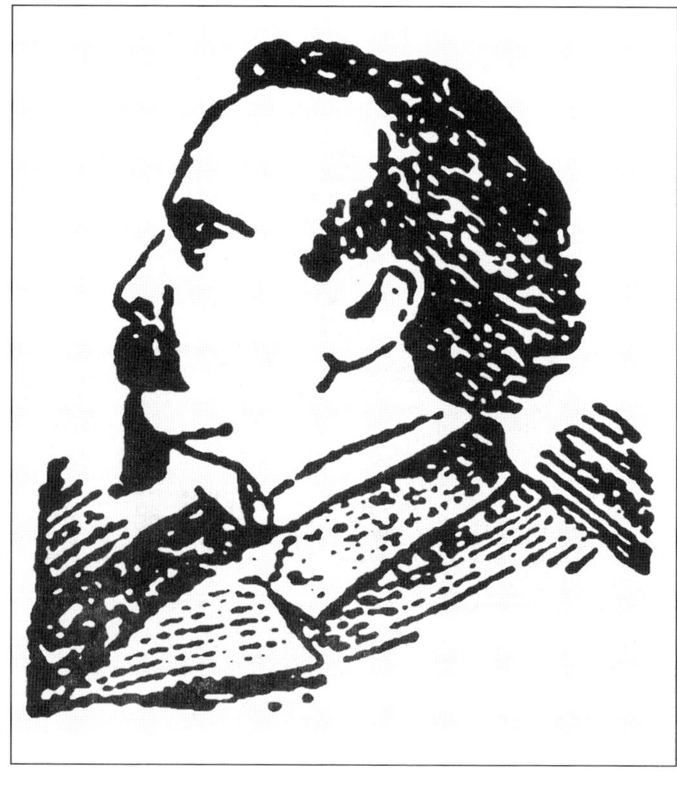

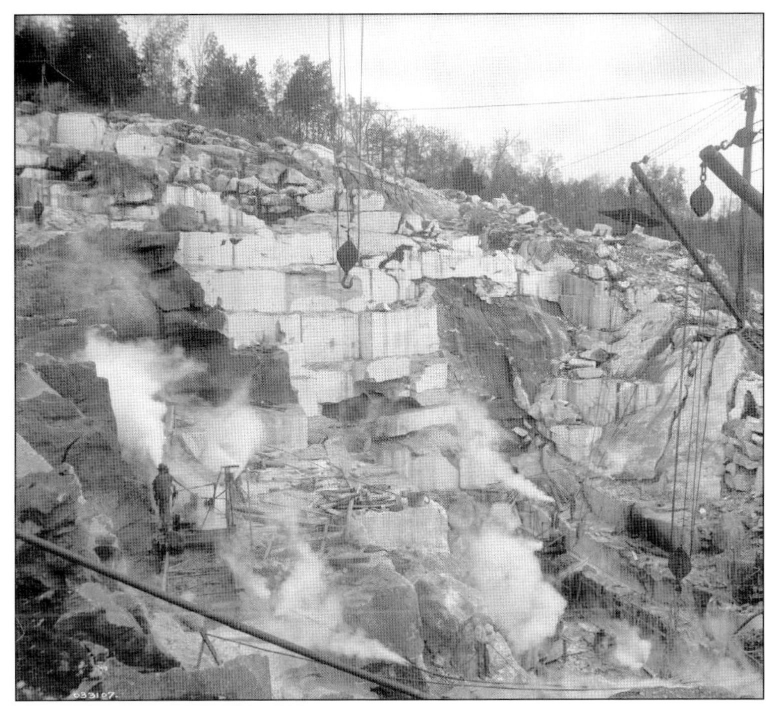

The construction bid pricing was based on using Indiana oolitic limestone for much of the exterior for economic reasons. That decision did not sit well with some, who argued that only materials from Georgia should be used in constructing the new capitol. Ultimately, the foundation would be of Georgia granite, and interior walls, floors, and steps would use Georgia marble. (LOC.)

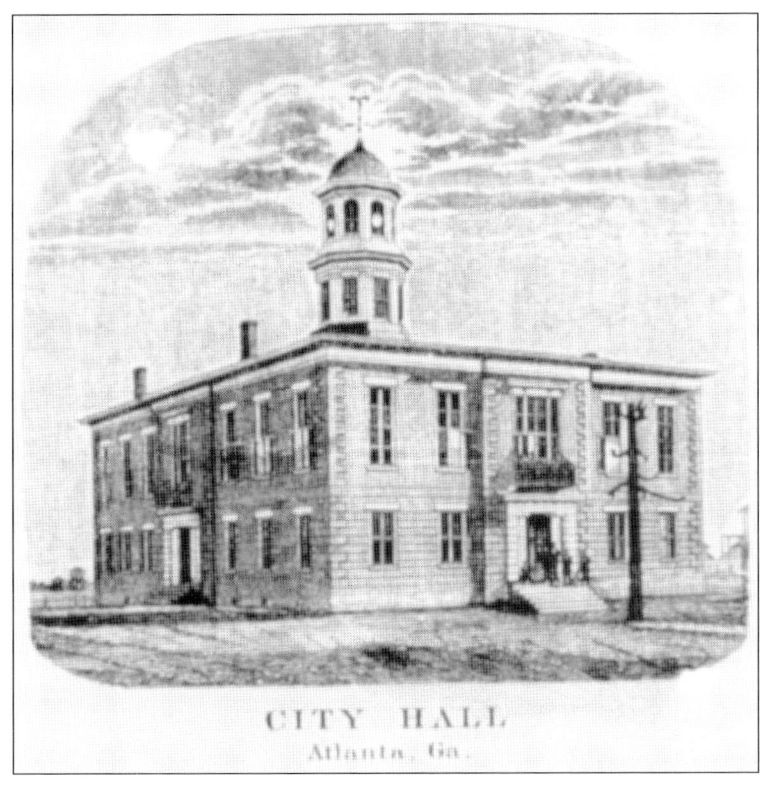

To make way for the new capitol, the city hall structure, which had occupied the spot for 30 years, had to be torn down. City offices had already been moved to the new chamber of commerce building on Hunter Street. The building was dismantled at a cost of $975.38, and an estimated 375,000 of its bricks were saved to be used in the new capitol. (GSA.)

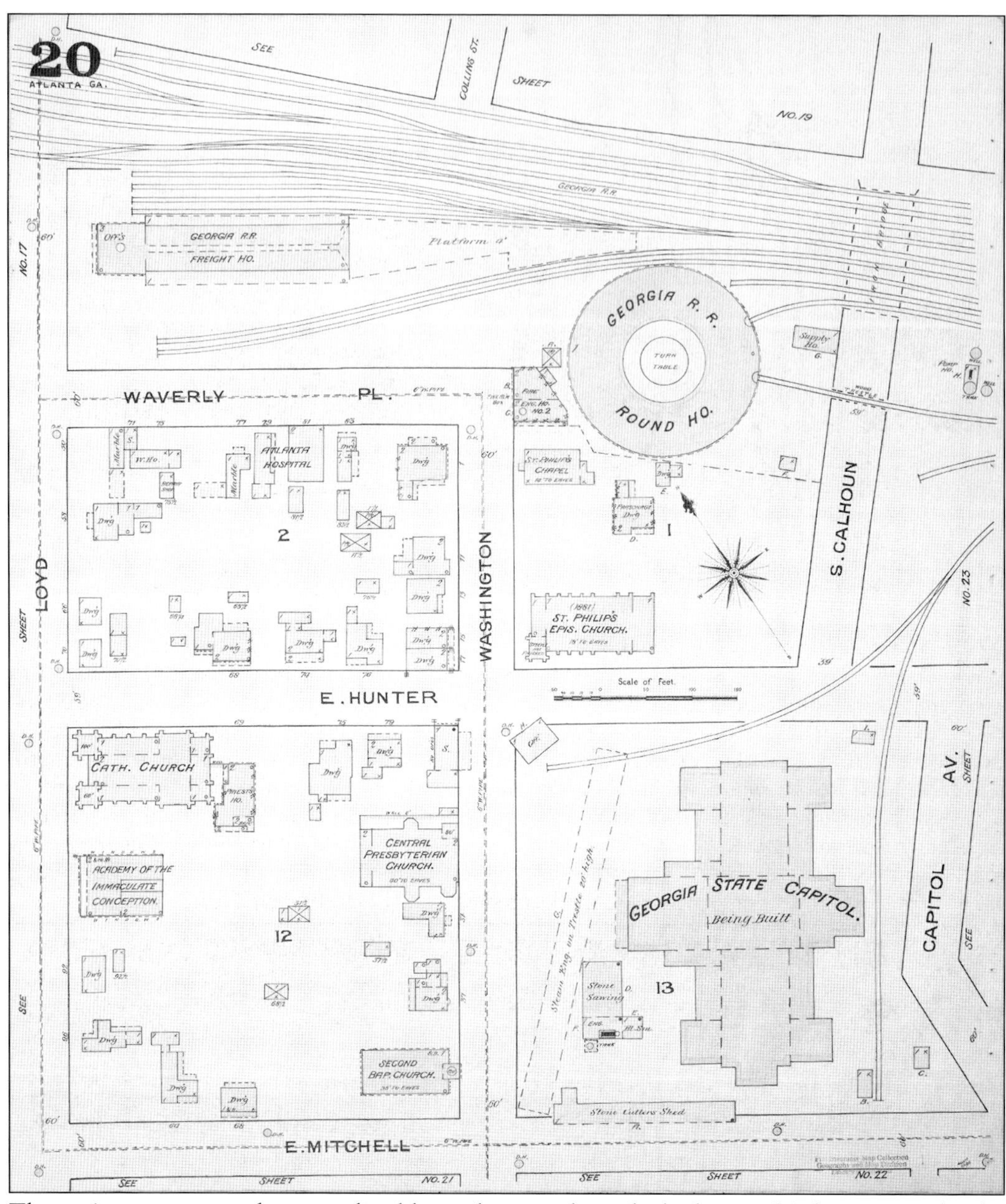

The site's proximity to the critical rail lines that ran through the heart of Atlanta proved to be important, as this 1886 Sanborn fire insurance map shows. Three rail tracks needed to be constructed linking the Georgia Railroad yard to the building site to help deliver materials, including the massive limestone, granite, and marble blocks. One rail line would enter at the corner of Hunter Street (now Martin Luther King Jr. Boulevard) and the newly renamed Capitol Avenue, running down the side of McDonough Street to Mitchell Street. A second track would go through the center of the building to the dome, and a third was to run around to the Washington Street side of the lot to a point where a line elevated about 20 feet off the ground was constructed to help deliver the stone into the structure. (LOC.)

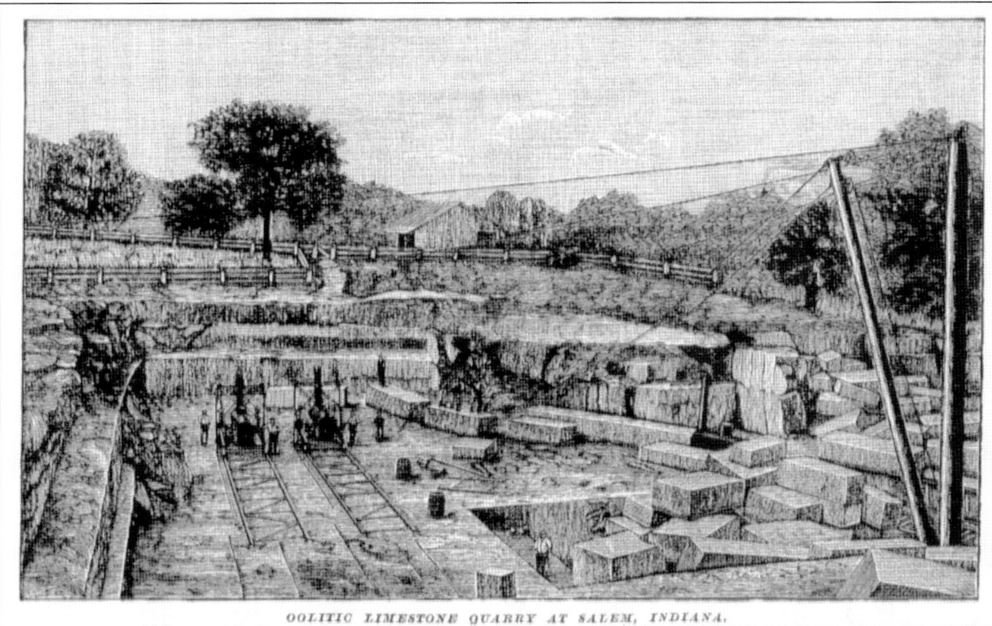

OOLITIC LIMESTONE QUARRY AT SALEM, INDIANA.

These etchings from the publication *Manufacturer and Builder* depict the cutting and transporting of blocks of oolitic limestone at the Salem Stone and Lime Company in southern Indiana to Georgia. A thin band of limestone ran from Salem north to near Spencer in what was named the Salem Formation and helped establish the area as a premier location for quarries. The Georgia Senate Committee on Public Property reported this limestone was chosen because of its strength, durability, and beauty, saying, "It possesses the most remarkable uniformity of grain and texture." The committee also admitted that cost was a consideration. There are no known photographs of the Georgia capitol grounds during its construction, but it was said to have a yard like the one in the below image to handle the arrival of the limestone. By 1900, Indiana limestone accounted for a third of all limestone quarried in the United States. (Both, Brenau Trustee Library.)

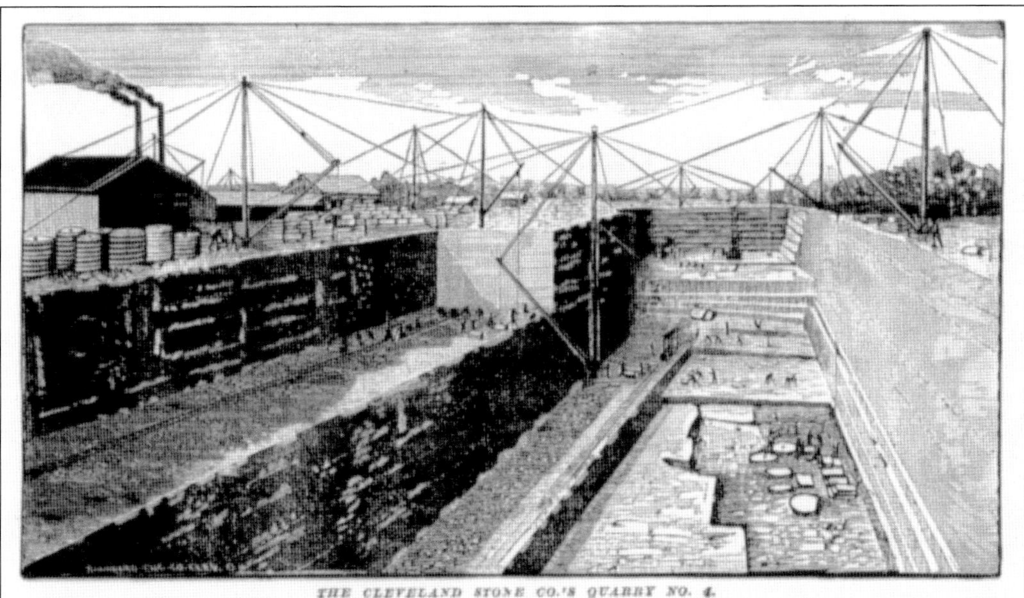

THE CLEVELAND STONE CO.'S QUARRY NO. 4.

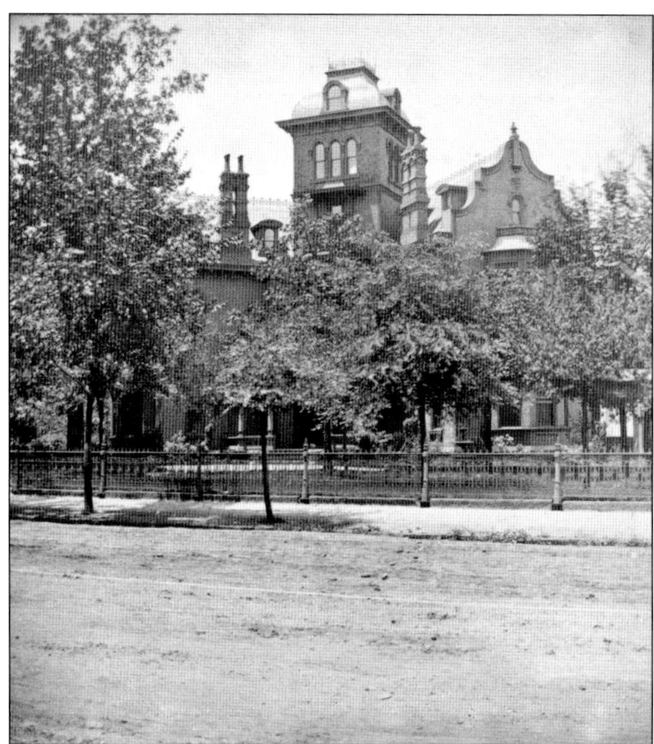

While the five-acre capitol site was very much a construction site after October 26, 1884, the neighborhood around it remained a mixture of churches, businesses, and grand homes, many similar to the governor's mansion a few blocks away. Excavation of the capitol grounds ran into some problems when a cistern, cesspool, and well were found. Foundation plans were revised and paid for through a contingency fund. (NYPL.)

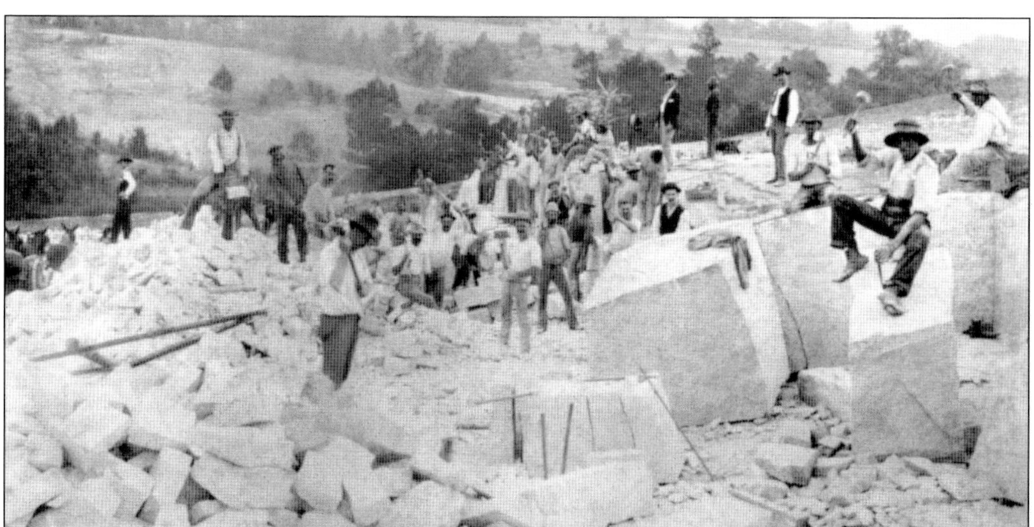

In the spring of 1885, the foundation of the capitol was taking shape. Records from the board of the Capitol Commission indicate that by mid-April, 175 wagon loads were arriving daily from quarries near Stone Mountain. Again, the specter of using only Georgia materials threatened to halt progress. The matter was laid to rest when it was determined that Georgia marble and granite would cost an additional $204,000 plus any other expenses incurred during a minimum six-month delay. (Stone Mountain Memorial Association.)

In preparation for the laying of the capitol cornerstone, sculptor Orion Frazee was provided with an imprint of the great seal of the state by Secretary of State Nathan C. Barnett so Frazee could cut a relief in the marble block. Frazee lived in Atlanta for only a short period and is best known for the death masks he created, including one of Jefferson Davis, president of the Confederacy. (AHC.)

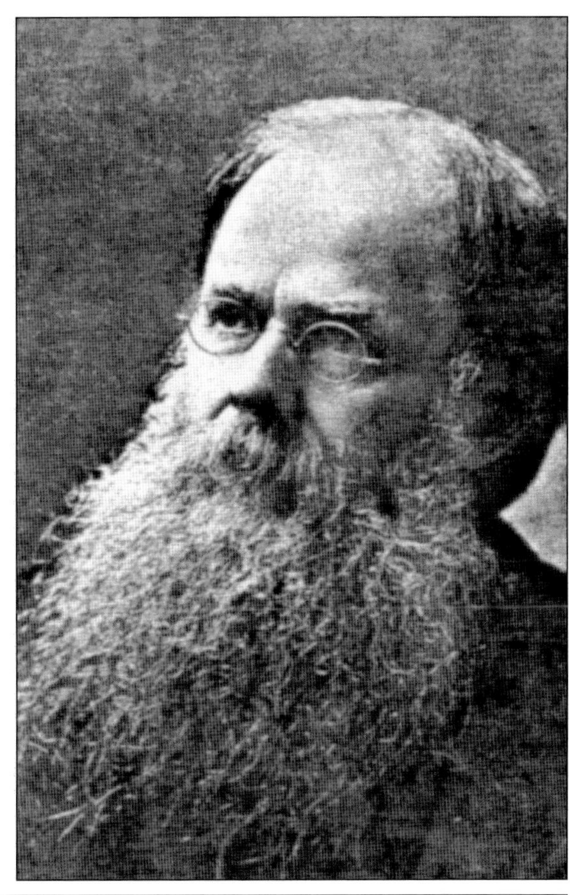

As the capitol began to take shape, brick from the old city hall was designated for use in the upper chambers while new brick was purchased from the Chattahoochee Brick Company. The rich clay along the Chattahoochee was ideal for brick manufacturing, and the company was producing about 50,000 bricks a day just for the capitol, largely through labor by prisoners forced to work in the controversial "lend, lease" practice. (AHC.)

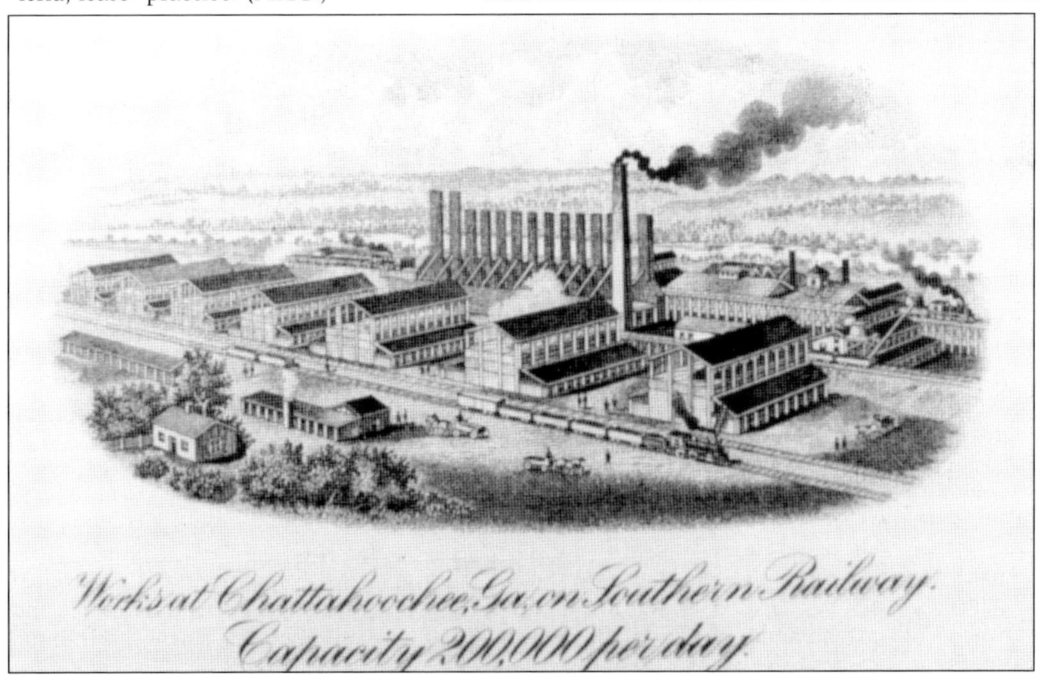

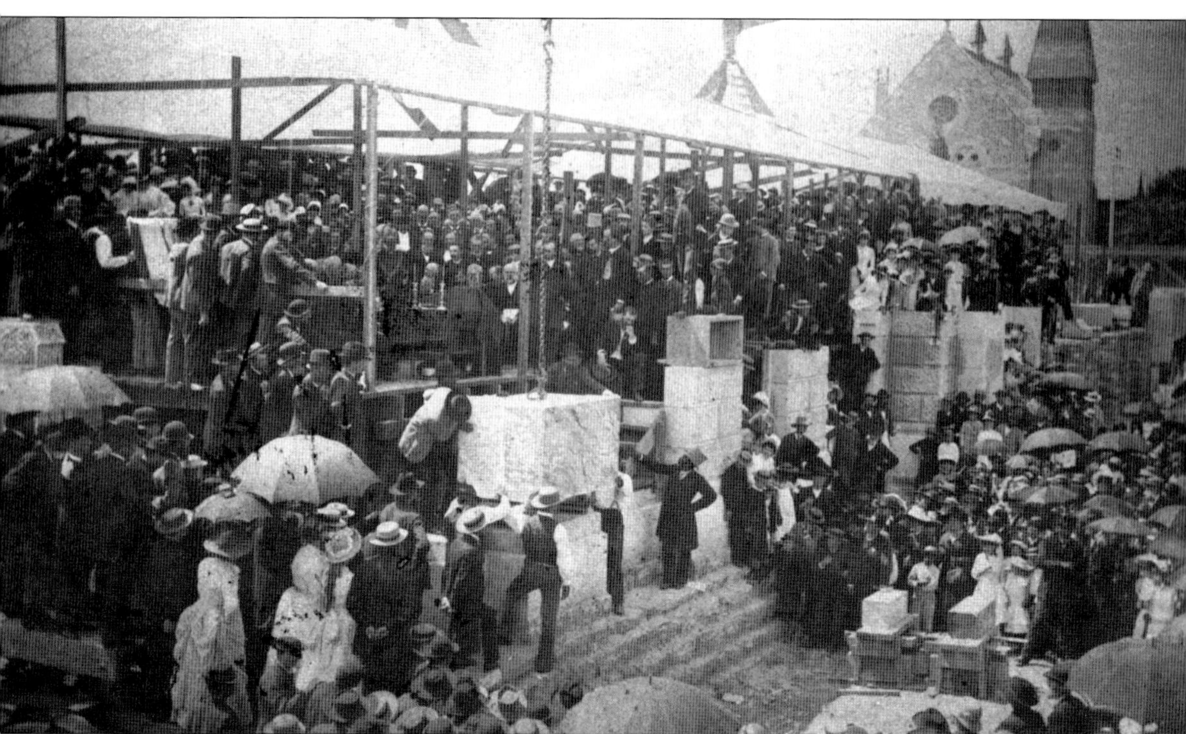

Much fanfare surrounded the laying of the cornerstone of the new Georgia State Capitol on September 2, 1885. Even though details of the event were reported in newspapers across the United States, few images exist to document the day. Hundreds can be seen crowded within the steel frame rising from the nine-foot-high granite blocks that formed the foundation. Invited guests included capitol commissioners from Indiana, South Carolina, Texas, and others. The festivities began with a half-mile procession from the temporary capitol building featuring city and state officials, the legislature, the governor, capitol commissioners, cavalry, infantry, and artillery units, as well as 1,200 Masons. The parade marched triumphantly onto the capitol grounds and ascended the stairs on Washington Street to walk through the growing structure's western entrance. At that point, the arches over the basement windows on the southwest end had been completed. Despite the festivities and the crowds, stonecutting continued throughout the day, although at some points, the proximity of the onlookers almost forced the work to a halt. (AHC.)

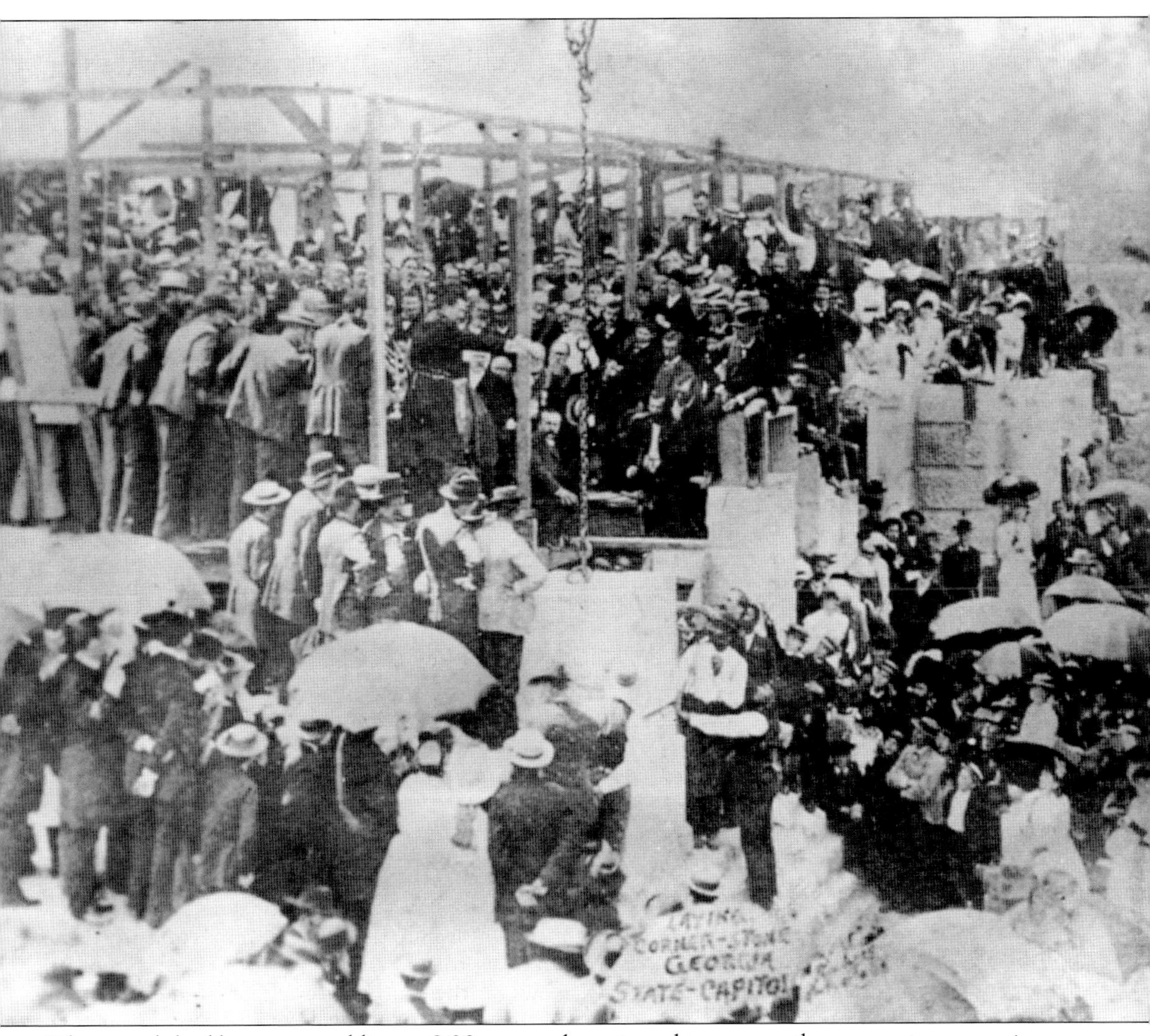

The crowds had begun assembling at 8:00 a.m. and continued to grow as the momentous occasion got underway with the 10:00 a.m. procession. The day was warm, and many in the crowd used umbrellas to shield themselves from the sun, while others avoided the shoulder-to-shoulder crowd and watched from nearby rooftops. An estimated 6,000 people were on hand to witness and listen as a chorus of 100 trained voices sang "My Country, 'Tis of Thee" to open the ceremonies. Governor McDaniel followed the song and welcomed the dignitaries and the crowd from atop the nine-foot-high granite foundation. This was a moment years in the making, and McDaniel commended the Georgia General Assembly for its planning of the day's proceedings, saying it had helped facilitate what he lauded as "appropriate ceremonies illustrative of the character of the building to be erected." (GSA.)

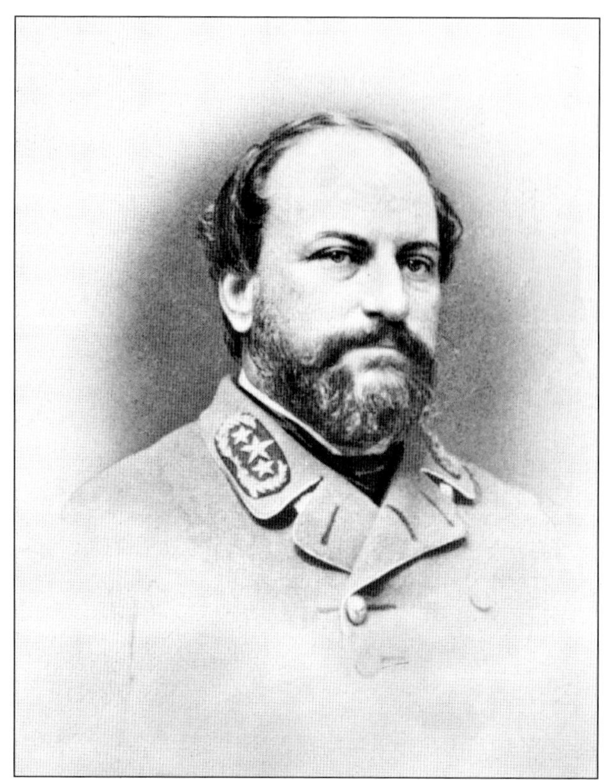

Alexander R. Lawton was the main speaker. Nationally recognized for his reconciliation efforts, Lawton was a former brigadier general in the Confederate army and had served in the state legislature. He had also notably helped organize Georgia's Ku Klux Klan. Lawton spoke of Georgia's history, making patriotic reference to the war and the present peace and prosperity of the country. He concluded by declaring, "There will be no flippant boast that Georgia is indeed the Empire of the South." (LOC.)

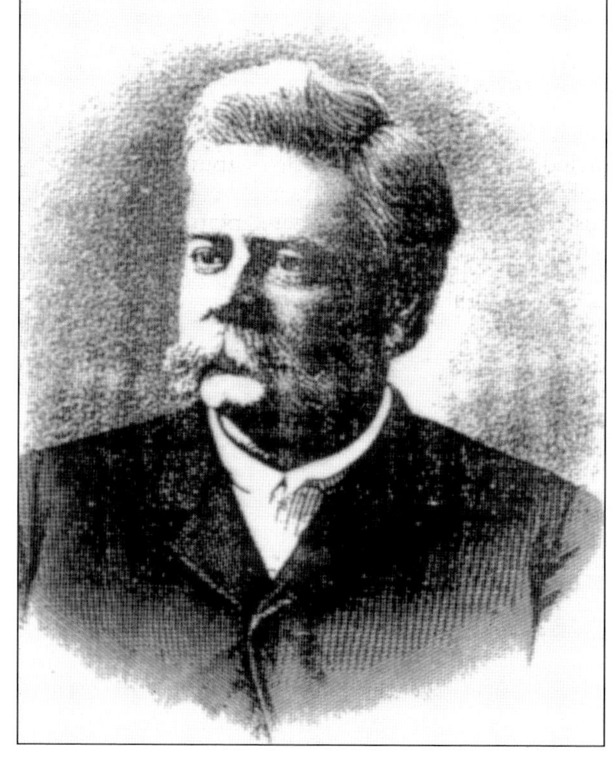

Dressed in a Masonic apron and chain collar, grand master John Davidson of the Masons of Georgia performed a Masonic ritual, pouring corn (symbolizing plenty), wine (for joy and gladness), and oil (for peace) to consecrate the stone as it was set into place. The location on the northeast corner was also traditional among Masons because it symbolizes passing from darkness (north) to light (east) and therefore ignorance to knowledge. (Grand Lodge of Georgia.)

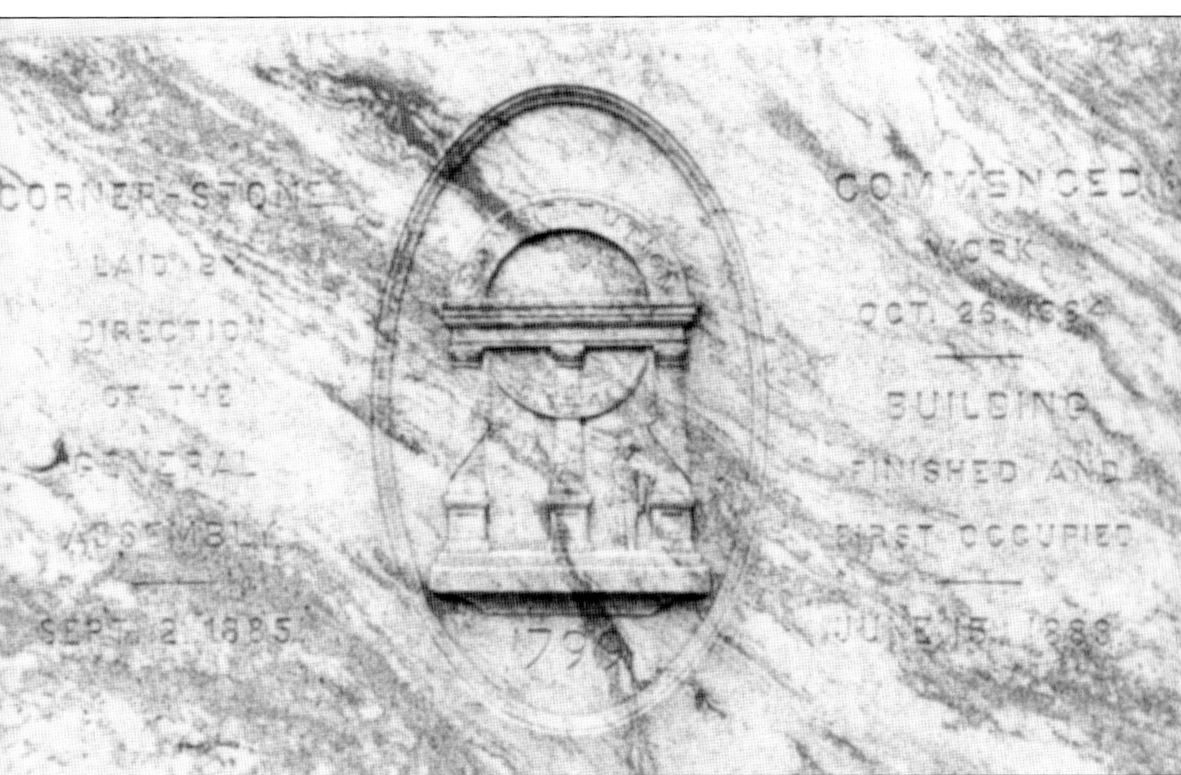

The cornerstone was made of marble from Pickens County and weighed over three tons. An 18-by-12-inch cavity had been carved in it to allow the placement of a copper box filled with mementos of the time. Sealed inside the vault were various government artifacts such as the code of 1882, a legislative manual, acts of the Georgia General Assembly from 1881 to 1884, and lists of governors, their staffs, legislators, judges, and commissioners as well as military rosters, several newspapers, and copies of the dedication ceremony program and accompanying speeches. Also included were a Bible, a bottle of Indian Springs water, a photograph of baseball player Patsy Cahill, and an already 100-year-old copper penny. Ironically, among the items placed inside for posterity were a copy of a rejected plan for the building and a brochure for the Salem Stone and Lime Company. The cost of the ceremony was paid out of the capitol budget and amounted to $498.53, plus $80.08 for the cornerstone itself. (Janice McDonald.)

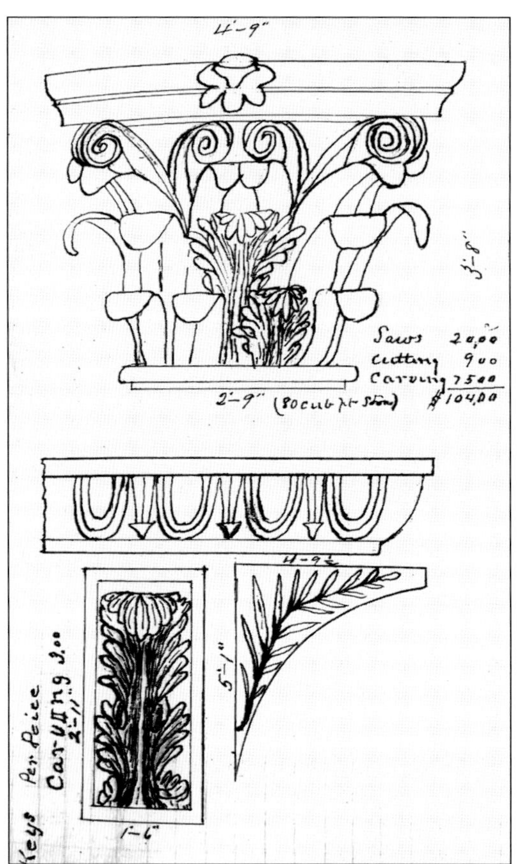

Contractors C.D. Horn and W.B. Miles kept meticulous records throughout the construction of the building. There were regular entries into their pocket-sized, leather-bound field record books. An entry in Horn's 1886 field notebook shows his attention to detail in recording the work being done, including not just the dimensions of these Corinthian columns but the cost of creating them. (AHC.)

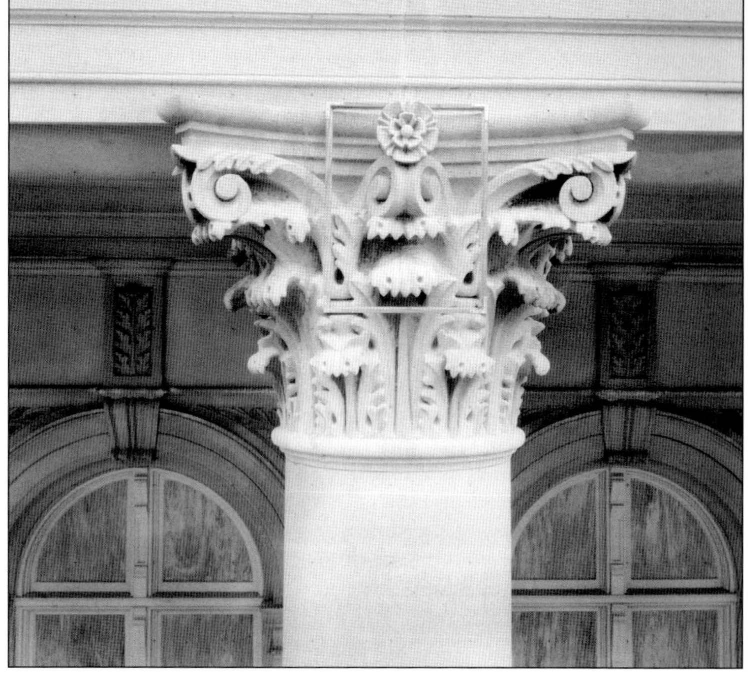

There are six columns at the western elevation, or main entrance, of the Georgia State Capitol that carry the Corinthian design depicted in Horn's drawing. The caps seen in the lower sketch of the previous image are repeated on the pilasters that surround the entire exterior of the capitol. The columns support the four-story portico and stand 272 feet tall. Similar caps appear throughout the building's interior. (LOC.)

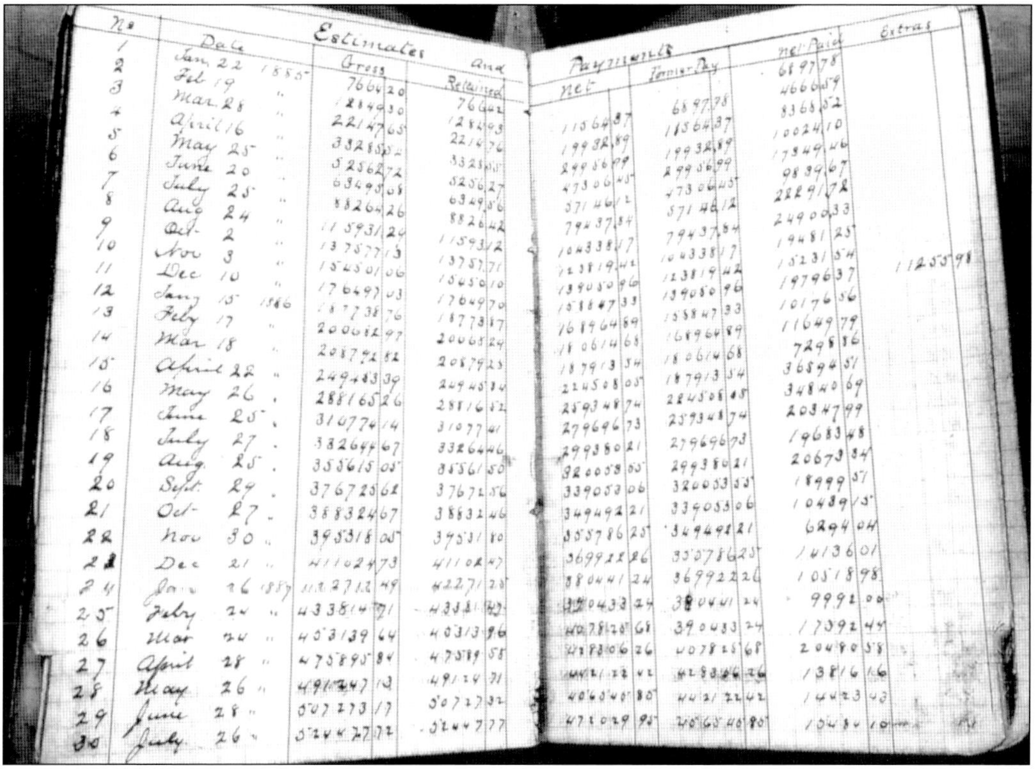

While Horn kept track of materials and labor, his partner W.B. Miles kept track of all the expenditures. They were well aware of the scrutiny they were under for making sure the capitol building project stayed within its budget. The men had met with lawmakers on numerous occasions to justify any changes in plans. These are pages from the field accounting book kept by W.B. Miles for 1887. After the Kimball Opera House fiasco, the pressure was on to make sure the building was not only well constructed but had what were considered many modern features. While the opera house had notoriously bad ventilation, the new building had three types of flues to handle hot and cold air as well as chimney smoke. Fans and air ducts in the basement pushed the air throughout the building. There was also an elevator, considered a real novelty at the time. Lavatories had hot and cold running water to all the sinks. Fireproofing was a priority, and a hollow clay fireproofing tile was used throughout the building. Even the domed roof was considered fireproof. (Both, AHC.)

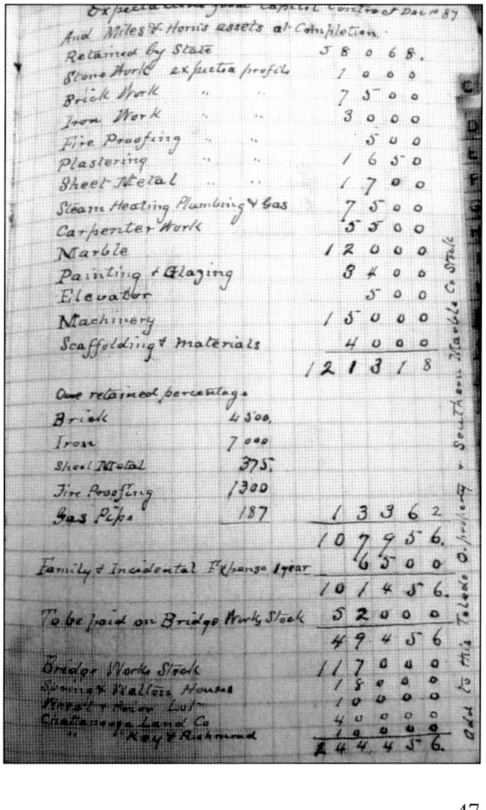

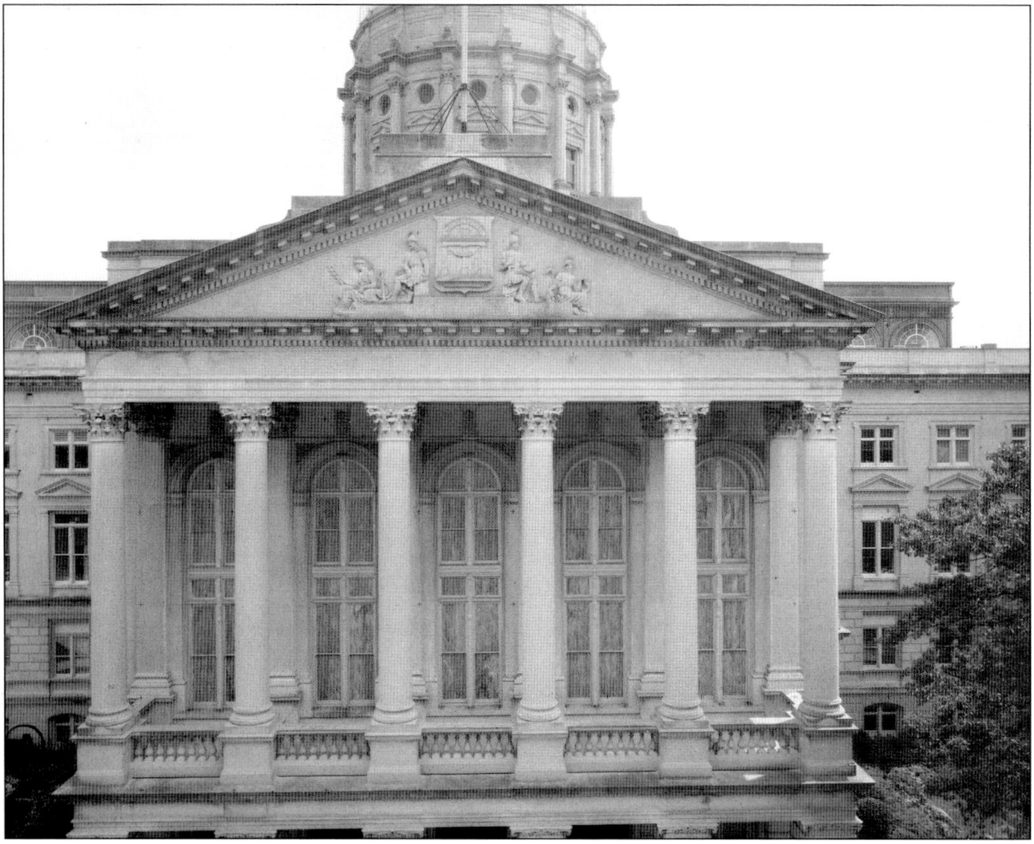

Having worked on the Vanderbilt mansion, sculptor George Crouch was contracted to do the ornamental work on the building, both inside and out. Due to growing expenses, the statuary that was originally planned for above the exterior entryways was eliminated. Crouch remained in Atlanta after completion of the capitol, gaining a reputation for his work carving monuments, headstones, and statuary for Oakland and Westview Cemeteries. (LOC.)

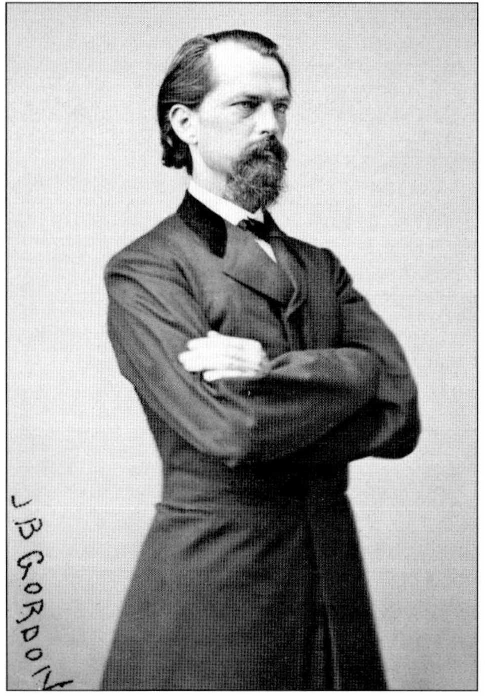

Gov. H.D. McDaniel did not seek reelection, and in November 1886, Georgia Civil War hero John B. Gordon became governor. McDaniel later said that no part of his official duties gave him as much pleasure as working with his Capitol Commission. As new governor, Gordon also became ex officio chairman. (LOC.)

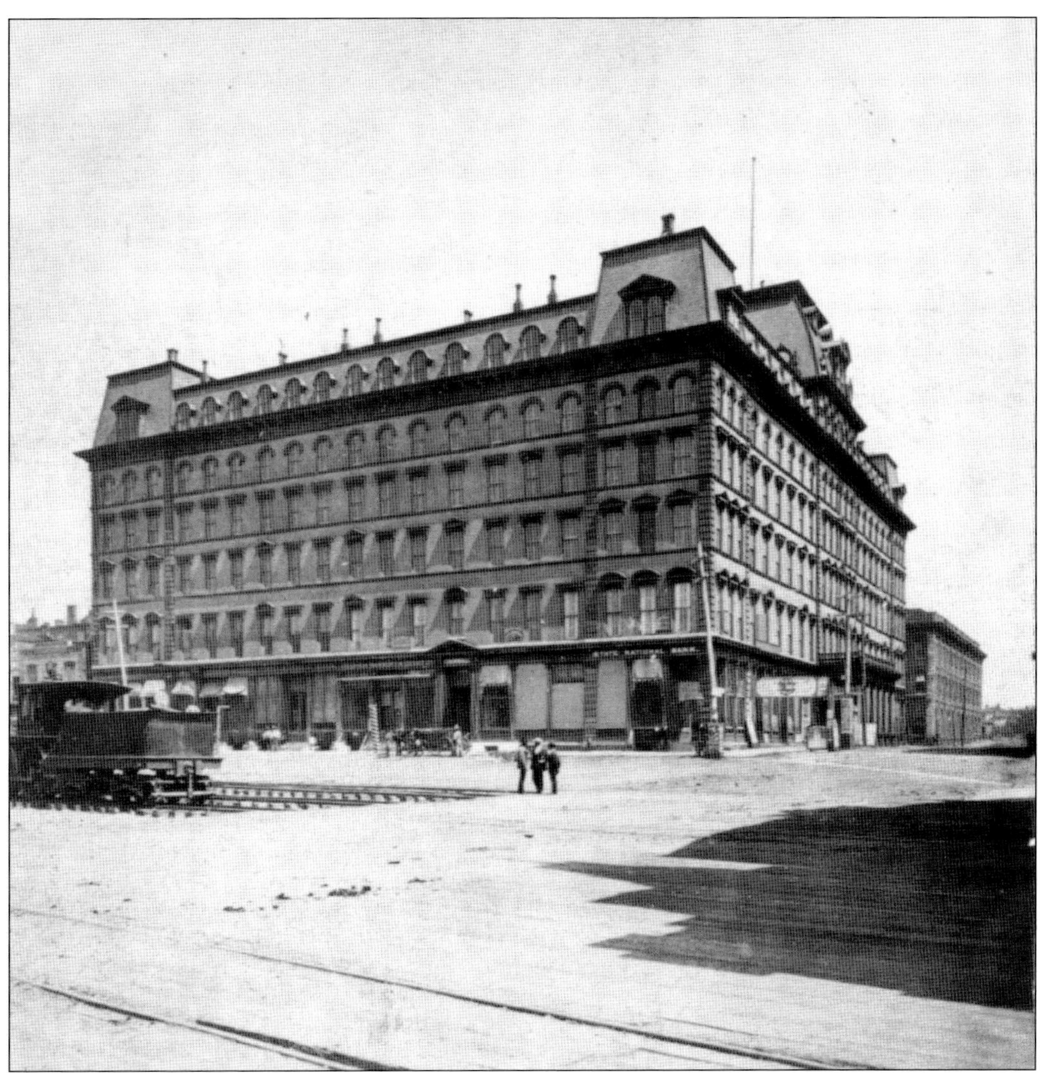

C.D. Horn met a violent death in August 1887 when he was shot breaking up a fight at the Kimball House Hotel between subcontractors A.B.F. "Bud" Veal and Samuel Hoyt Venable. The loss of Horn created a possible problem for the Capitol Commission, which was concerned it would need a new bond with Miles. Fortunately, it did not, and Miles continued to oversee the final phases of construction. After being granted a brief extension on construction, final inspection of the capitol took place on February 26, 1889. The closing tally showed the project had come in under the $1 million budget. The $999,881,57 total cost included $27,500 for salaries for the commissioners, $25,000 for the architects, $10,626 for superintendents' salaries, $20,000 for additional land, $10,645 for frescoing, and $897,210.48 in labor and materials. On February 28, W.B. Miles was given a check for $118.43. (NYPL.)

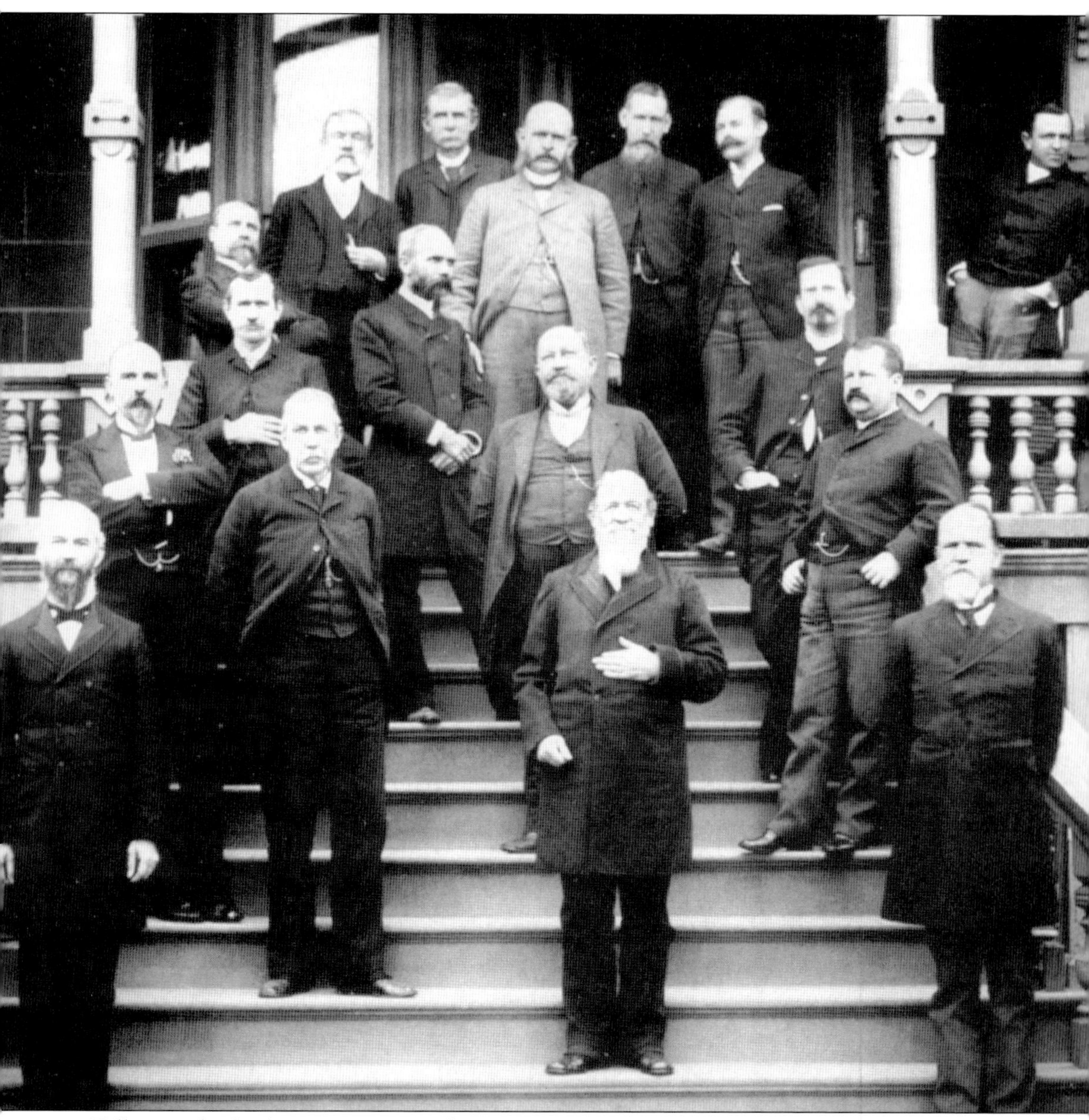

Following the final inspection, capitol commissioner Evan P. Howell invited his fellow commission members, former governor Henry McDaniel, current governor John Gordon, and several other dignitaries to his Westend home for a celebration and elegant midday dinner. The centerpiece for the dining table was an intricately detailed, three-foot-long papier-mâché model of the capitol, complete with the carvings of the exterior stonework and lights illuminating the interior. It was created by architects Edbrooke and Burnham. Standing on the Howell home steps are, from left to right, (first row) former governor Henry McDaniel, Phil Cook (with hand across his waist), and Gov. John B. Gordon; (second row) Commissioner W.W. Thomas; (third row) Commissioner E.P. Alexander, host E.P. Howell, and Atlanta mayor Tom Glenn; (fourth row) two unidentified and Commissioner A.L. Miller. The men in the last two rows and on the porch are unidentified. (Georgia Capitol Museum.)

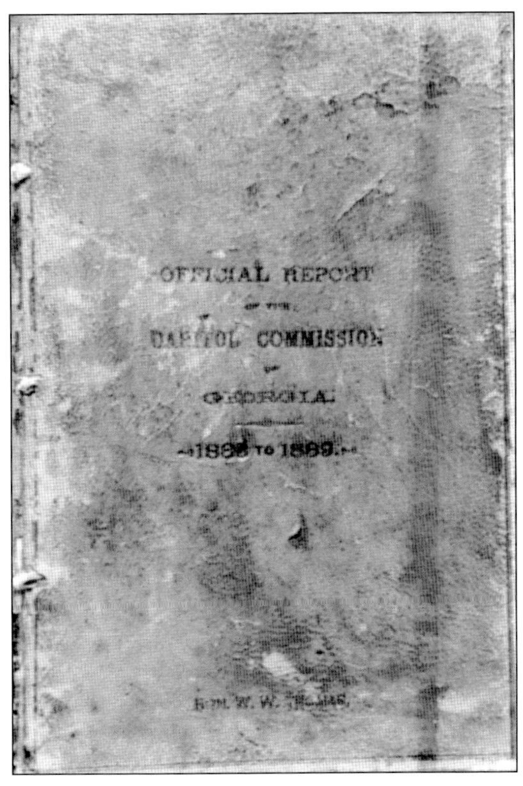

This leather-bound book in the Georgia Capitol Museum archives is the official report of the proceedings of the Capitol Commission for 1888–1889. This particular copy belonged to Commissioner W.W. Thomas of Coweta County. Each of the commissioners was given a copy with their name embossed on it as a tribute to their work in delivering the capitol to the people of Georgia. (Georgia Capitol Museum.)

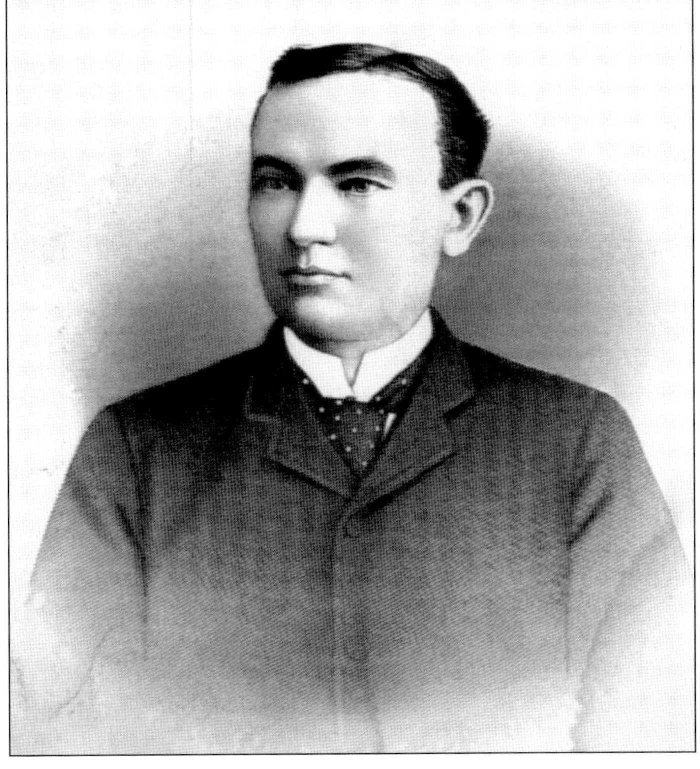

With the capitol completed, it was time to furnish it. An attorney and former solicitor general, Georgia Senate president Fleming DuBignon served on the new commission to supervise the specifications, bidding, and contracts. Other commission members included Governor Gordon, Speaker of the House Clay, Rep. J.L. Lamar, and Sen. Frank Rice. The furnishing budget was $83,000, and the goal was to have the building ready by May. (AHC.)

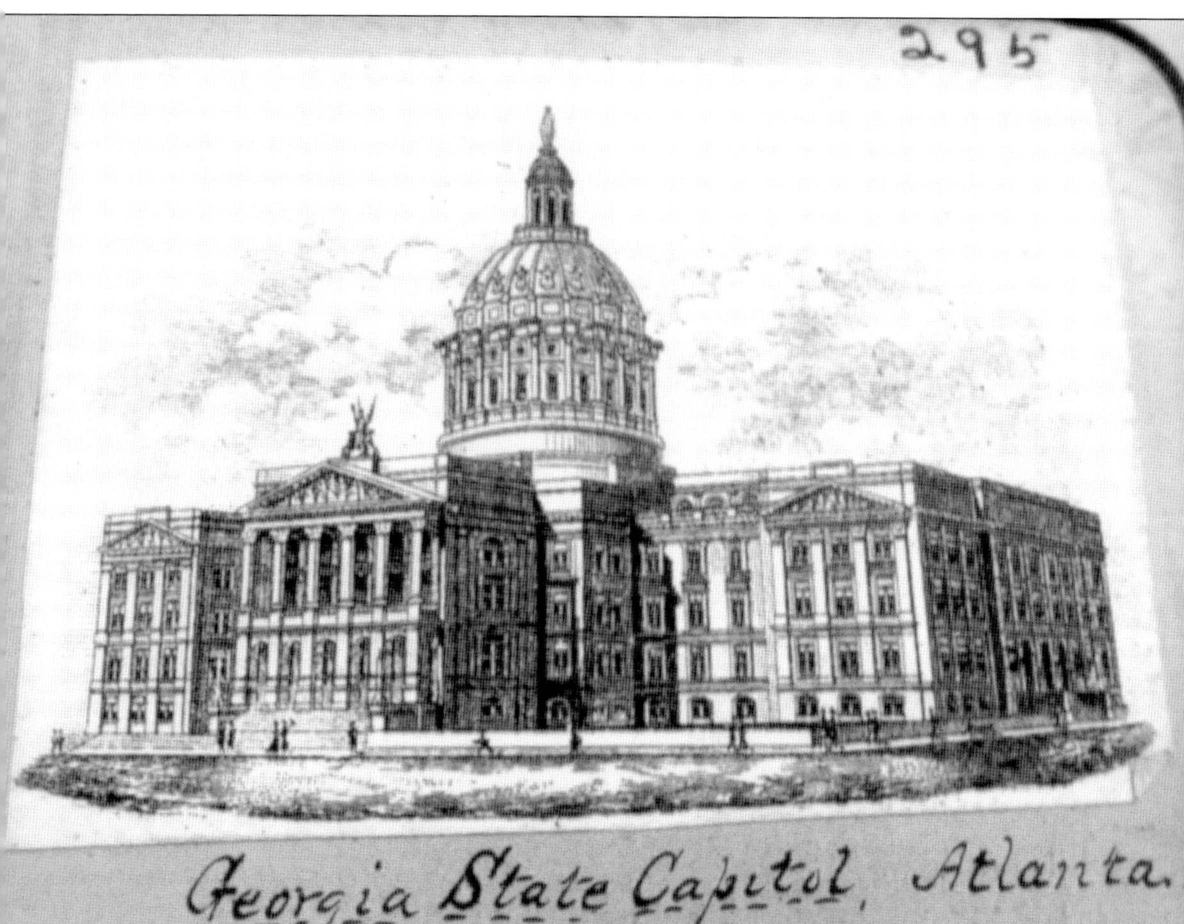

This image, based on Edbrooke and Burnham's original architectural drawing, was pasted in the back of Miles's field book as a reminder of the ultimate goal of his four-year effort. On July 4, 1889, thousands again gathered at the new Georgia State Capitol as Commissioner Evan P. Howell formally presented the completed building to Gov. John B. Gordon, who accepted it. Gordon then passed it on to the Georgia General Assembly, who accepted it through Senate president Fleming DuBignon and House Speaker Pro Tempore Martin Calvin. Former governor Henry McDaniel was on hand as Howell praised him, saying the people of Georgia owed McDaniel a debt of gratitude. He added that McDaniel "gave his attention night and day to the work necessary for the faithful performance of this work. It was his watchful eye in drawing the contract and appointing such men as Alexander, Crane, Thomas, and Miller that made this building one worthy of the people of Georgia." (AHC.)

Three

The Georgia State Capitol Building

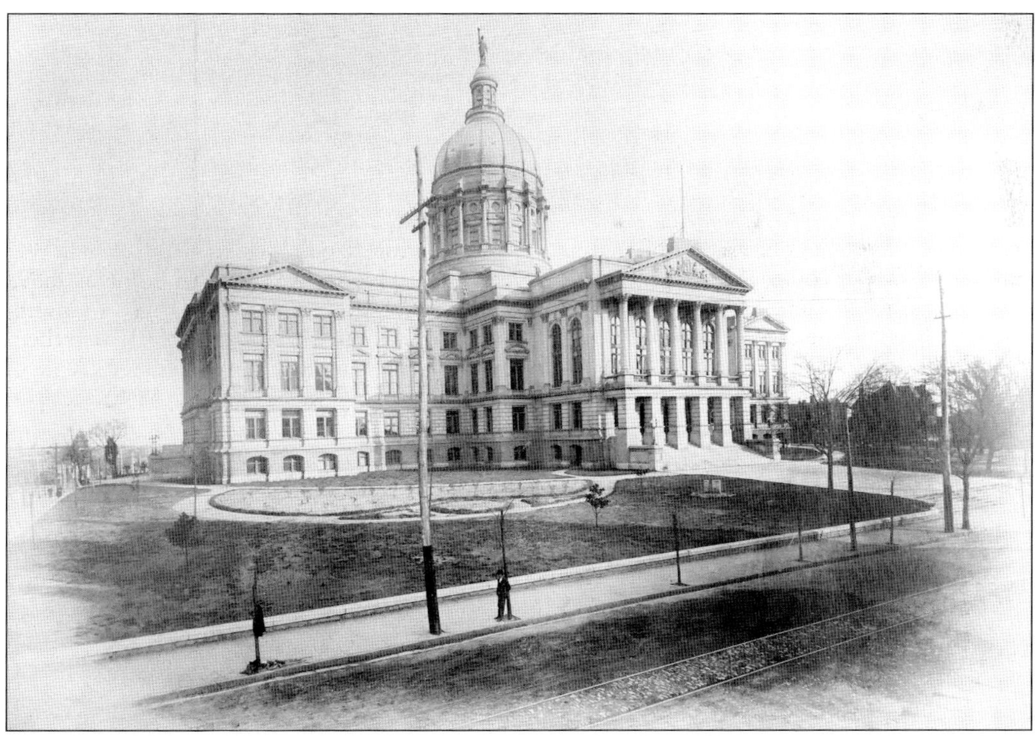

The finished capitol measured 347 feet from north to south through its center and 272 feet, 8.5 inches from east to west through the portico entrance. The ground floor covered an entire acre of the five-acre plot of land designated Capitol Square. From the basement to the top interior of the 48-foot-wide dome measured 172 feet. (Judith Vanderver Photography.)

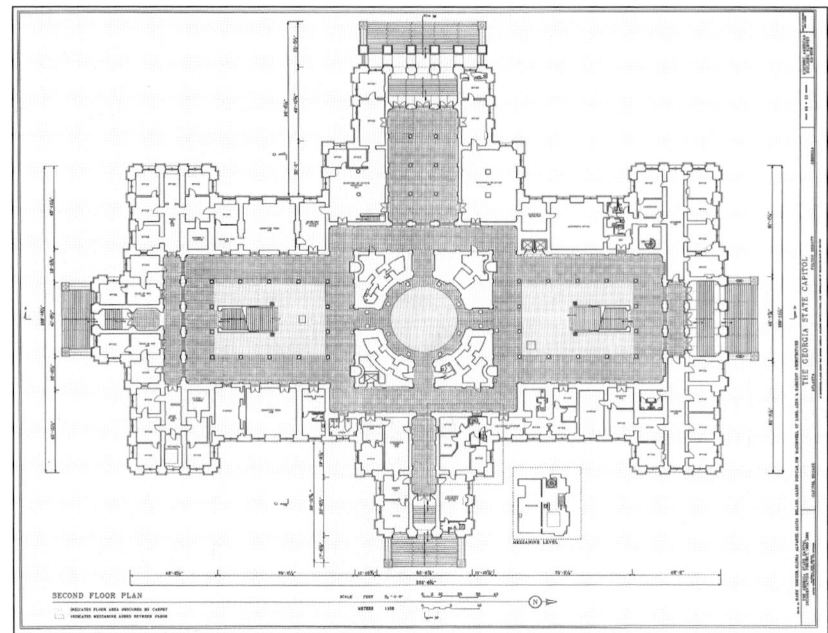

These architectural drawings are part of a series of documents submitted to a 1996 Historic American Buildings Survey. Above is the second floor, which was considered the main floor. After the capitol opened for business and to the public in 1889, most would enter through the west entrance, at the top of the diagram. The shaded areas depict the multistoried open areas such as the north and south atria and the dome at the center. The third-floor plan below shows the contrasting sizes of the chambers of the Senate and the House of Representatives. Both chambers were two stories in height to allow a gallery to sit above and observe the debates. Although the general layout of the building is four rectangles surrounding a central square, none of the arms mirror one another and all have their own distinct sizes and features. (Both, LOC.)

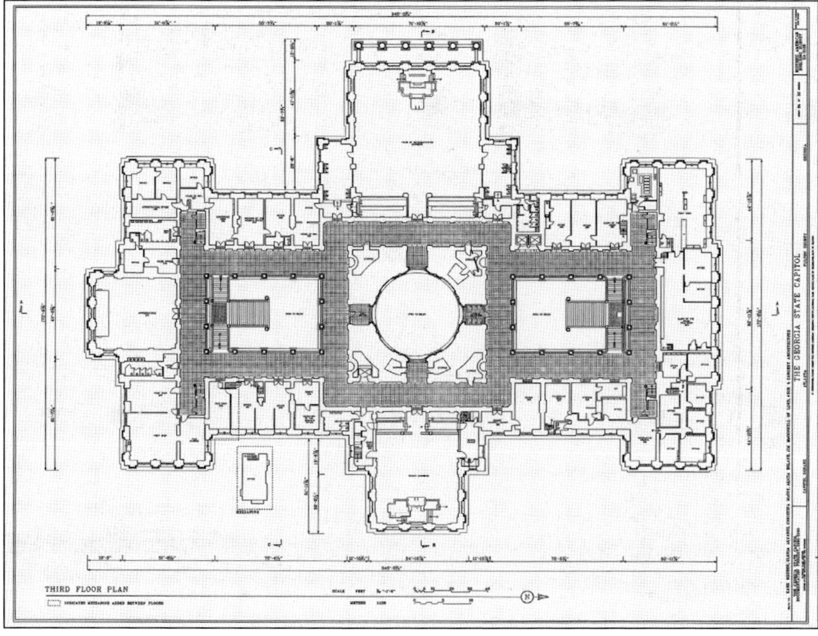

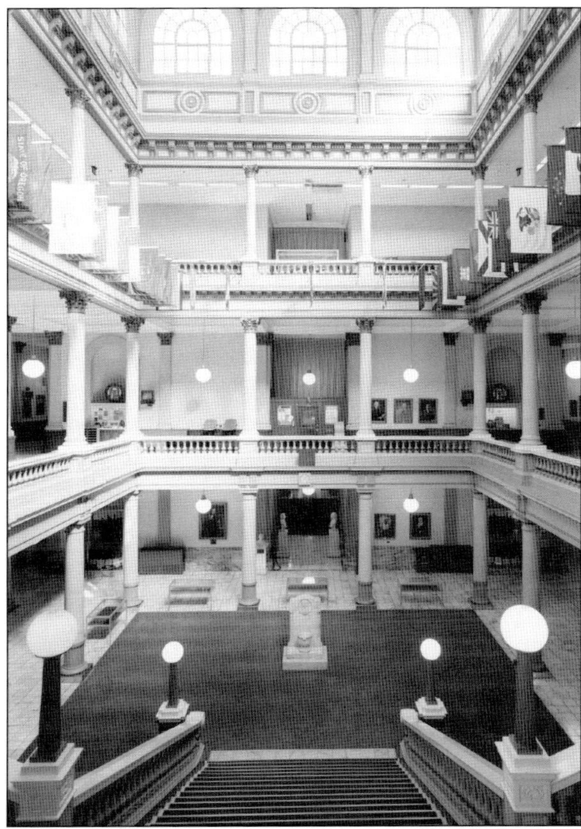

During the day, the capitol is generally filled with natural light through large, flowing, galleried lobbies. The north and south wings both feature what were referred to as light shafts. Each of the wings has large rectangular shafts that measure 50 feet wide by 70 feet long and 12 feet high on the roof of the capitol, sitting on either side of the rotunda, which is also open. The walls of the roof shafts have a series of windows that allow light to pass through to three lower floors. The configuration of the shafts over the two largest wings helps optimize the use of natural light throughout the day. (Both, LOC.)

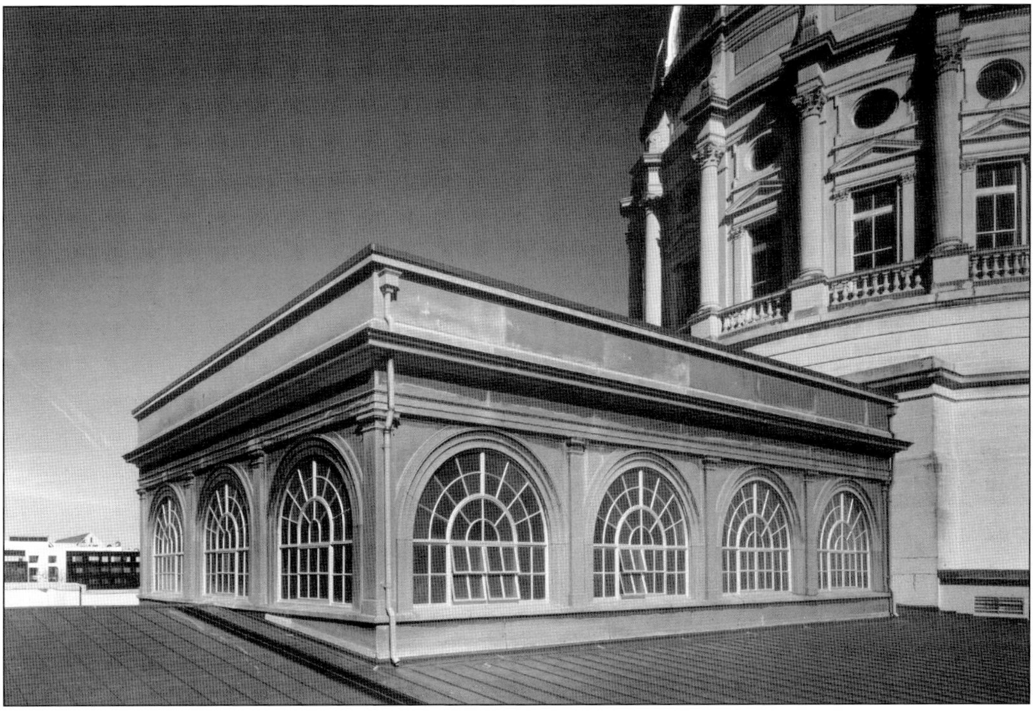

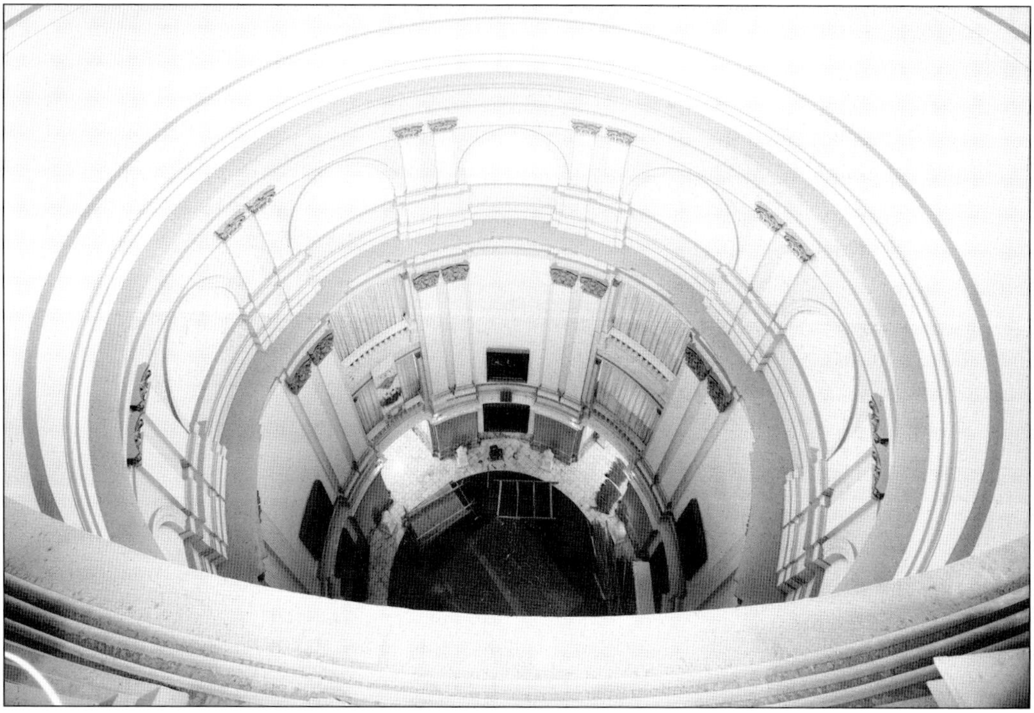

The rotunda at the center of the Georgia State Capitol is three stories high, soaring 172 feet above the main floor. The round vault is surrounded by clerestory windows, with the dome itself rising 75 feet above the level of the roof. Though originally designed to be constructed of stone, plans changed to save money. Metal-clad brick walls were used instead to form the dome and then covered with metal and painted to look like stone. (LOC.)

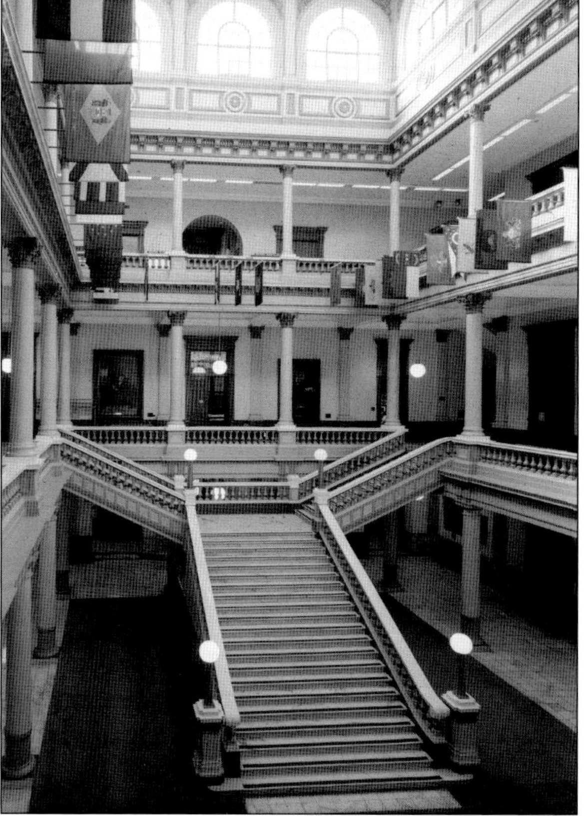

The open east and west arms of the building each feature sweeping marble staircases leading from the main floor to the second- and third-floor galleries. These two floors feature a colorful contrast of four-foot-high pink marble wainscoting juxtaposed against the white marble floors. The pink marble is known as Etowah pink or Etowah floris and was supplied by the American Marble Company of Kennesaw, Georgia. (LOC.)

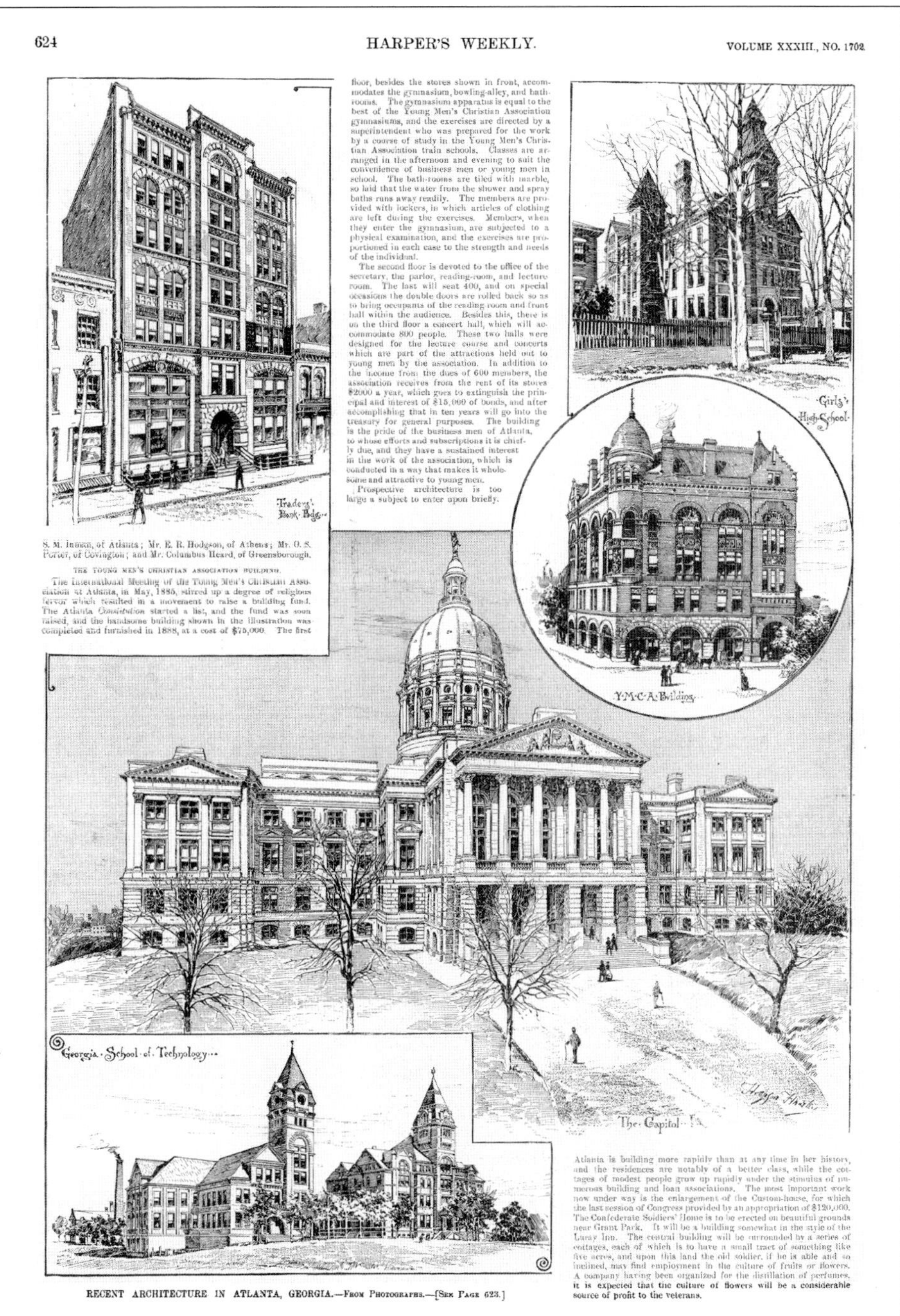

624 HARPER'S WEEKLY. VOLUME XXXIII., NO. 1702.

S. M. Inman, of Atlanta; Mr. E. R. Hodgson, of Athens; Mr. O. S. Porter, of Covington; and Mr. Columbus Heard, of Greensborough.

THE YOUNG MEN'S CHRISTIAN ASSOCIATION BUILDING.

The International Meeting of the Young Men's Christian Association at Atlanta, in May, 1885, stirred up a degree of religious fervor which resulted in a movement to raise a building fund. The Atlanta *Constitution* started a list, and the fund was soon raised, and the handsome building shown in the illustration was completed and furnished in 1888, at a cost of $75,000. The first floor, besides the stores shown in front, accommodates the gymnasium, bowling-alley, and bath-rooms. The gymnasium apparatus is equal to the best of the Young Men's Christian Association gymnasiums, and the exercises are directed by a superintendent who was prepared for the work by a course of study in the Young Men's Christian Association train schools. Classes are arranged in the afternoon and evening to suit the convenience of business men or young men in school. The bath-rooms are tiled with marble, so laid that the water from the shower and spray baths runs away readily. The members are provided with lockers, in which articles of clothing are left during the exercises. Members, when they enter the gymnasium, are subjected to a physical examination, and the exercises are proportioned in each case to the strength and needs of the individual.

The second floor is devoted to the office of the secretary, the parlor, reading-room, and lecture room. The last will seat 400, and on special occasions the double doors are rolled back so as to bring occupants of the reading room and front hall within the audience. Besides this, there is on the third floor a concert hall, which will accommodate 800 people. These two halls were designed for the lecture course and concerts which are part of the attractions held out to young men by the association. In addition to the income from the dues of 600 members, the association receives from the rent of its stores $2000 a year, which goes to extinguish the principal and interest of $15,000 of bonds, and after accomplishing that in ten years will go into the treasury for general purposes. The building is the pride of the business men of Atlanta, to whose efforts and subscriptions it is chiefly due, and they have a sustained interest in the work of the association, which is conducted in a way that makes it wholesome and attractive to young men.

Prospective architecture is too large a subject to enter upon briefly.

Atlanta is building more rapidly than at any time in her history, and the residences are notably of a better class, while the cottages of modest people grow up rapidly under the stimulus of numerous building and loan associations. The most important work now under way is the enlargement of the Custom-house, for which the last session of Congress provided by an appropriation of $120,000. The Confederate Soldiers' Home is to be erected on beautiful grounds near Grant Park. It will be a building somewhat in the style of the Luray Inn. The central building will be surrounded by a series of cottages, each of which is to have a small tract of something like five acres, and upon this land the old soldier, if he is able and so inclined, may find employment in the culture of fruits or flowers. A company having been organized for the distillation of perfumes, it is expected that the culture of flowers will be a considerable source of profit to the veterans.

RECENT ARCHITECTURE IN ATLANTA, GEORGIA.—From Photographs.—[See Page 623.]

An 1889 issue of *Harper's Weekly* carried a feature called "Recent Architecture in Atlanta." While the article spoke of the growing Georgia School of Technology, the new YMCA building, and the Girl's High School, the main focus was on the new Georgia State Capitol. The piece outlined the various features of the building, gushing over the fine furnishing. But it focused a great deal on what it reported to be "a matter of general regret among Georgians." Old questions were again raised about why Indiana limestone was brought in to construct the capitol when "exquisite" Georgia marble and granite was so readily available nearby. (Georgia Historical Society.)

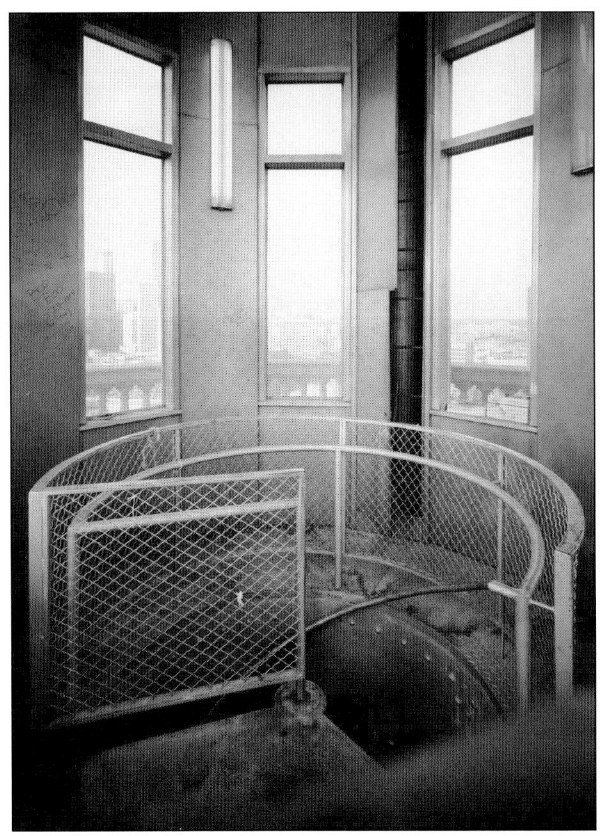

For decades, visitors were allowed to climb to the top of the dome and look out over the city. This was a daunting task, involving not only climbing the four stories to the base of the rotunda, but then negotiating a small spiral staircase to the top of the cupola. The payoff was a 360-degree view of Atlanta. In all, visitors had to navigate three sets of stairs with 232 steps. Still, climbing to the top of the dome proved to be a popular attraction with as many as 400 people a day making the ascent. In the photograph below taken from the cupola, the Georgia Railroad freight depot is in the foreground next to the Union Depot with the Kimball House Hotel in the distance farther along the tracks. (Left, LOC; below, AHC.)

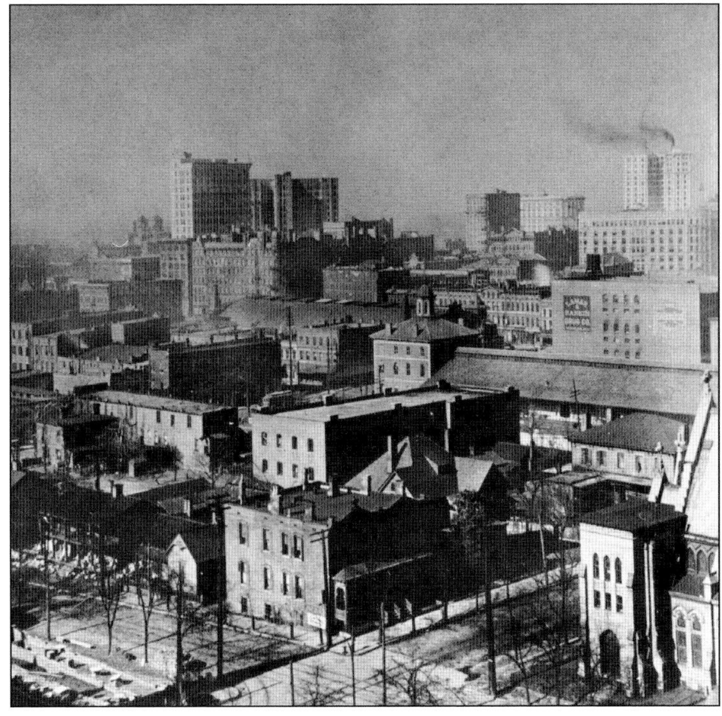

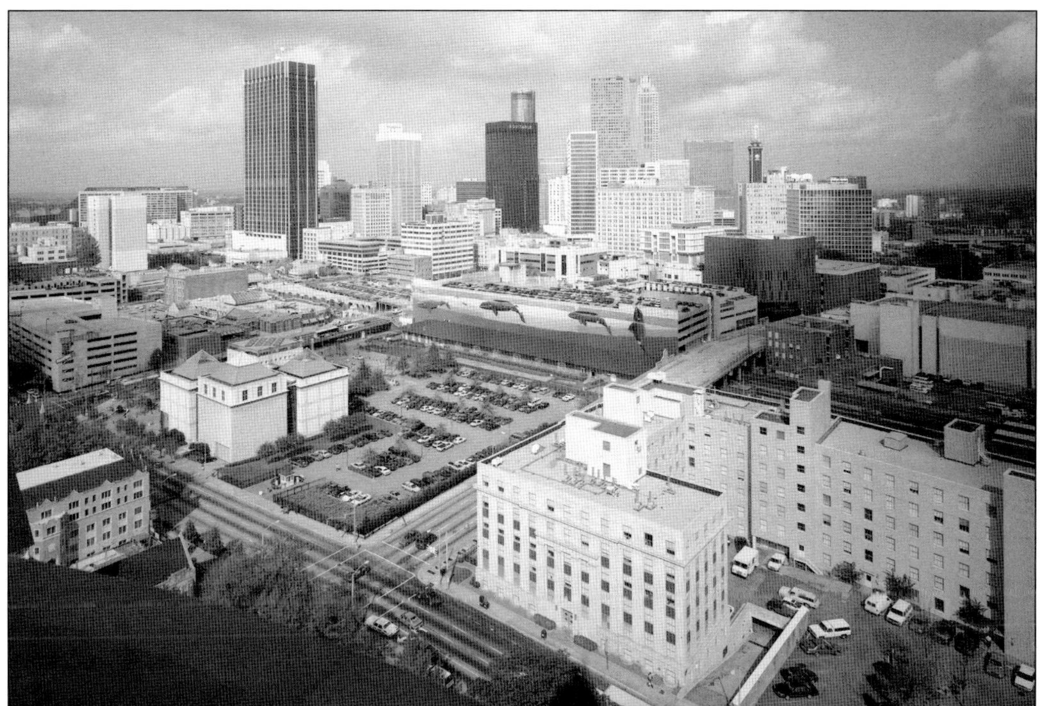

More than 100 years later, this would be the view that visitors to the dome would get if they were still allowed to make the climb. Tours were discontinued in the early 1900s for safety reasons. The Georgia Railroad freight depot's distinctive long building is still visible in this 1996 photograph, although the depot's cupola was destroyed by fire in 1935. (LOC.)

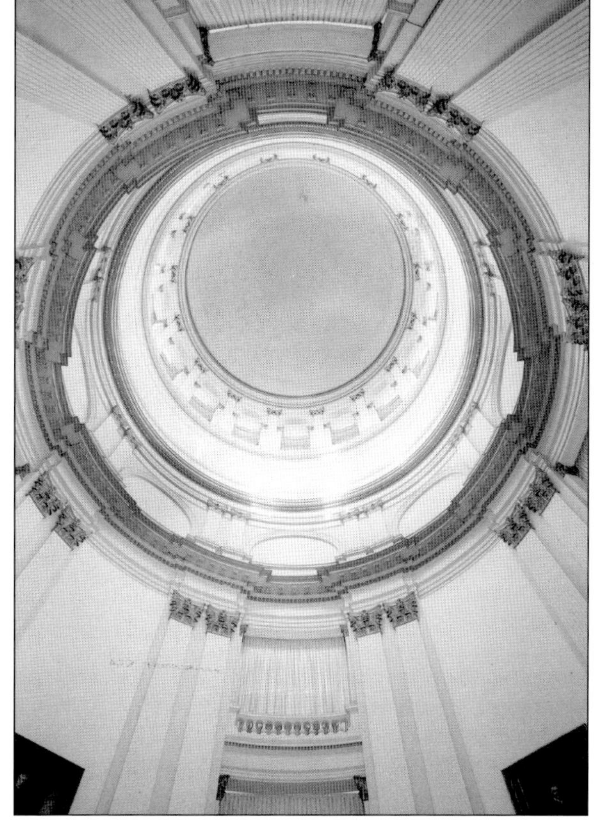

Capitol commissioners had considered painting the rotunda with an elaborate mural. In another effort to stay within budget, the idea was scrapped. They opted instead to use paint and lighting to accentuate the dome's curvature. Graduated lighting was used, fading from brighter at the base to darker in the center. (LOC.)

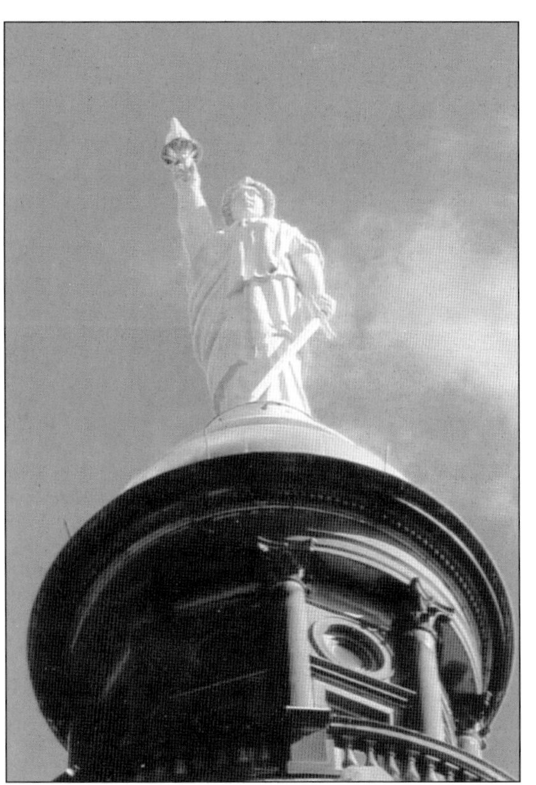

Atop the capitol dome is a 26-foot-tall figure of a woman. Originally called *Goddess of Liberty*, the statue is now known as Miss Freedom. Made of copper, she is painted white and carries a torch in her right hand and a sword in her left. It is unclear if her torch was lit in the early days, although records indicate electric wiring was intended to be run to the torch. (GSA.)

Fires destroyed many of the capitol's construction documents, so there are no details of Miss Freedom's origins or even the engineering it took to put the 1,600-pound statue in place. She was likely created by the W.H. Mullins Company of Salem, Ohio, which later exhibited at Atlanta's 1895 Cotton States and International Exposition. Founded in 1872, the company specialized in statuary with similar composition. A company catalog shows statues bearing a strong resemblance to Miss Freedom. (Salem Historical Society.)

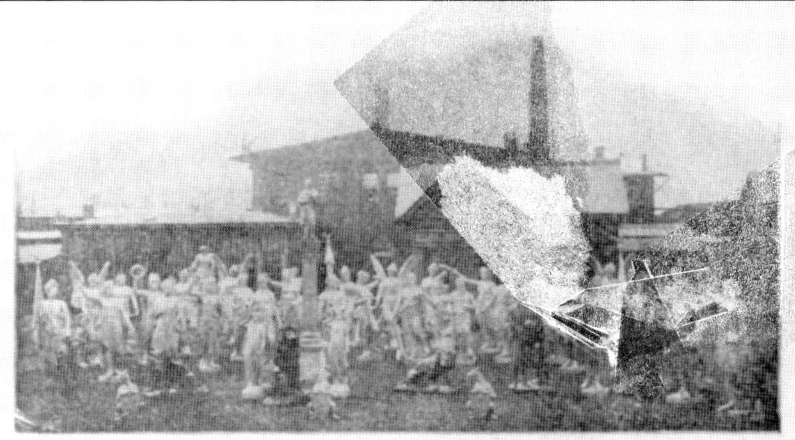

Benjamin Harvey "Ben" Hill (1832–1882) was a lifelong politician who served as a member of the Georgia House of Representatives, served in the Civil War, and was later elected to the US Senate. During the Civil War, he became a spokesperson for Confederate president Jefferson Davis. A reported 50,000 people packed the area of what is now Hardy Ivy Park near the capitol when Davis helped unveil a marble statue in Hill's honor on May 1, 1886. (GSA.)

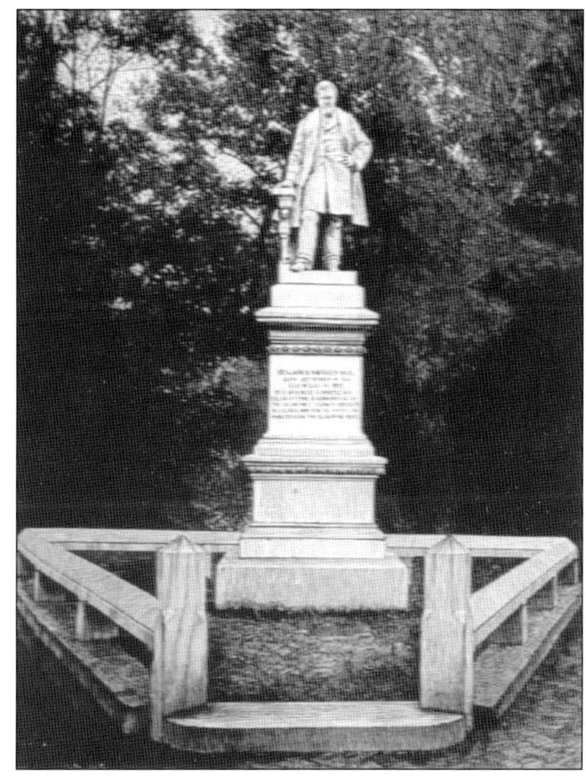

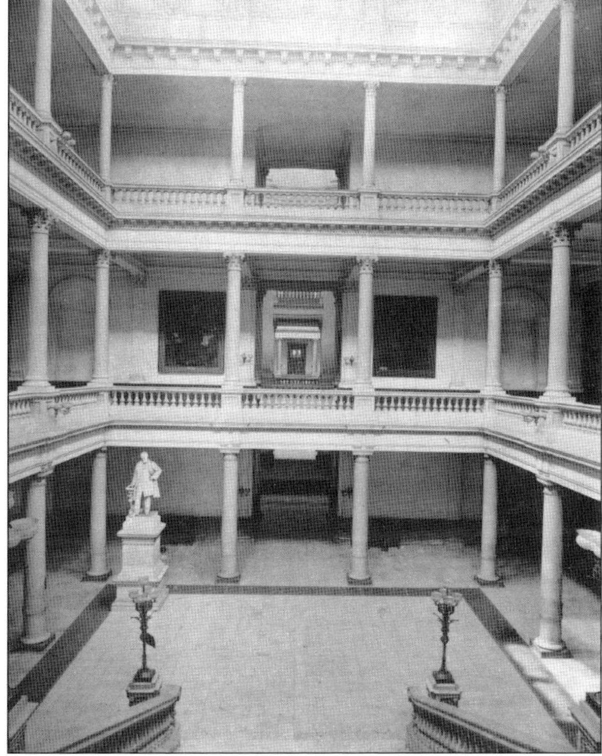

Soon after the state government began its occupancy of the capitol, Gov. John Brown Gordon made a call to move the Hill statue from outdoors to a place of more prominence—the atrium of the capitol. On December 9, 1890, the General Assembly passed a resolution to move the statue. The marble statue was carved by the prominent sculptor Alexander Doyle. (AHC.)

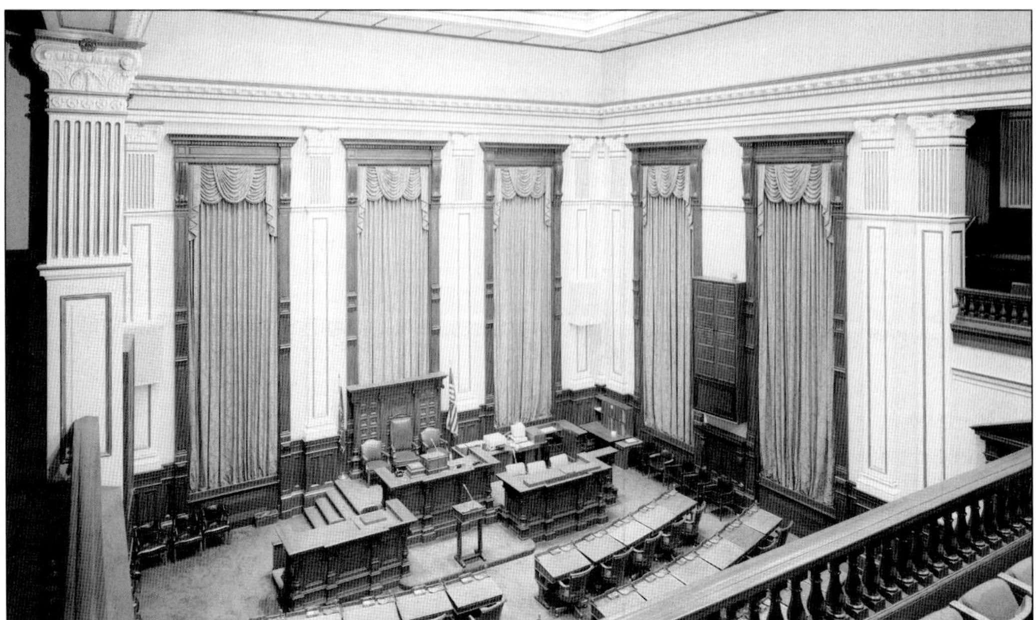

While the public areas in the building were mostly two-toned stone and marble, inside the legislative chambers was another matter. They were extravagant with chandeliers, warm oak panels, and Florentine Renaissance motifs. The new Senate chambers were in the west arm of the capitol and configured much as the old Senate chambers had been. The lawmakers were able to easily find their seats the first day and go right to work. (LOC.)

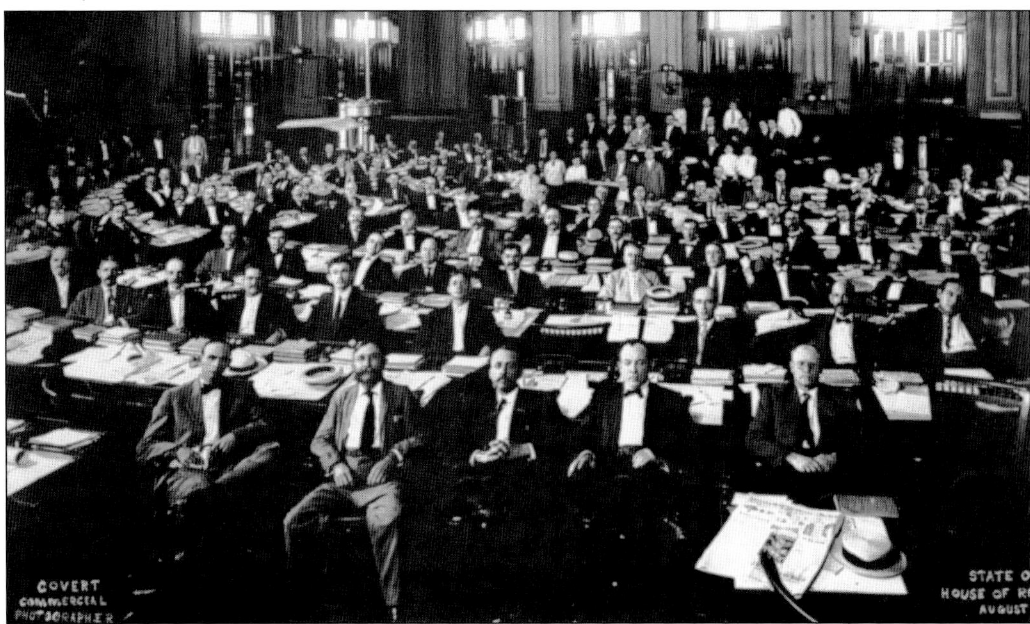

Furniture in both chambers was oak, cherry, and maple to match the finished wood. Each chair could swivel so the members could view any section of the chamber. The Senate chambers featured a paint scheme the *Atlanta Constitution* called "rich and beautiful beyond description" but pointed out it was "less toward the gorgeous than the house." The original furnishings called for 500 spittoons to reduce tobacco stains. (Georgia Building Authority.)

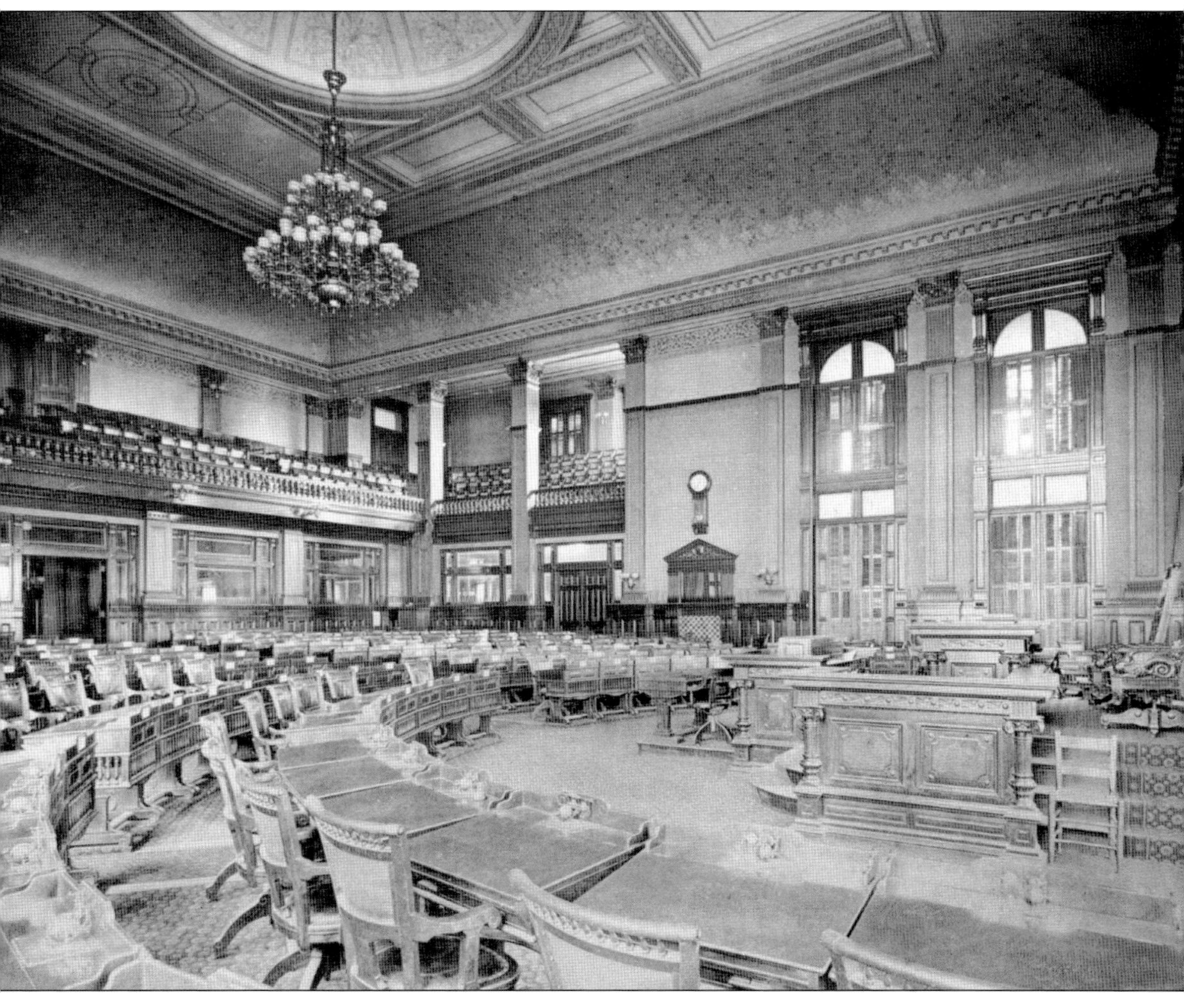

When the House of Representatives took their seats in their new chamber for the first time in July 1889, it was an entirely new configuration. Seat placement in the House chamber was chosen through a lottery system. The well of the House of Representatives, in the east arm, was much larger than the Senate because it had three times as many members. It was also showier, with rich colors of red and gold and a cherry finish to the wood. While the speaker's podium had its own lights, from the dome hung a large chandelier appointed with 90 lights. There was handsome drapery and carpet specified as "best body Brussels." (AHC.)

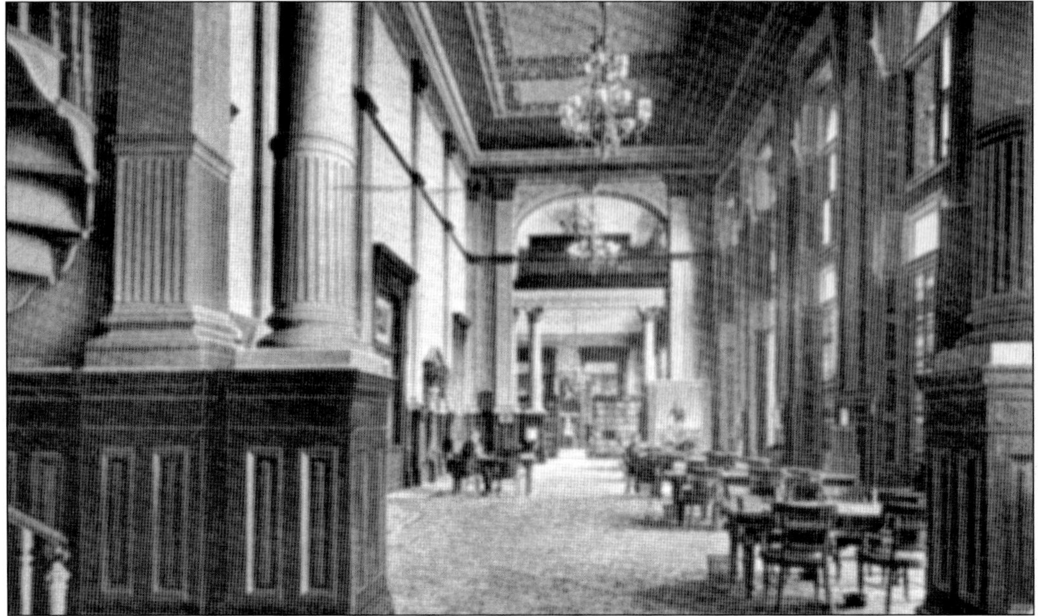

The State Library was a source of pride, celebrated by many as the best law library in the southern states. It contained an estimated 65,000 volumes when it opened. Among the columns were updated editions of law books as well as federal reports and miscellaneous works of government and state documents. It also had copies of Supreme Court of Georgia reports in addition to each state's statutes. (Janice McDonald.)

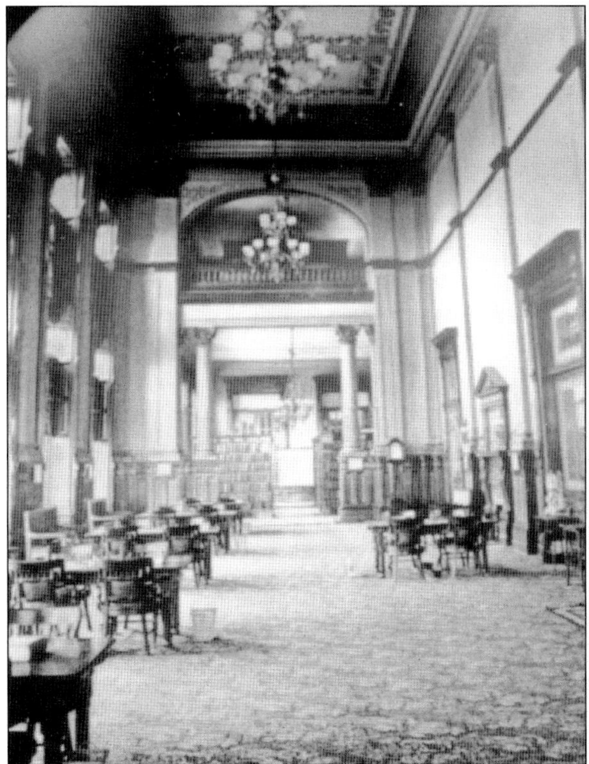

Located off the north atrium, the library was 70 feet long and almost 29 feet wide, boasting 39-foot ceilings. By 1914, the state librarian estimated that in addition to the volumes on the shelves, there were another 100,000 stored in the basement. The State Library was removed during the 1956 renovations and the space was divided into three floors. The old location now houses the clerk of the House and the Legislative Council. (Janice McDonald.)

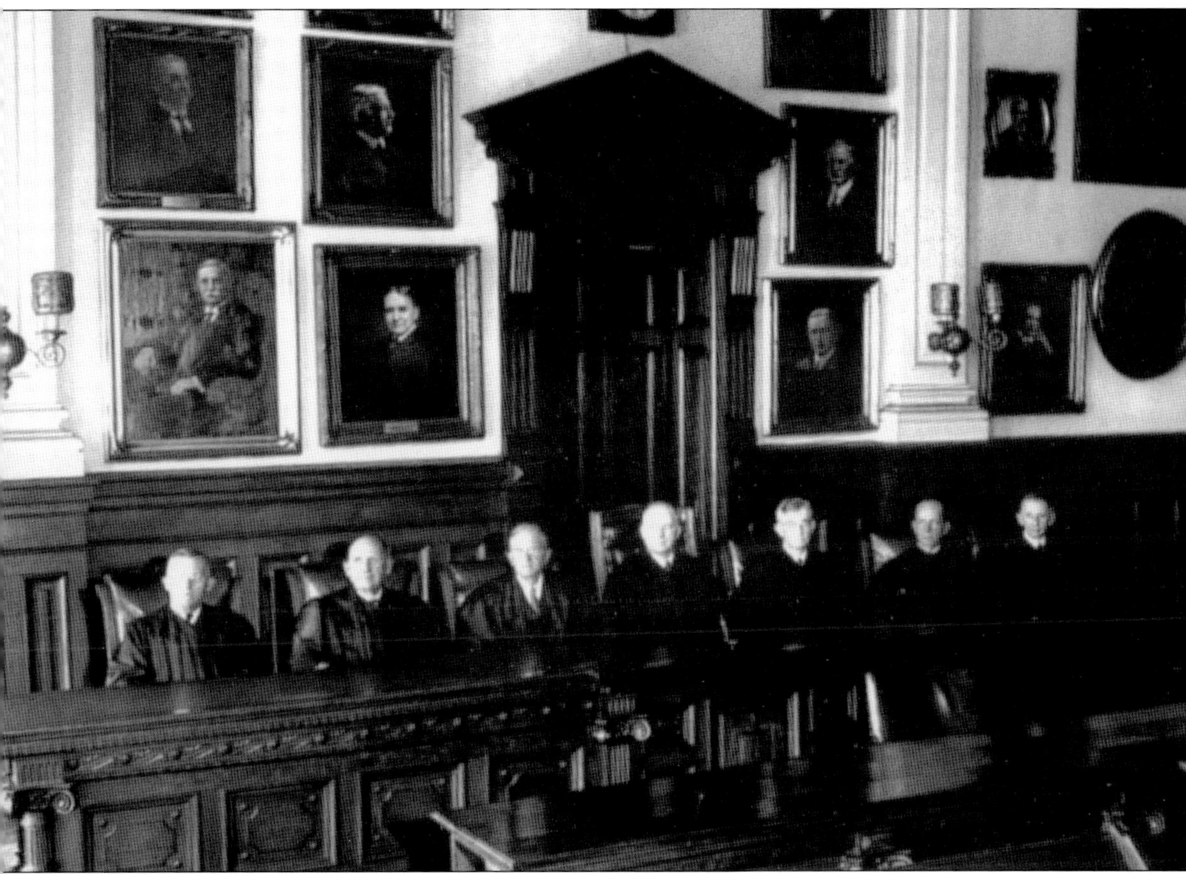

The library was next to the Supreme Court of Georgia to grant easy access. The courtroom was finished in a similar fashion to the library with white oak but also had frescoes much like those of the Senate chamber. Judges sat behind a massive desk on an elevated platform two feet above the floor. The original chamber contained four tables, a reporters' table, and four settees that were 12 feet long and could seat six people each. This photograph is of the justices on the bench in 1949. From left to right are Justice T.S. Candler, Justice W.Y. Atkinson (presiding), Chief Justice W.H. Duckworth, Justice R.C. Bell, Justice T. Grady Head, and Justice J.H. Hawkins. Bell served as chief justice from 1943 to 1946 and was the last person elected by the people as chief justice. (GSA.)

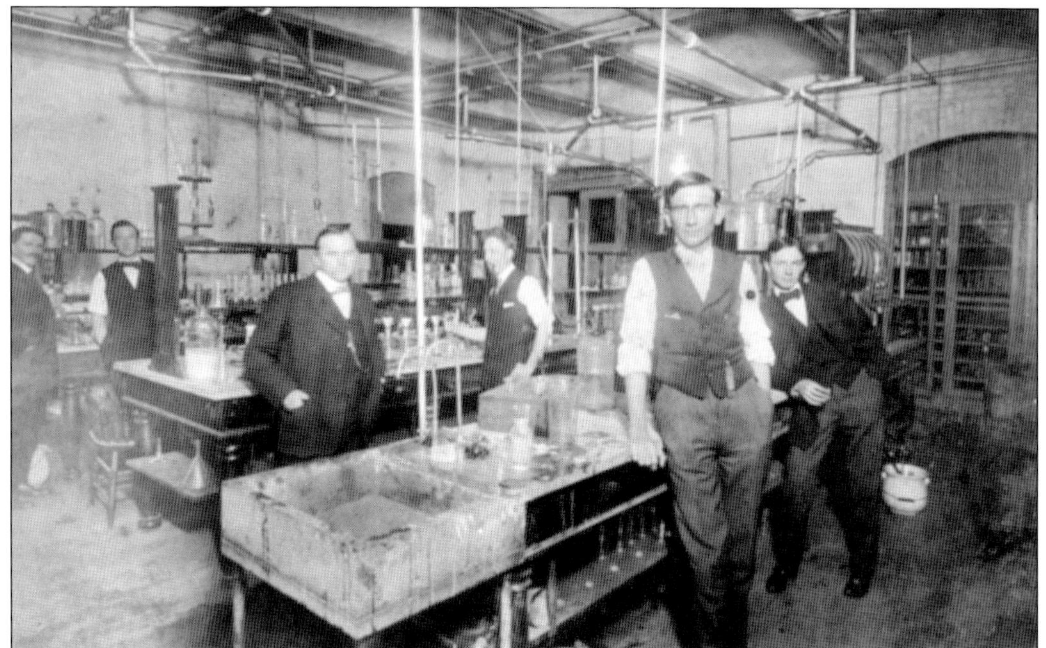

The early capitol also housed laboratories overseen by the Department of Agriculture. This 1908 photograph shows assistant state chemist Samuel Herbert Wilson in front leaning on a lab bench with several unidentified coworkers. A graduate of the Georgia School of Technology, Wilson was hired in 1907 and was elevated to state chemist in 1919. He was also director of the state oil laboratory. (GSA.)

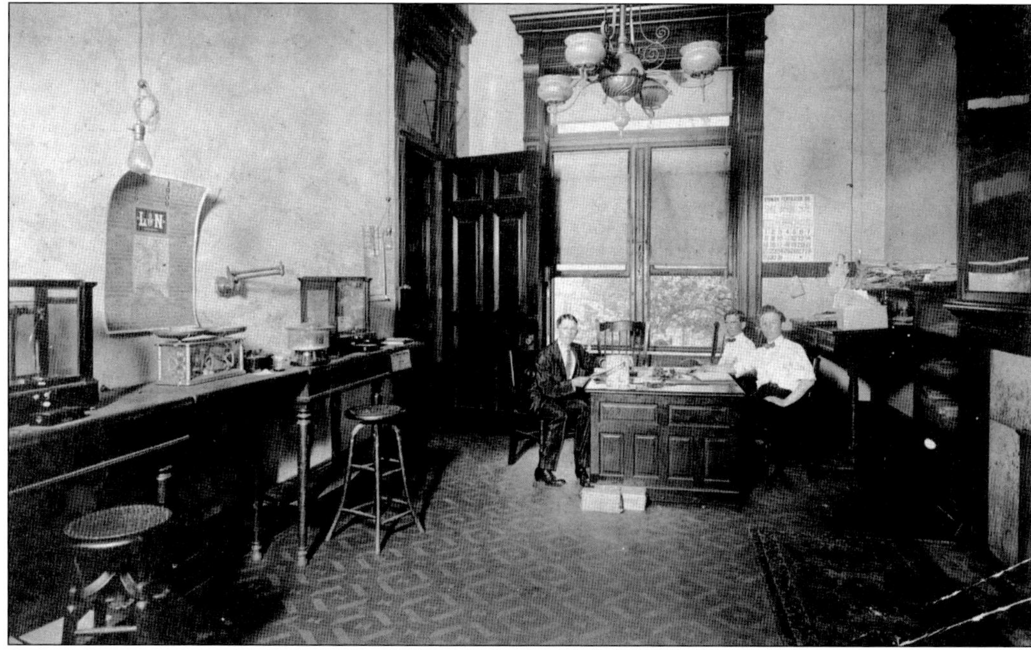

The laboratory and the offices of the state chemist were on the first floor. Dr. R.E. Stallings was the official state chemist when this photograph was taken in 1907. Pictured in the office are, from left to right, Stallings and assistant chemists R.C. Holtzclaw and Samuel H. Wilson. (GSA.)

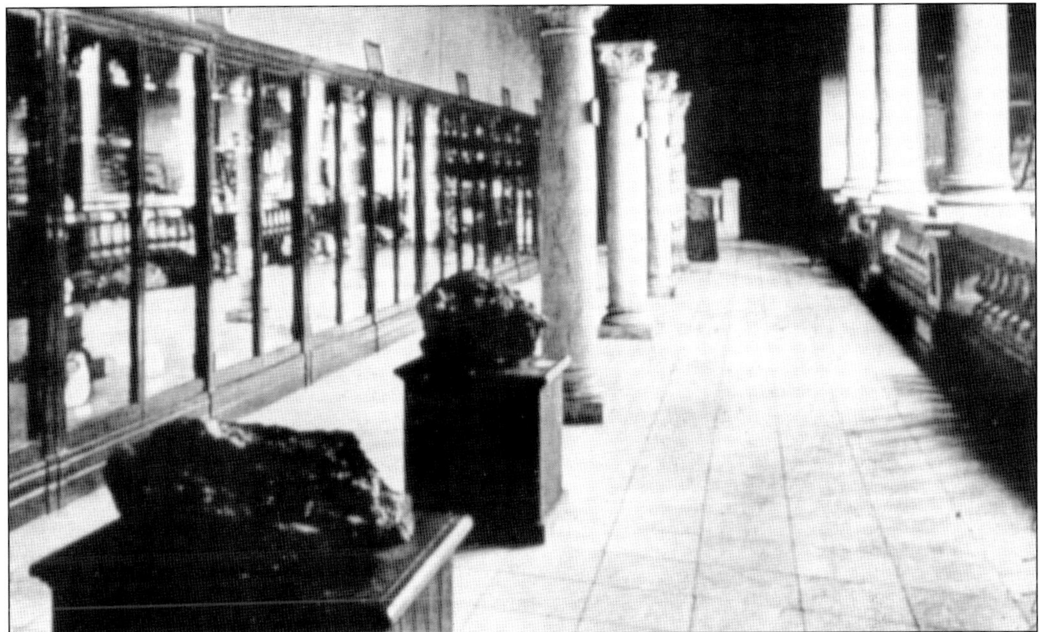

The office of state geologist was resurrected the same year the capitol was completed. The state geologist began a concerted effort to collect and preserve minerals, plants, and soils that could not only show Georgia's scientific and economic resources but would also help keep track of and maintain its natural and cultural history. In 1890, a part of the capitol building was chosen to temporarily house a museum for these collections. (GSA.)

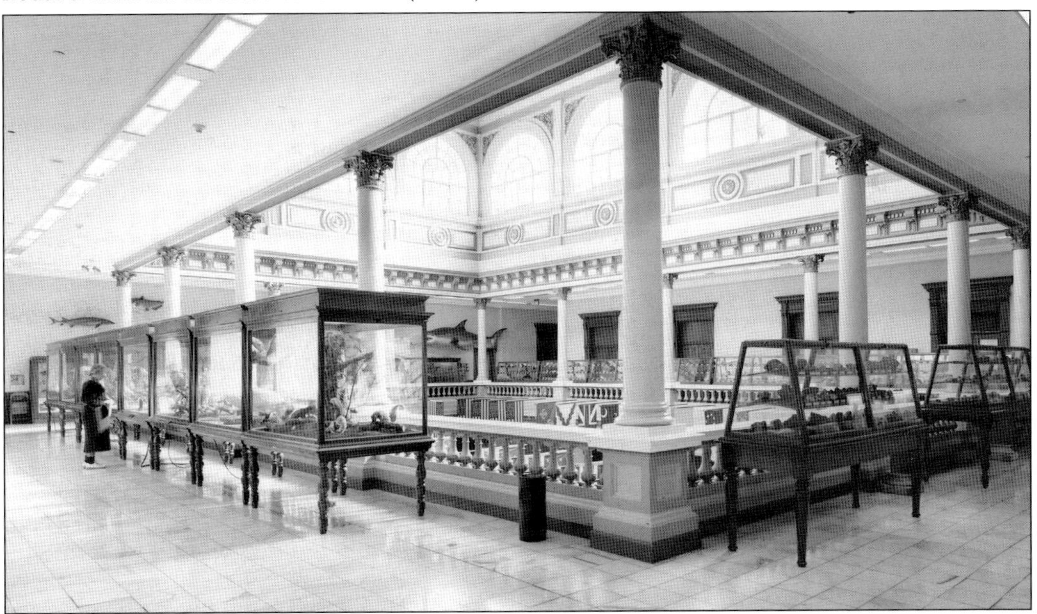

While the museum was originally labeled as temporary, the Georgia Capitol Museum has steadily expanded. In 1955, the General Assembly officially created the Georgia State Museum of Science and Industry, transferring the collections from the hands of the Department of Mines and Mining. The museum's displays are exhibits in the atria of the capitol and include a significant number of artifacts, including original materials, historic flags, and works of art. (LOC.)

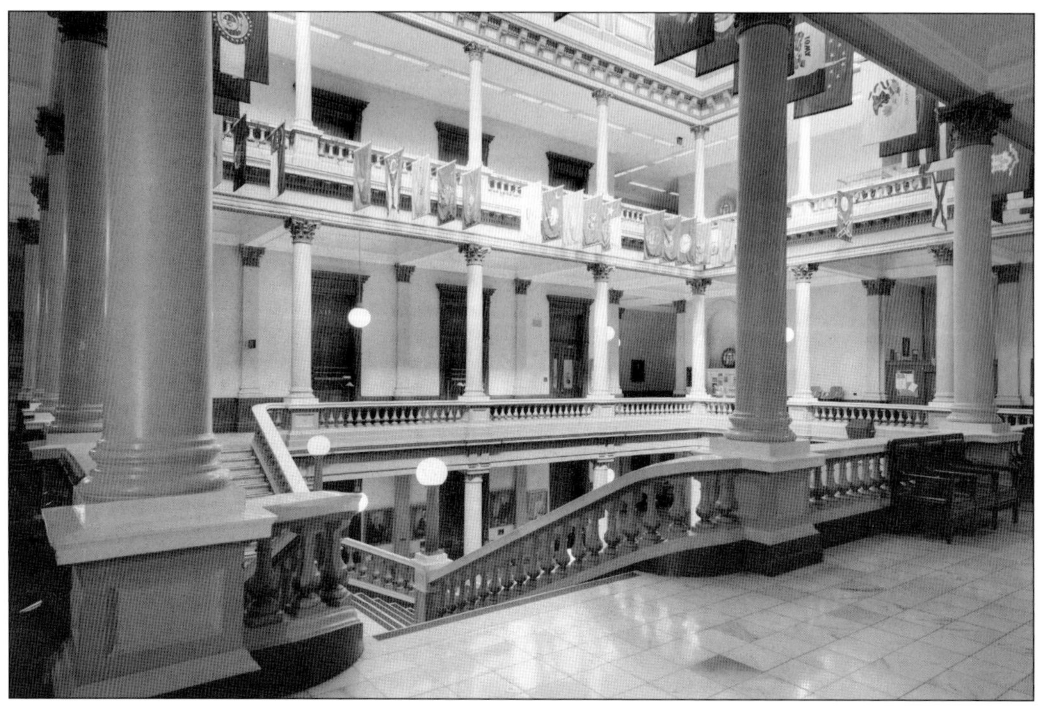

While the columns on the exterior of the building are Indiana limestone, the ones throughout the interior were created using cast-iron forms. The durable columns were then painted to match the marble interior. The Corinthian capitals that form their decorative tops are plaster. (LOC.)

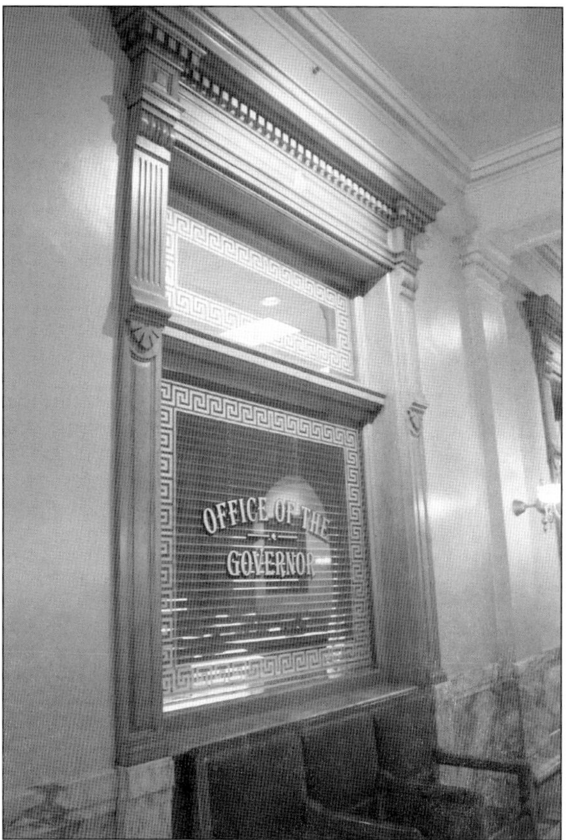

The governor's suite is in the northwest corner of the first floor of the building, near the main western entrance. *Harper's Weekly* described it as "a dream of beauty." The original layout included four offices, a reception area, a vault, and the extravagance of a private lavatory. Having undergone several modernization efforts, which changed its appearance and layout, the exterior now looks much like it did originally. (Janice McDonald.)

For all the planning that went into the capitol itself, the landscaping was less involved. In 1890, a total of $18,000 was appropriated for landscaping, which included walkways, sidewalks, retaining walls, and some plantings. The statues that would later be erected have often been funded through public initiatives. (AHC.)

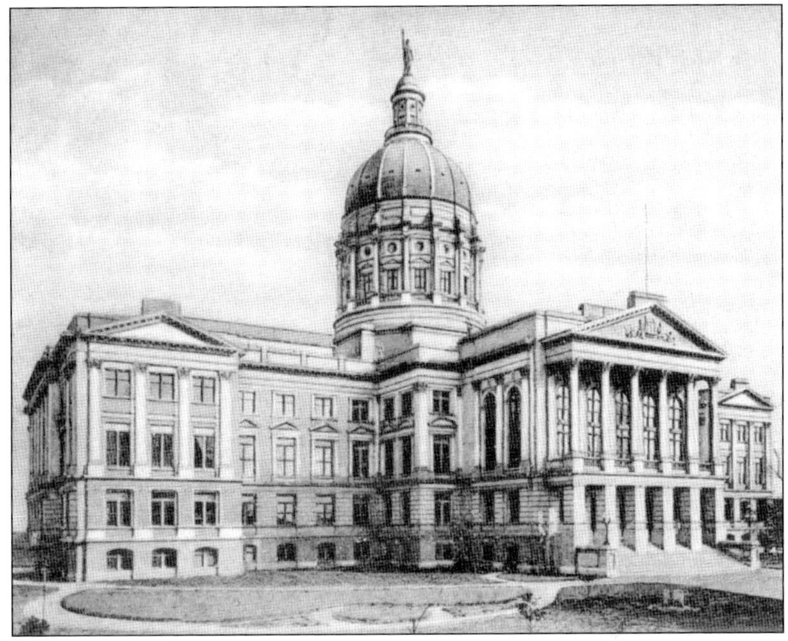

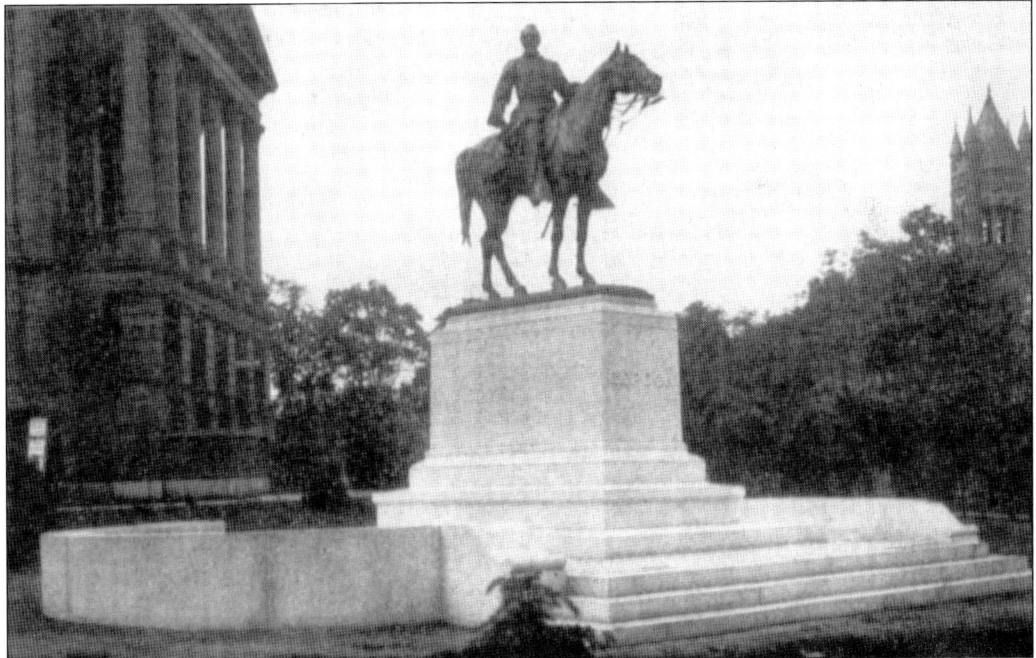

John B. Gordon was governor at the time the capitol was dedicated, and he later served as a US senator. His equestrian statue on the north side of the capitol grounds was unveiled on May 25, 1907. The $25,000 it cost to sculpt and erect it was split between Confederate veterans and an appropriation by an act of the Georgia legislature. The bronze sculpture was created by Solon Borglum, whose brother Gutzon Borglum carved Mount Rushmore. (GSA.)

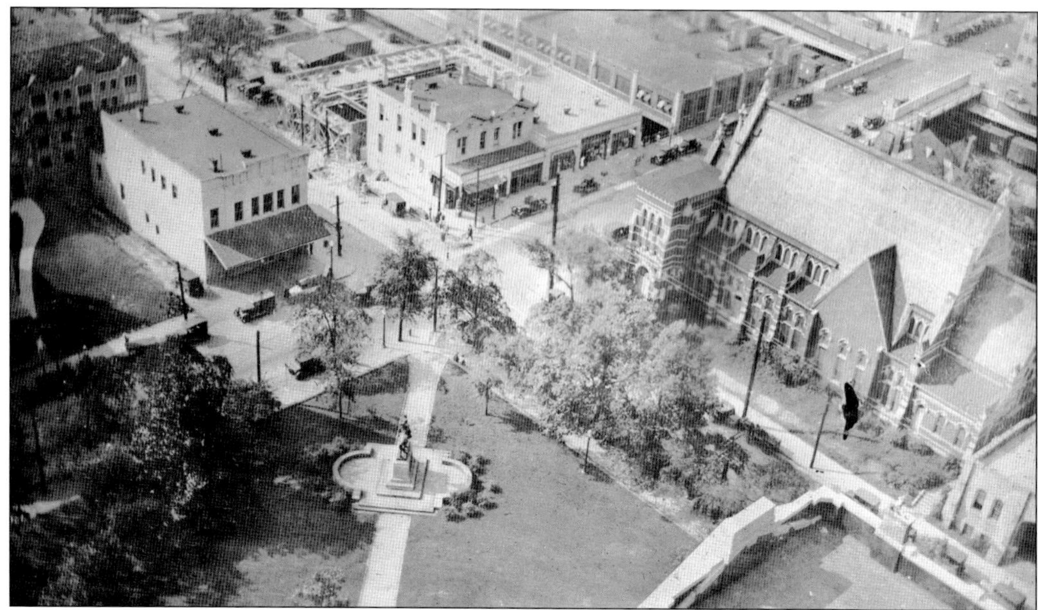

This 1928 photograph taken from the capitol roof shows the neighborhood with the statue of Governor Gordon at center. Trinity Episcopal Church was still at Washington and Hunter Streets, while a store occupied the space later taken over by the expansion of Central Presbyterian Church. Gordon's connection to the Confederacy and his support of the Ku Klux Klan made keeping his statue and his legacy on the grounds a controversial issue. (GSU.)

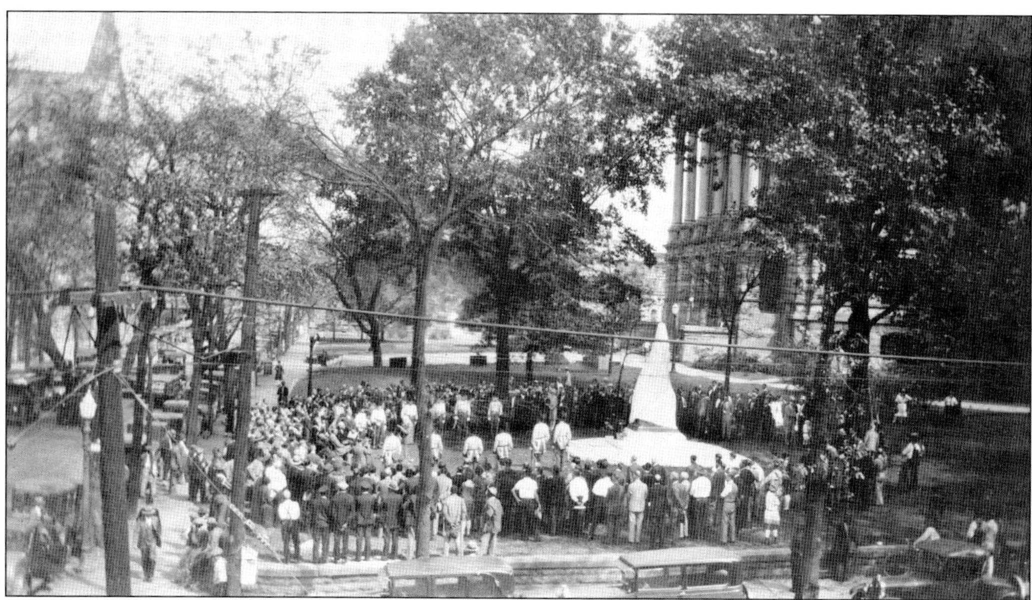

A statue honoring both Joseph E. Brown, Georgia's governor during the Civil War, and his wife, Elizabeth, was unveiled in 1928. Although a firm secessionist during the war, Brown defied many of the Confederacy's wartime policies, including the draft. The statue's position on the southwestern corner of the grounds has it facing the Second Baptist Church, which the Browns helped build and attended. (GSA.)

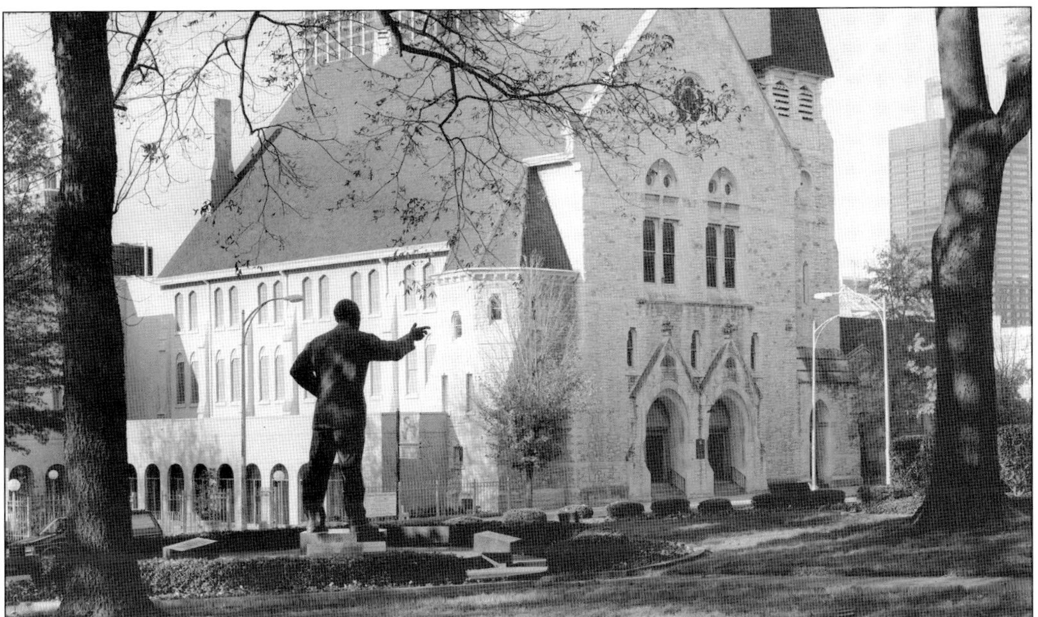

As the years progressed, more memorials began to find their way onto the capitol grounds. In 1975, governor and US senator Richard B. Russell's statue was dedicated on the southwest corner, not far from the Browns. Russell had served briefly as the speaker of the Georgia House of Representatives before running for governor. He left the office after winning a seat in the US Senate. The Russell Senate Office Building in Washington, DC, was named in his honor. (LOC.)

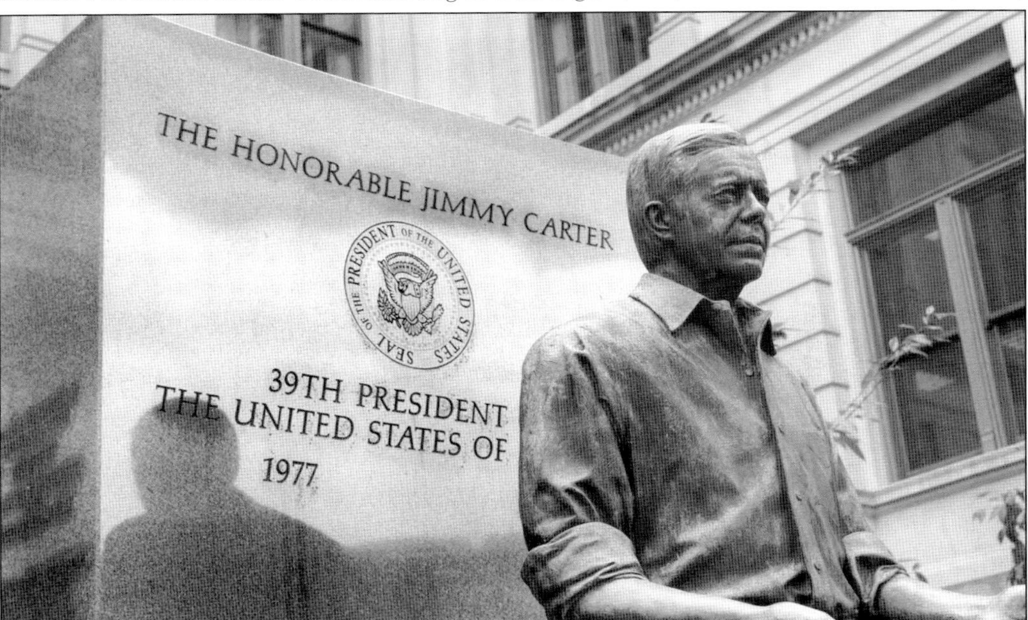

In 1994, a statue honoring Jimmy Carter, the 39th president of the United States, became the eighth statue to be dedicated on the capitol grounds. Located beneath the windows of the governor's office, it depicts the former Georgia governor in a less formal manner with his sleeves rolled up. Inscriptions on the granite benches of the plaza carry tributes to his many accomplishments, including "conservationist," "poet," "global citizen," and "man of faith." (Janice McDonald.)

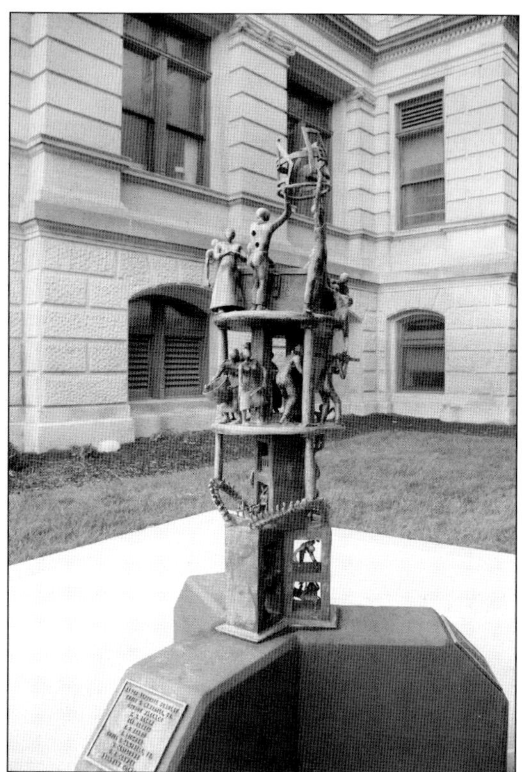

Near the eastern entrance to the capitol is a distinctive monument called *Expelled Because of Color*, erected in March 1976. The statue honors 33 African American legislators who won their seats in the General Assembly during the 1868 election—the first election blacks were allowed to vote in. Though legally elected, the men were expelled from the legislature. The following year, the Supreme Court of Georgia ruled in their favor, and they were reinstated in 1870. (Janice McDonald.)

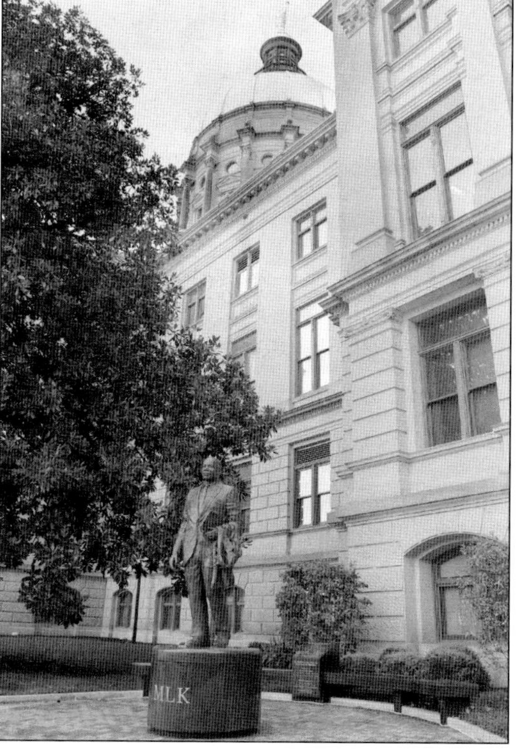

Following the assassination of civil rights leader Dr. Martin Luther King Jr., Gov. Lester Maddox refused to allow Dr. King's body to lie in state at the capitol and denied requests to lower flags to half-staff. In 2017, Dr. King was honored on the capitol grounds with the placement of a statue that overlooks Liberty Plaza. The unveiling took place on August 17, the 54th anniversary of his "I Have a Dream" speech. (Janice McDonald.)

Four

The Capitol Neighborhood

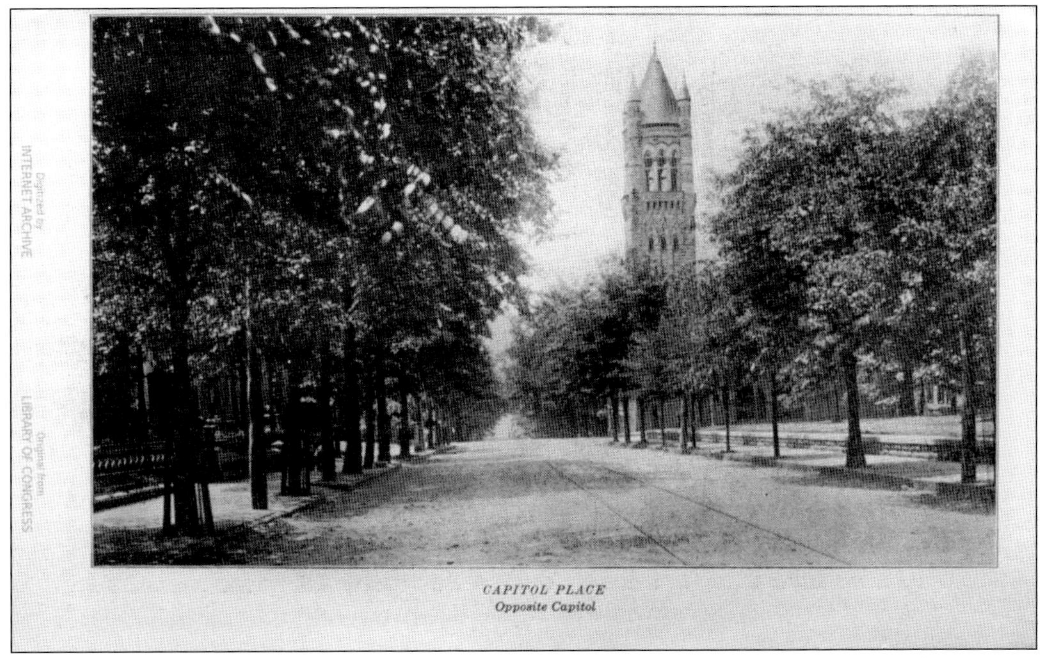

Published in 1907, an illustrated guidebook called *Atlanta Up-to-Date* reported how the city was thriving, including descriptions of the new, tall buildings that had been constructed as well as the beautiful residences of downtown Atlanta. Washington Street and Capitol Avenue skirted the capitol grounds on the east and west and were lauded as "two of Atlanta's oldest residence streets" with "stately and substantial homes." (GSA.)

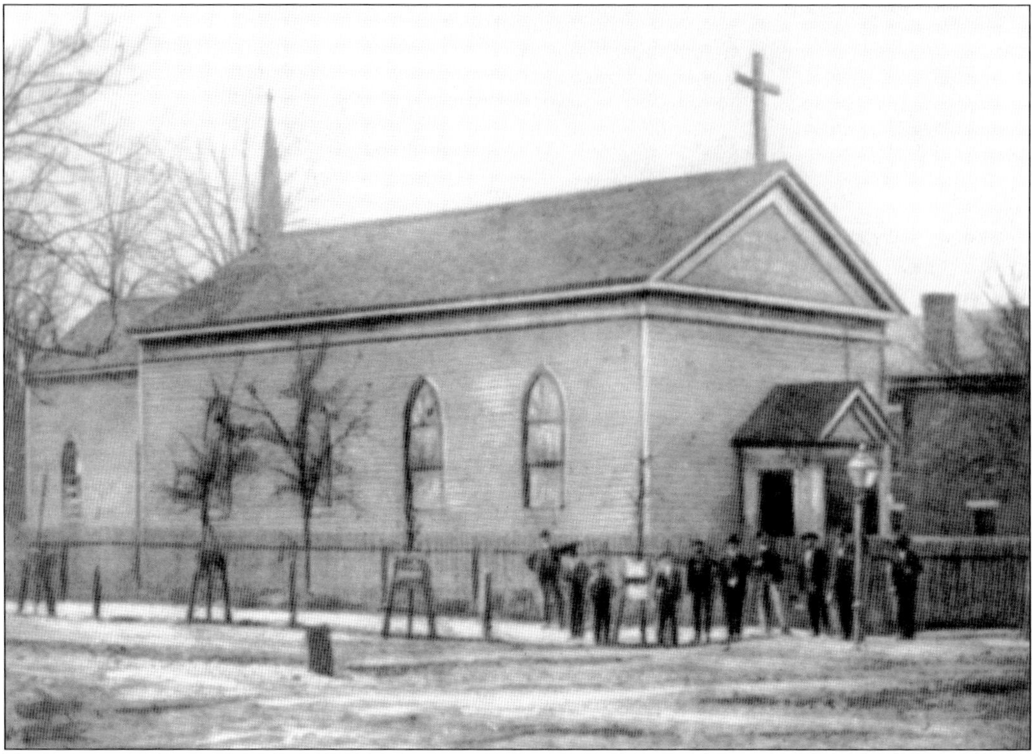

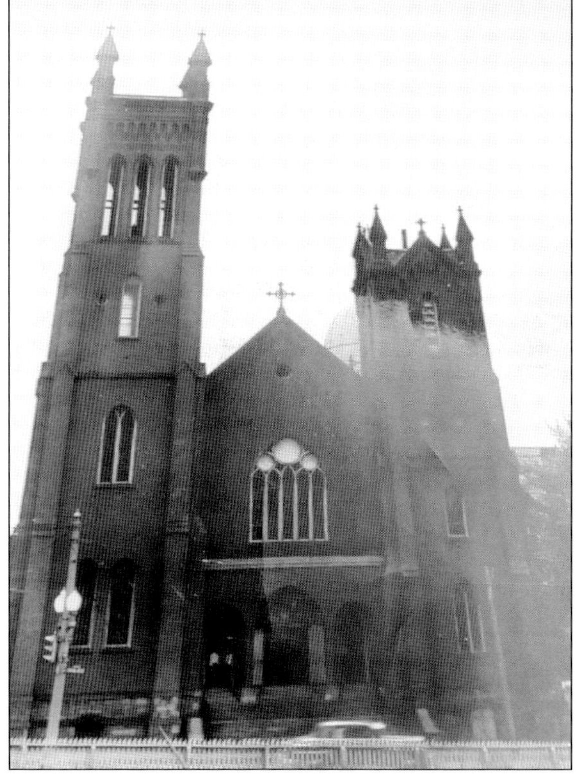

The Church of the Immaculate Conception built its first chapel in 1848 at the corner of Washington and Hunter Streets to help serve the growing Roman Catholic population of Atlanta. During the Civil War, it was used as a hospital. Fr. Thomas O'Reilly is credited with saving all the churches in the city by threatening to excommunicate any Catholic Union soldier involved in destroying the structures. (AHC.)

The Church of the Immaculate Conception survived the war but was damaged. Plans were made for a larger Gothic Revival–style brick structure, which was completed in 1873. Father O'Reilly's body is interred in a crypt beneath the main altar. The church was restored in 1954 and dedicated as the Shrine of the Immaculate Conception in 1958. The oldest church in Atlanta, it was listed in the National Register of Historic Places in 1976. (AHC.)

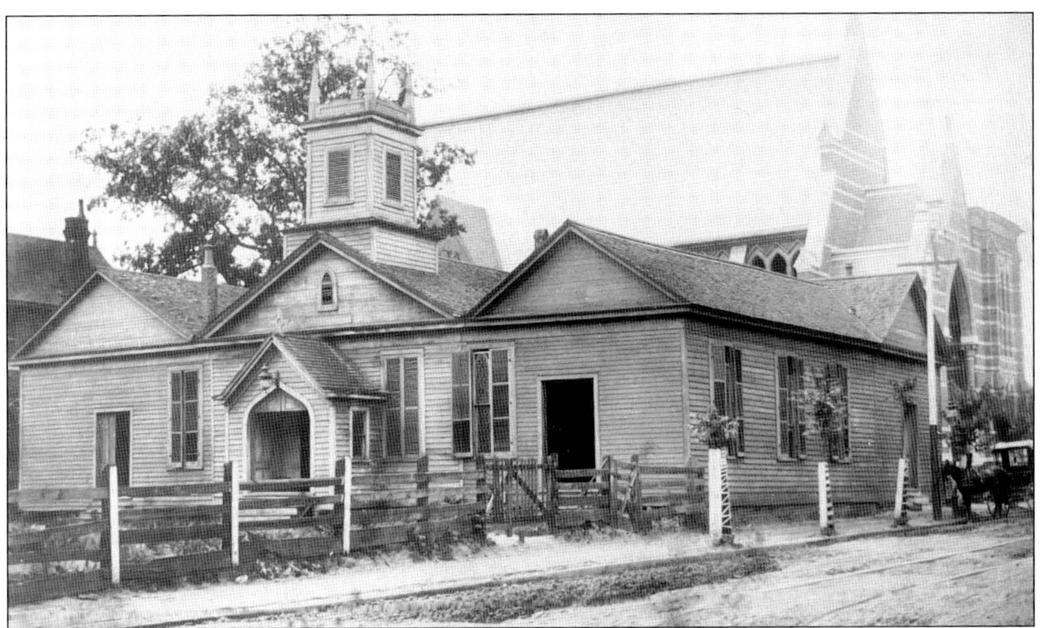

The first St. Philip's Episcopal Church was consecrated in 1848, erecting its first house of worship on the corner of Hunter and Washington Streets, facing Washington. By 1876, it had grown to have the largest Episcopal congregation in Georgia, prompting the 1890s addition of the wings shown here to accommodate the congregants. The St. Philip's property was adjacent to Fire Engine House No. 2, which was next to the Georgia Railroad roundhouse. (St. Philip's Cathedral.)

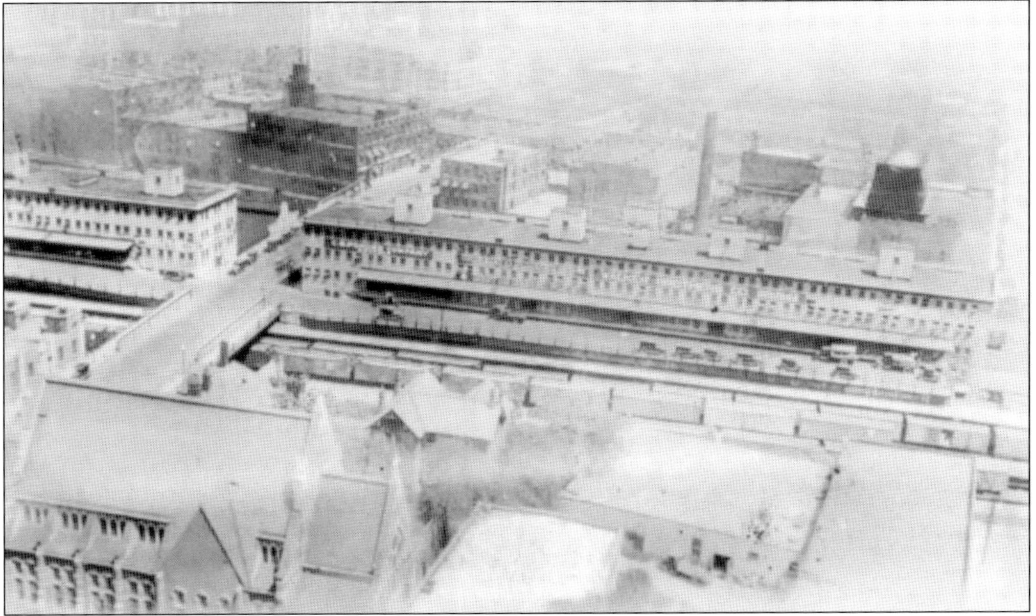

By 1916, when this photograph was taken from the roof of the capitol building, the roundhouse had been demolished and the firehouse moved. The roof of St. Philip's is in the foreground, but there is increased traffic downtown, including more and more automobiles. Washington Street had been elevated onto a bridge over the city's growing railroad gulch, obscuring much of the front of St. Philip's. The congregation ultimately moved in 1933. (AHC.)

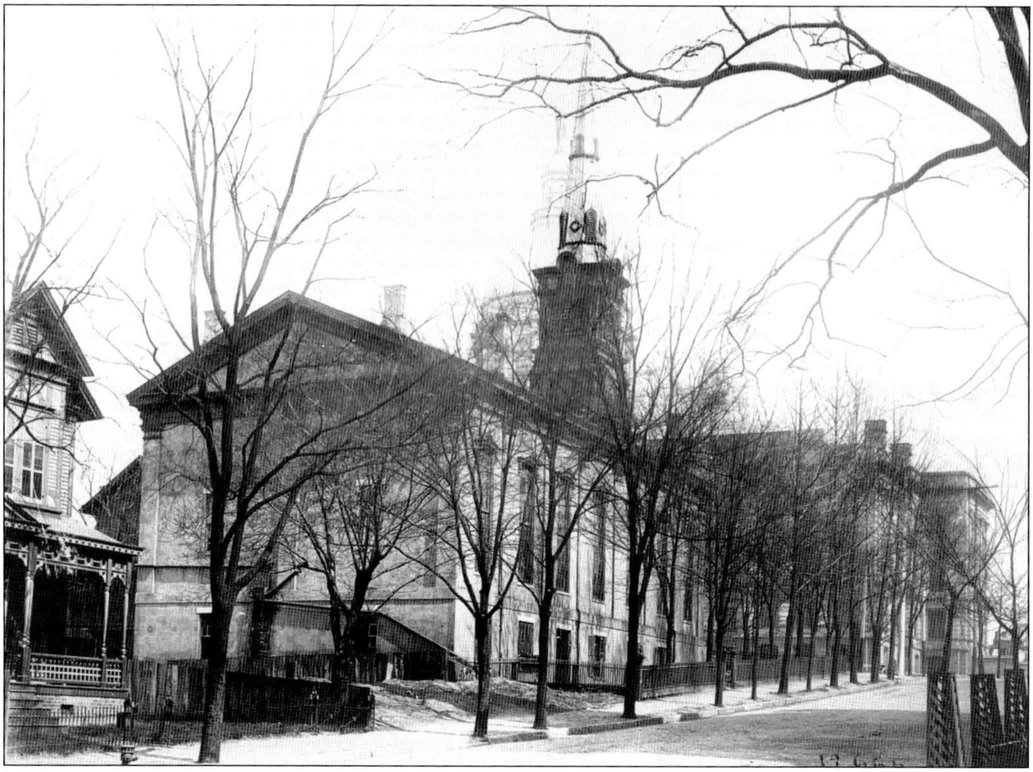

The five-acre square block of the capitol site had churches on three sides. Second Baptist Church was constituted on September 1, 1864. Its 19-member congregation purchased property on the corner of Washington and Mitchell Streets, building their church at a cost of $14,000. Central Presbyterian Church was constructed next door to Second Baptist in 1860. (AHC.)

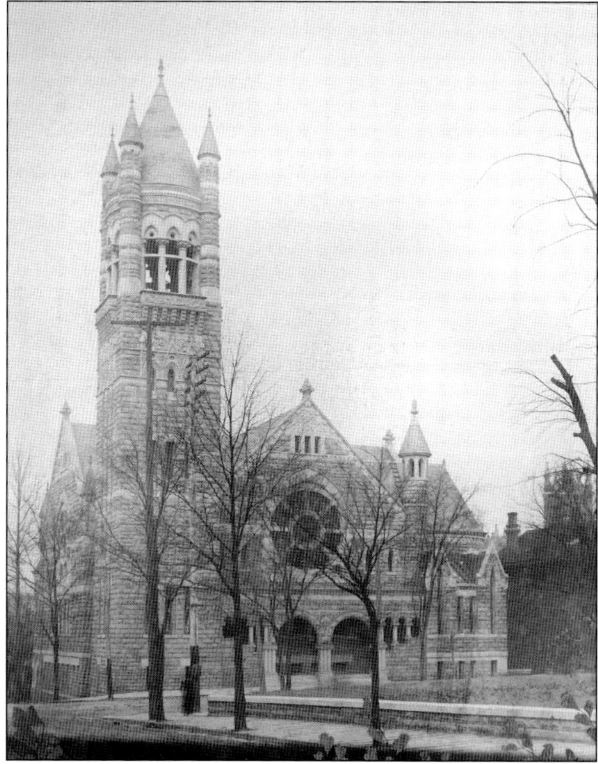

Following the Civil War, both churches expanded their sanctuaries, taking on entirely new looks. Second Baptist Church built a distinctive bell tower that could be seen across the city. The church later updated it. Central Baptist Church took over the property in 1934. After almost a century, the Baptists chose to relocate to the suburbs for more space, selling their lot to the neighboring Central Presbyterian Church in 1960. (Judith Vanderver Photography.)

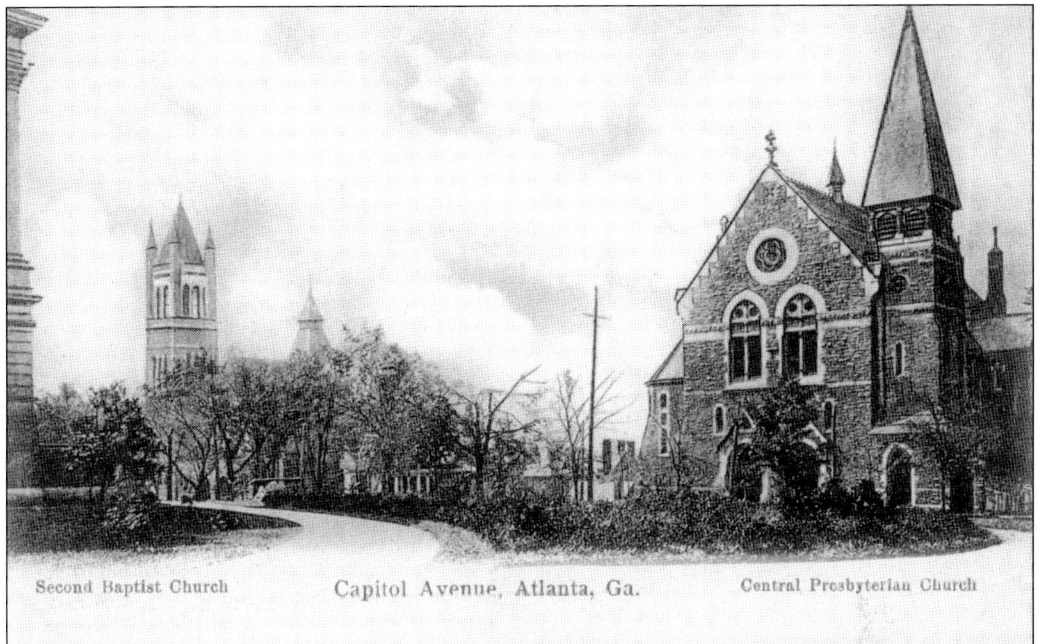

Central Presbyterian Church's present Gothic-style building was dedicated just one month after the capitol's cornerstone was laid in 1885. The building was listed in the National Register of Historic Places in 1986. As Atlanta's residential population shifted away from the increasingly busy downtown area, many churches like Second Baptist and St. Philip's followed their members to the suburbs. Central Pres, as it was called, began referring to itself as "the church that stayed." (Janice McDonald.)

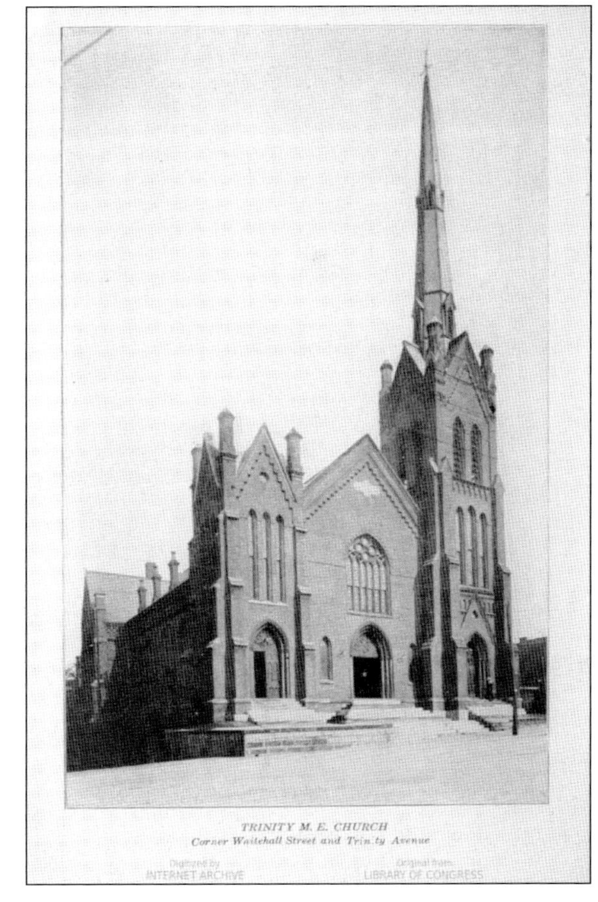

Trinity United Methodist Church was first founded in Atlanta in 1853, eventually erecting a church on Mitchell Street directly across from city hall on a site now occupied by the Georgia Department of Transportation building. This illustration shows the second church, which was on the corner of Whitehall and Peters (now Trinity Avenue) Streets. In 1912, Trinity moved again, this time a block away to the corner of Washington and Peters Streets. (GSA.)

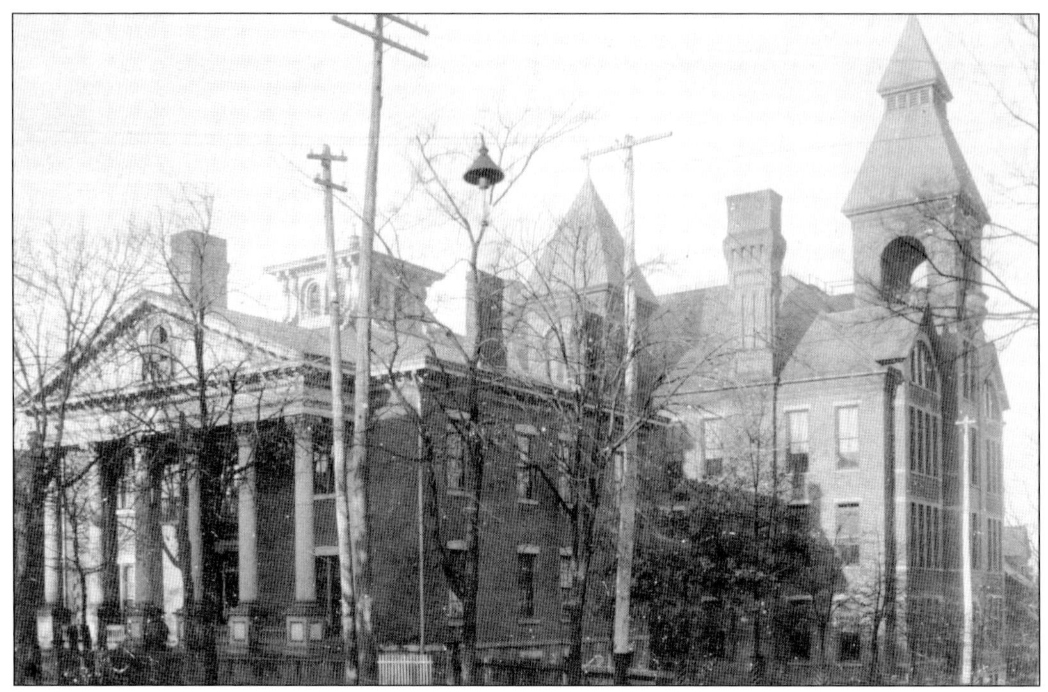

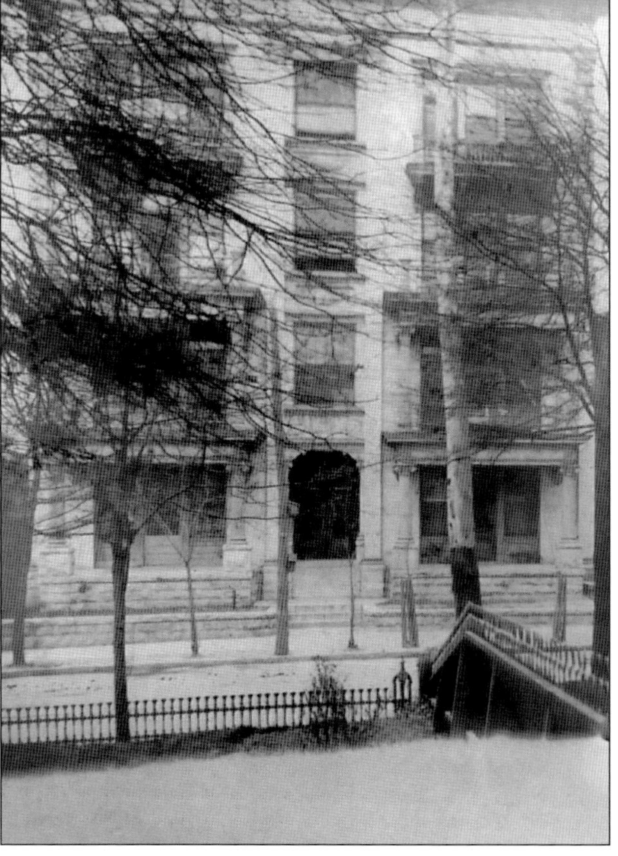

Across Mitchell Street from Second Baptist Church on the corner of Mitchell and Washington Streets was Girl's High School. Part of Atlanta's original public school system, it opened in 1872 in the former Neal mansion, seen here on the left. Of the seven Atlanta Public Schools created, this was the only one exclusively for girls. The demand for more female education prompted an expansion, requiring the addition of a much larger building on Mitchell Street adjacent to the mansion. (Janice McDonald.)

Next door to the Girl's High School at 87 Washington Street was the Tallulah Apartment building. The four-story building had been a large private home and was converted to what was considered one of downtown's better apartment accommodations. Most of the tenants worked nearby and were professionals such as clerks, lawyers, and even some small company presidents. (Janice McDonald.)

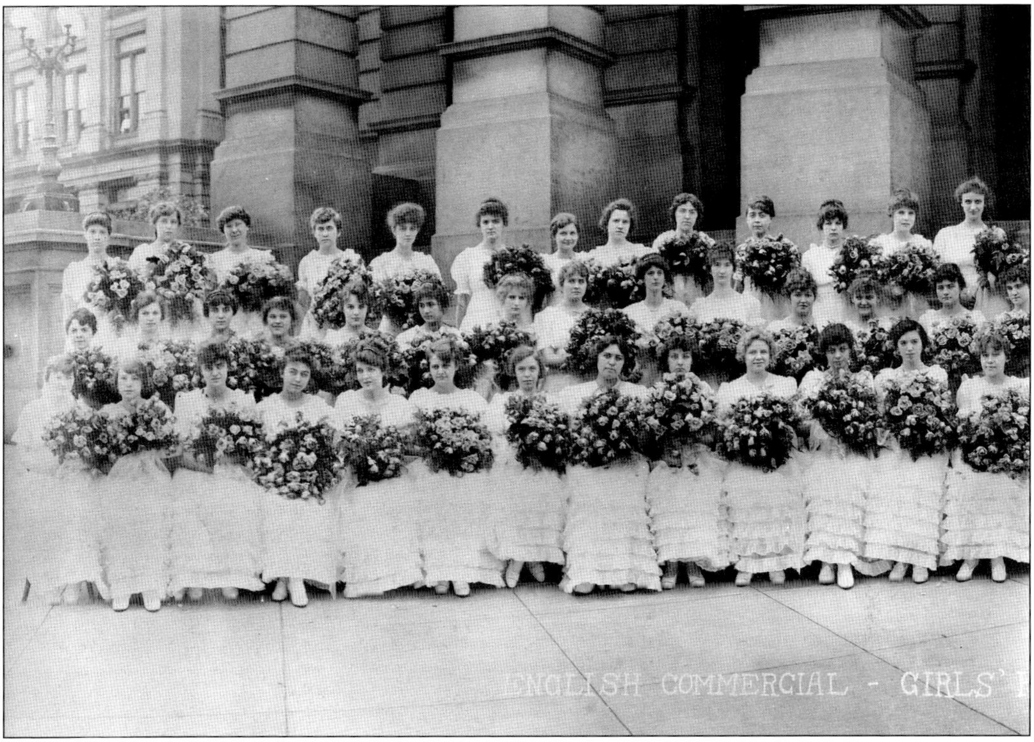

This 1915 graduation ceremony on the steps of the Georgia State Capitol building was a combination of classes from the Girl's High School and the English Commercial High School. English Commercial was founded in 1889 and focused on business-related studies such as stenography, accounting, banking, and typing courses to help prepare students for the job market. (GSA.)

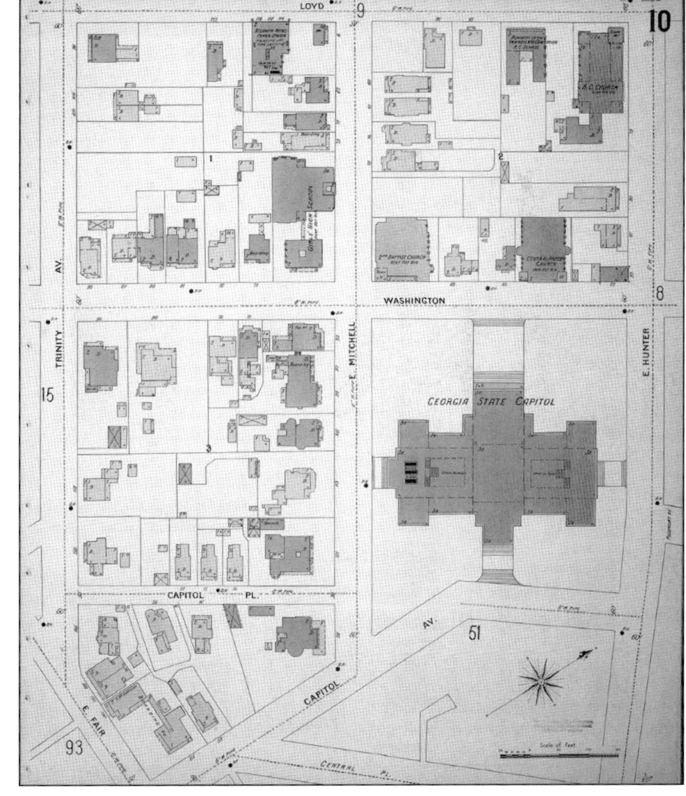

In 1866, surveyor Daniel Sanborn began creating detailed fire insurance maps of several cities, which were regularly updated to show structures, their uses, and how they were constructed to help assess fire risk. This 1899 Sanborn map shows that the neighborhood around the new capitol was still largely homes, churches, and schools. (LOC.)

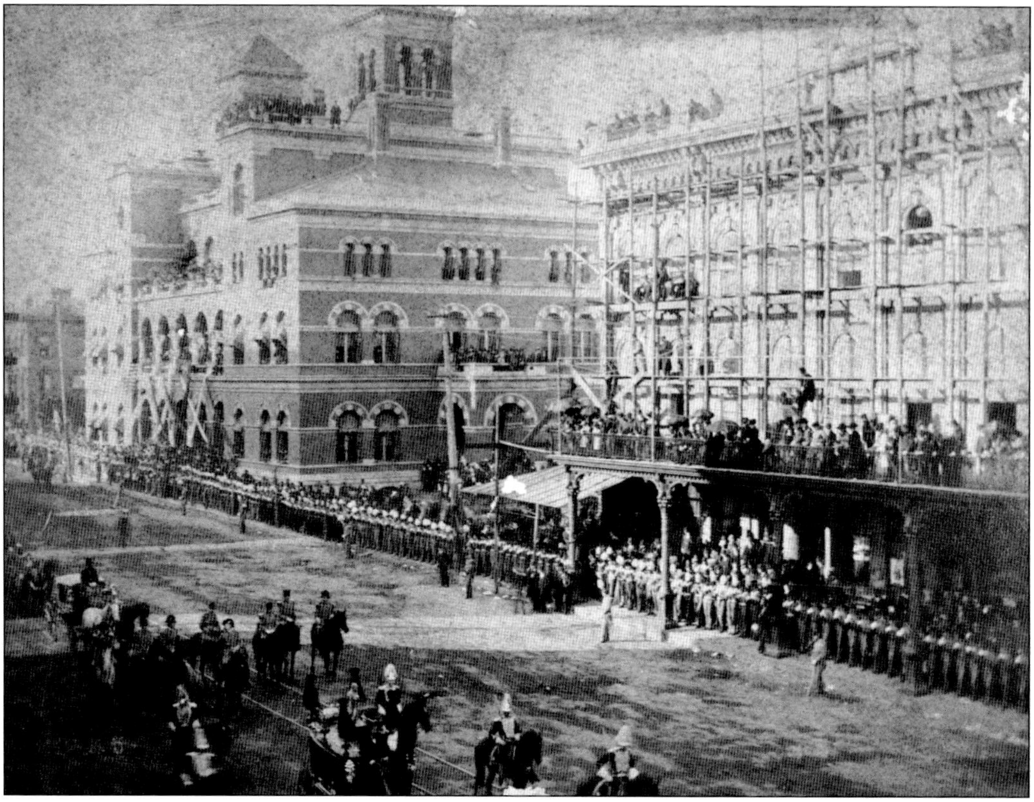

Gov. Alexander H. Stephens's funeral on March 8, 1883, was a solemn parade whose path led from the state capitol at the Kimball Opera House up Marietta Street past the US Customs House to Oakland Cemetery. Stephens died just four months after being sworn into office. The customs building was constructed in 1878 at Marietta and Forsyth Streets and was also home to Atlanta's main post office. (GSA.)

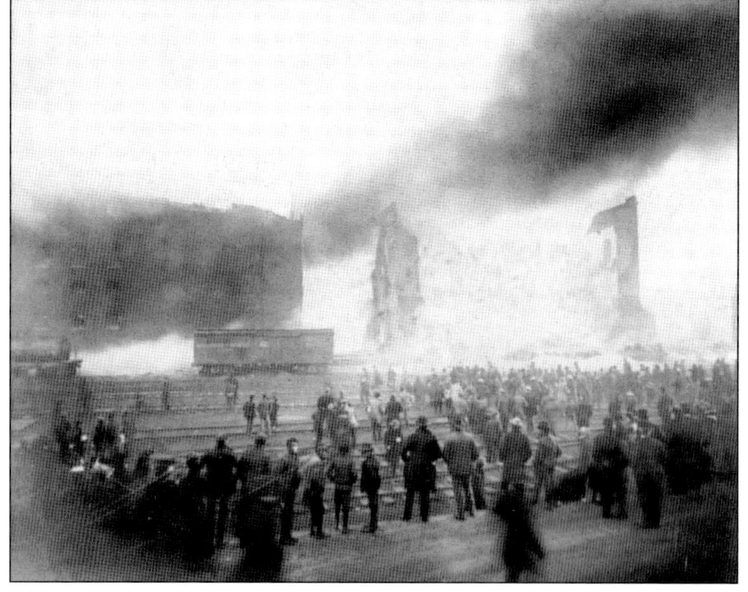

In 1896, the grand Markham House Hotel burned and was a complete loss. Adjacent to Union Terminal, the 107-room hotel was the largest in the city. The Markham House had a large second-floor balcony that allowed speakers to reach crowds, making it a central part of city activities. When Pres. Rutherford B. Hayes visited Atlanta in 1877, he spoke from the balcony of the Markham House. (AHC.)

When Atlanta city government vacated the original city hall in 1886 to make way for construction of the capitol building, city offices moved to the chamber of commerce building at South Pryor Street. The mayor's office and general council chamber were on the fourth floor. It was across the street from the Fulton County Courthouse, which had been expanded three different times as the county's needs grew. (GSA.)

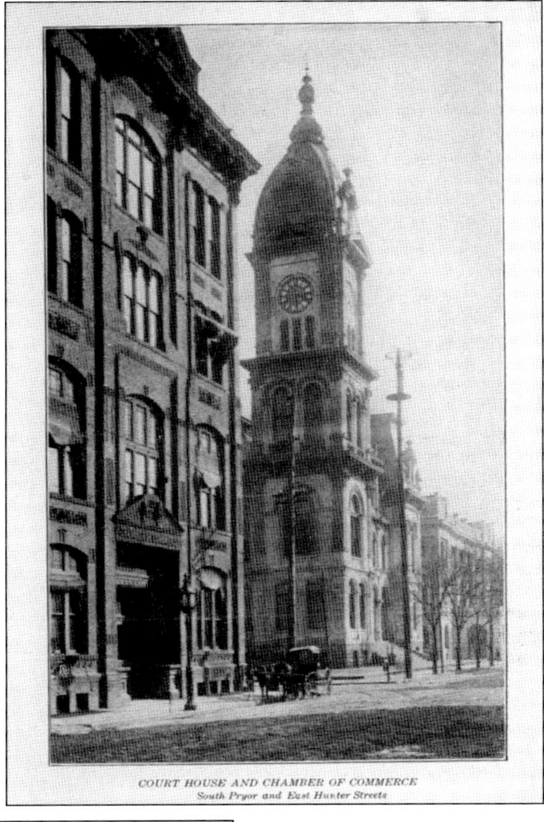

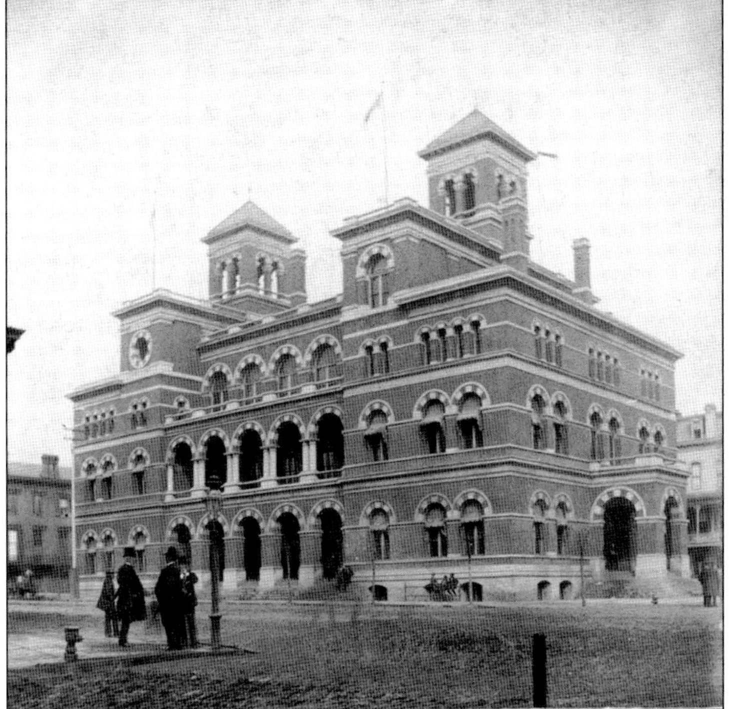

In 1911, Atlanta mayor Robert Maddox helped purchase the US Customs House and US Post Office from the federal government, and the building became the new city hall. The grand structure on Marietta Street housed Atlanta city government for less than two decades. It was demolished in 1930 soon after city offices moved to a new building. (NYPL.)

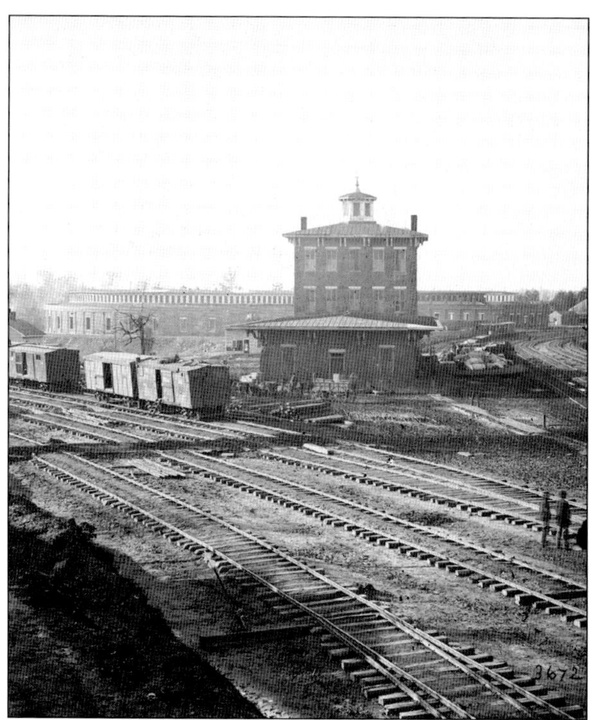

The Georgia Railroad freight depot still stands two blocks from the Georgia State Capitol. Completed in 1869, it originally had a three-story office building attached that was topped with a cupola. Fire destroyed that building in 1935. The depot served as the main freight depot for the Georgia Railroad, which was founded in 1833 in Augusta. The Georgia Railroad connected to the Atlantic & Western Railroad in Atlanta when it was known as Marthasville. (LOC.)

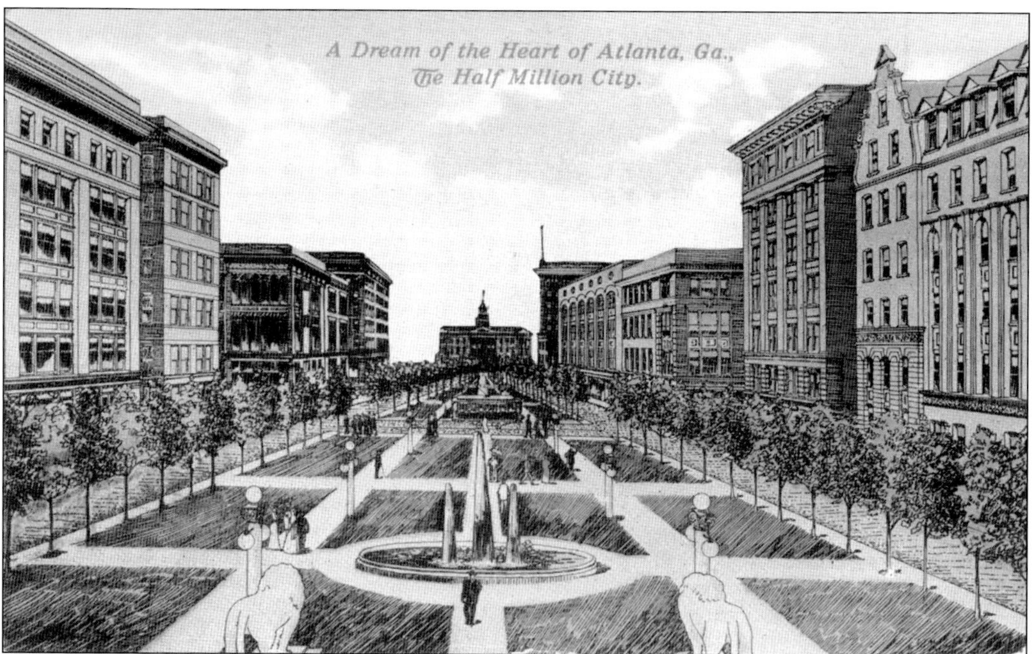

This is a conceptual drawing from 1909 for a "civic park" at the western entrance to the Georgia State Capitol. The president of the Atlanta Architectural Haralson Bleckley League first proposed what was known as Park Plaza near the state capitol as part of a comprehensive city beautification and development plan. His planned public space would be directly west of the capitol building, with state, county, and city government buildings around the park. The plan never materialized. (Janice McDonald.)

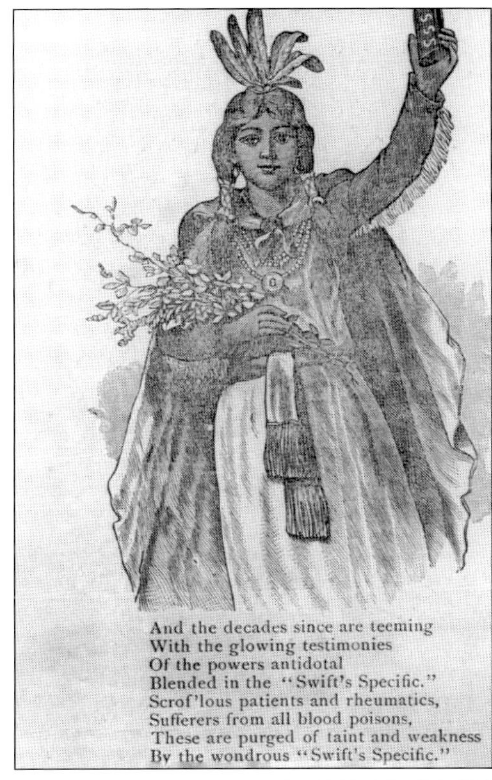

Swift's Specific was a popular tonic in the late 1800s manufactured in a laboratory at the corner of Hunter and Central Streets, just two blocks from the Georgia State Capitol. The company brochure from 1888 tells the story of a Creek Indian chieftain's daughter named Uanita who created a natural potion from "blossoms, roots and grasses of the wildwood" to produce an elixir to help cure her father of a blood illness. (National Library of Medicine.)

Swift Specific's Atlanta labs claimed to make tonic based on Uanita's secret formula, which she had shared with a white preacher she married. Charles Swift founded the Swift Specific Company in Atlanta in 1879 and marketed the elixir as an all-natural cure for everything from blood disorders and skin ailments to cancer. Doctors were reportedly on staff to maintain the tonic quality, and the company did a booming mail-order business. (GSU.)

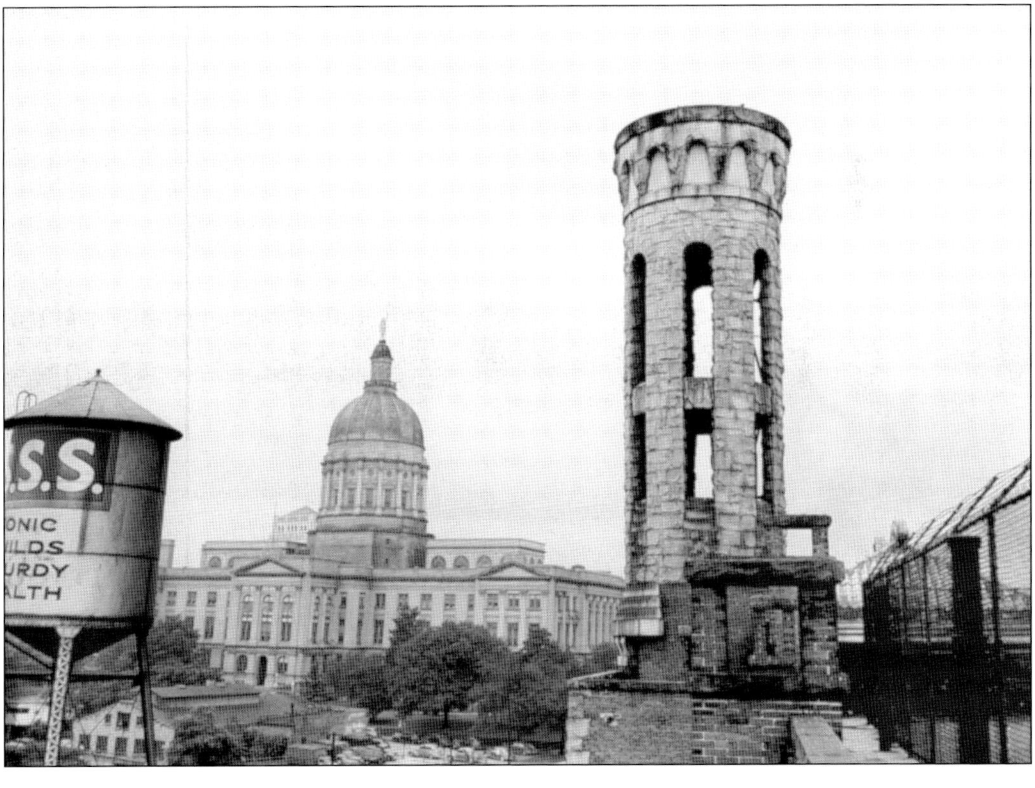

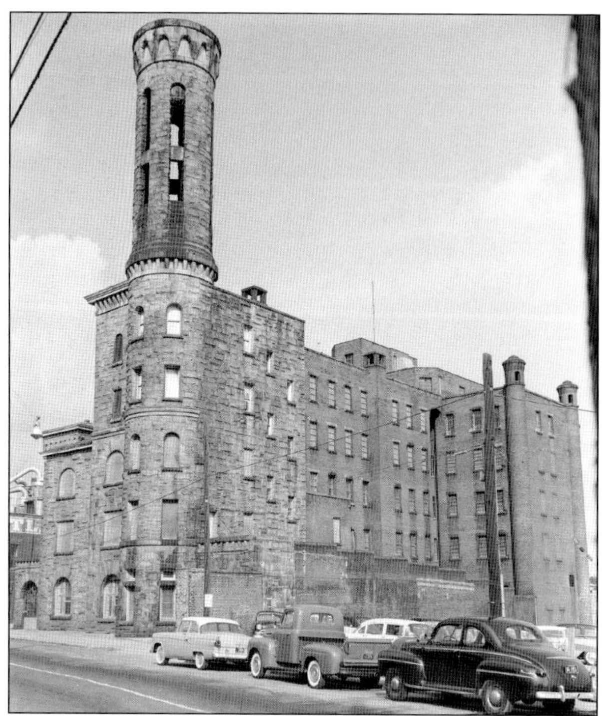

Next door to Swift was the Fulton County Jail, known as "Fulton Tower" for its distinctive 100-foot-high Romanesque stone pillar chimney. The detention center was built in 1898 at a cost of $175,000 to replace the original jail on Frasier Street. In 1960, all 440 inmates were moved across town to a newer, more modern jail, and Fulton Tower was abandoned. It was torn down in 1962. (AHC.)

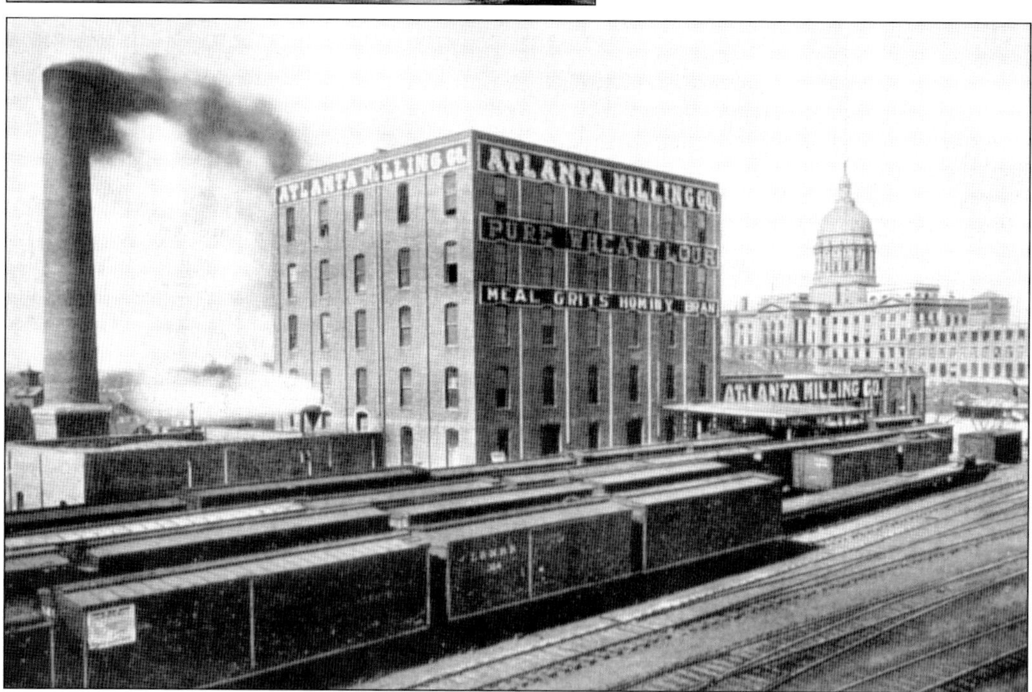

The Atlanta Milling Company replaced the Woodward Lumberyard in 1911 along the tracks two blocks from the capitol and stood next to the Fulton County Jail. Known for its Capitola brand of flour, Atlanta Milling Company's advertisements professed that the flour was a "scientific blend of the finest winter wheat" and that it had "unparalleled quality at once the best bread flour in the world." (GSA.)

Construction on the new 275,000-square-foot Fulton County Courthouse began in 1911, and the nine-story stone and concrete building took over three years to complete, costing $1.25 million. Over the arches at the main entrance on Pryor Street in the center of the building are six giant semidetached Corinthian columns. The facade is decorated with ornamental terra-cotta and granite. The now connected Justice Center was completed in 1993. (Janice McDonald.)

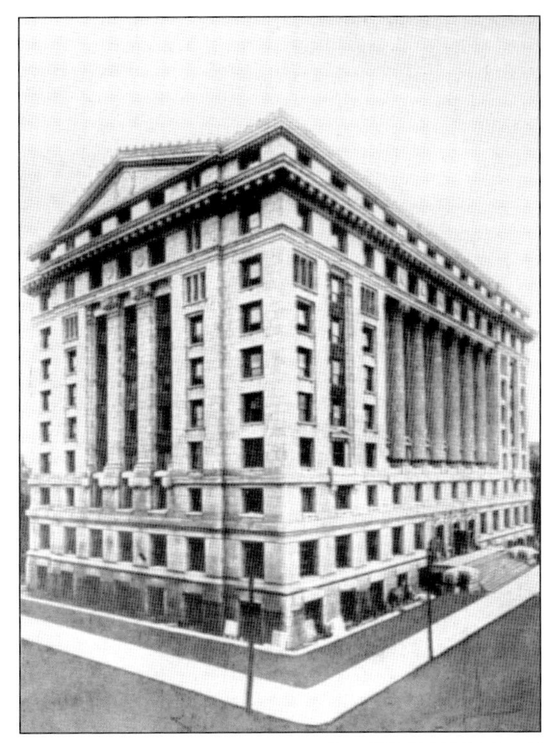

This 1950s aerial photograph of the capitol gives a good overview of the neighborhood. The Fulton County Jail and Swift Specific are just to the right of the capitol dome. The busy rail yard area on the left is where the 20-story James H. "Sloppy" Floyd Veterans Memorial Building and the Georgia State MARTA station now stand. (GSA.)

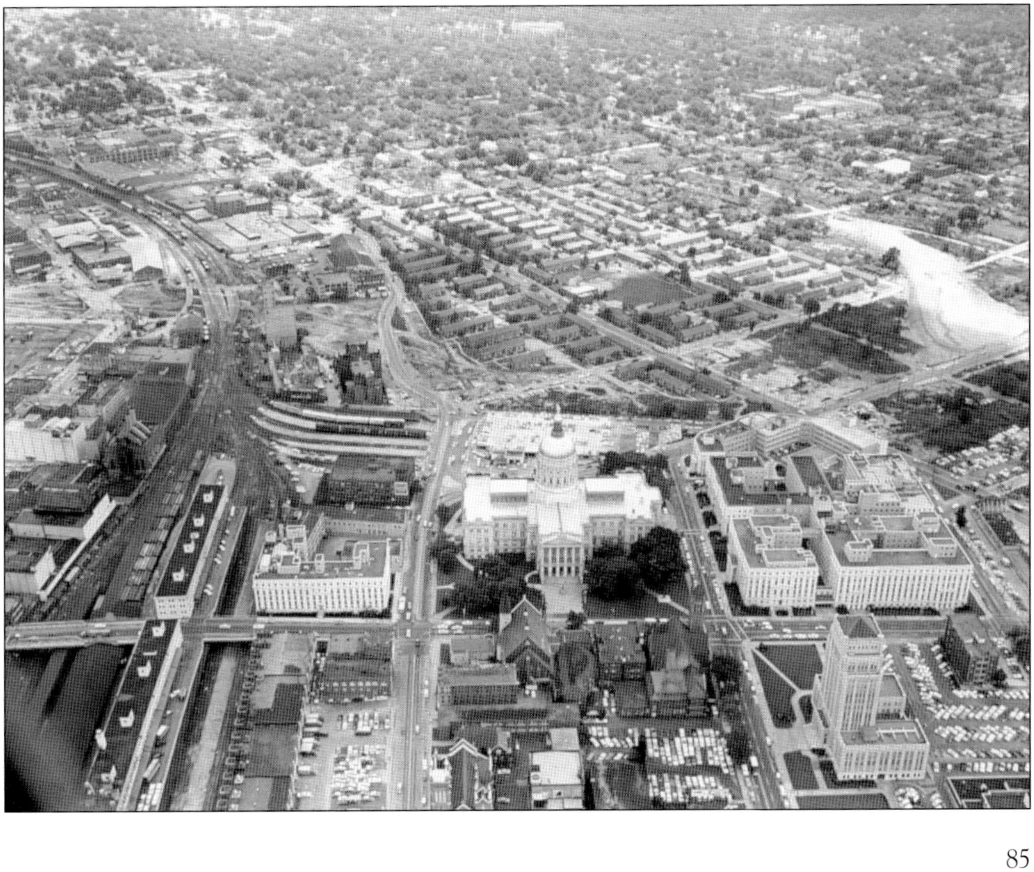

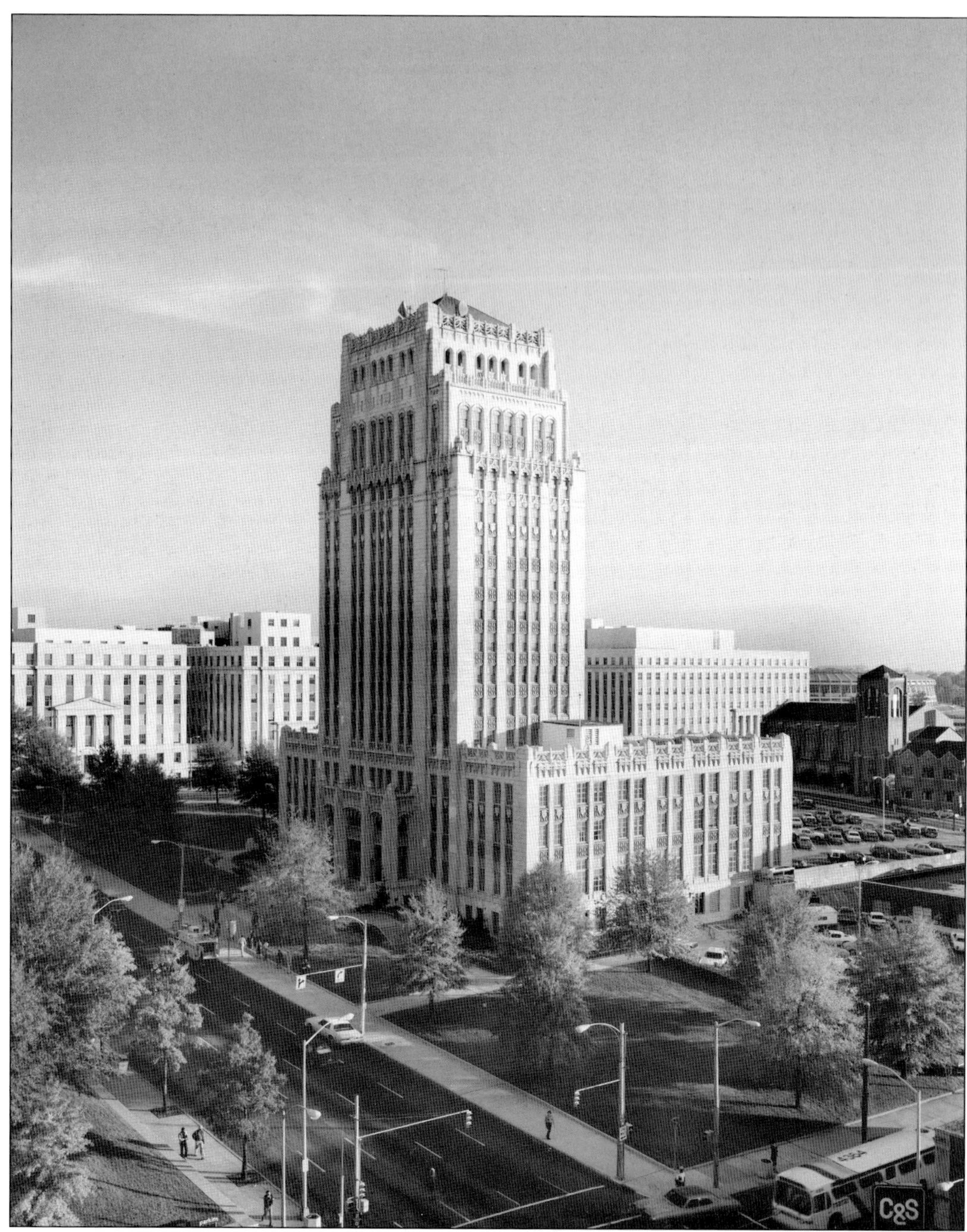

Atlanta's third city hall officially opened in 1929. A $1 million bond was passed to finance the construction. G. Lloyd Preacher was commissioned to design it. Standing 11 stories high, the neo-Gothic Art Deco tower was constructed of cream-colored terra-cotta tiles with green terra-cotta above the windows. The base and crown of the building are highly decorated with a balustrade, and the main entrance is designed with Georgia marble. For this project, the city secured half of the entire block between Washington and Pryor Streets along Mitchell Street, taking over the property once occupied by Girl's High School, which moved to a new facility in the Grant Park neighborhood in the 1920s. (LOC.)

City hall's ornate Art Deco lobby was constructed using various native Georgia marble for many of the surfaces. Pillars support the coffered ceilings, and there are flanking staircases on either side of a wall of elevators. Ogee arches are over both doors, and elevators with pinnacles, decorative crochets, and a delicate frieze are seen throughout the building. An annex with a multistoried atrium was added to the building in 1986. (LOC.)

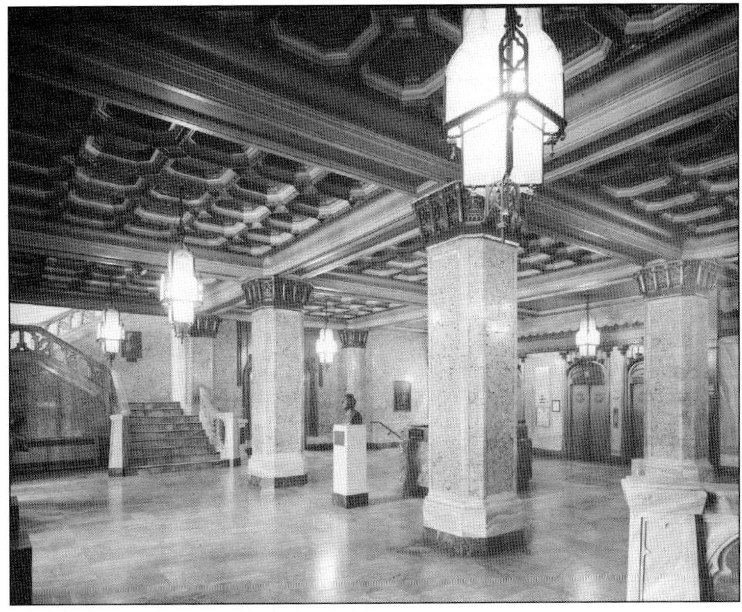

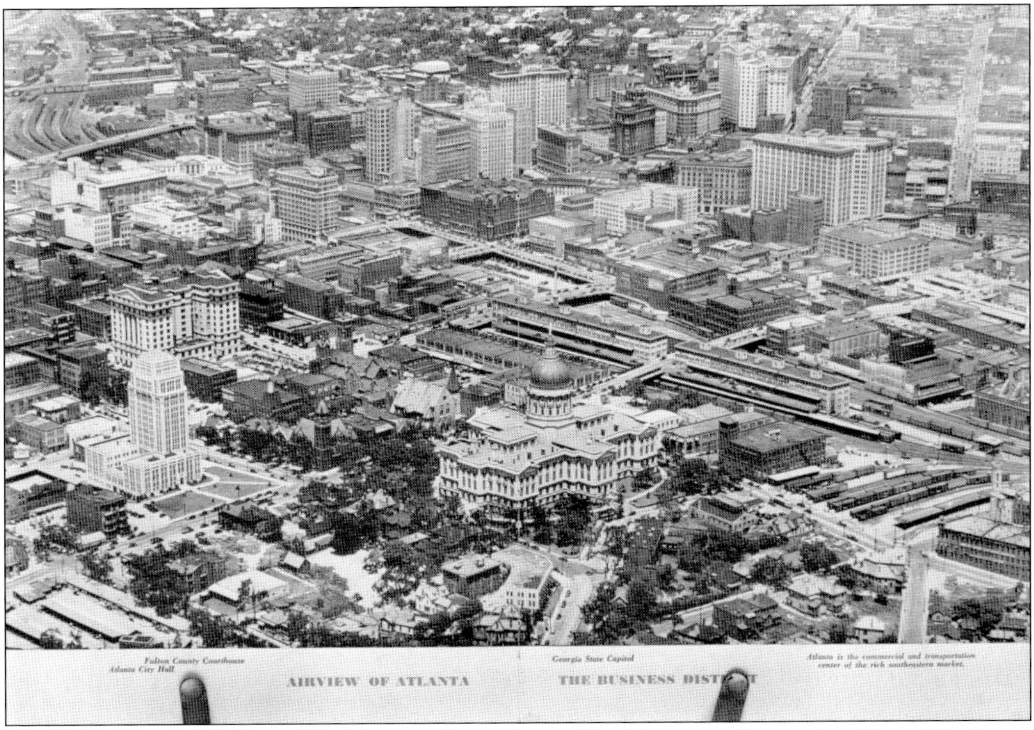

Changes in the area around the Georgia State Capitol building are obvious in this aerial view of downtown from 1941. City hall still stands out on its own, and viaducts all but cover the railroad gulch through the heart of the city. By 1956, the grand mansions just to the south (left) of the capitol on Washington and Mitchell Streets were long gone, replaced with the judicial building housing the State Library, which had moved out of the capitol along with the Supreme Court of Georgia and Court of Appeals. (GSU.)

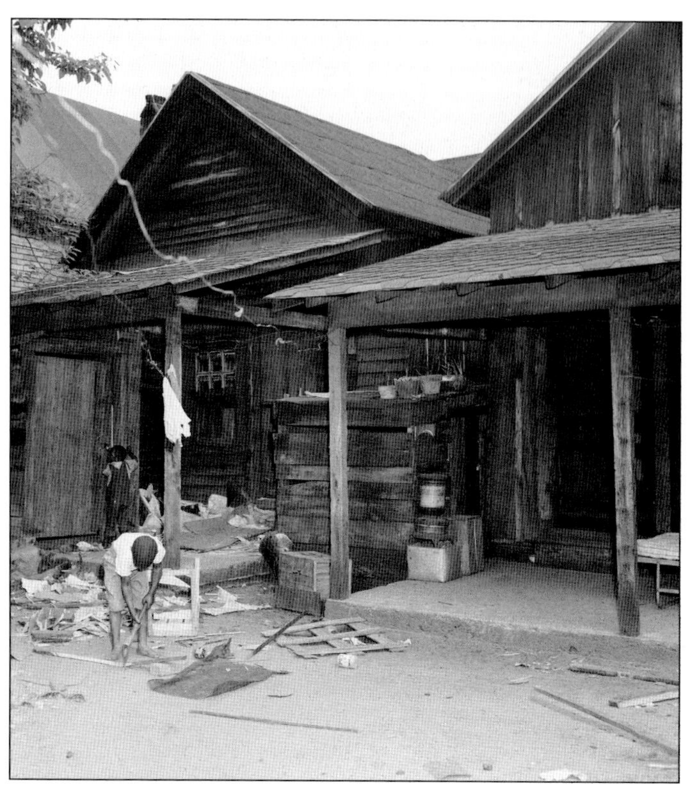

Less than two blocks east of the capitol were several blocks of what were described on Sanborn fire maps as "Negro shanties." They were bordered by East Hunter Street, now Martin Luther King Jr. Boulevard, and Fair Street, now Memorial Avenue. These were areas of abject poverty and for decades were where the poorest of poor lived. Crowded and often without electricity, many of the structures could barely be called buildings. Those who lived here often worked as laborers, maids, and cooks. In 1938, the Atlanta Housing Authority was created and began to clear the slums and build public housing. By 1941, Capitol Homes had been created where the shanties once stood. (Left, Franklin D. Roosevelt Library and Museum; below, LOC.)

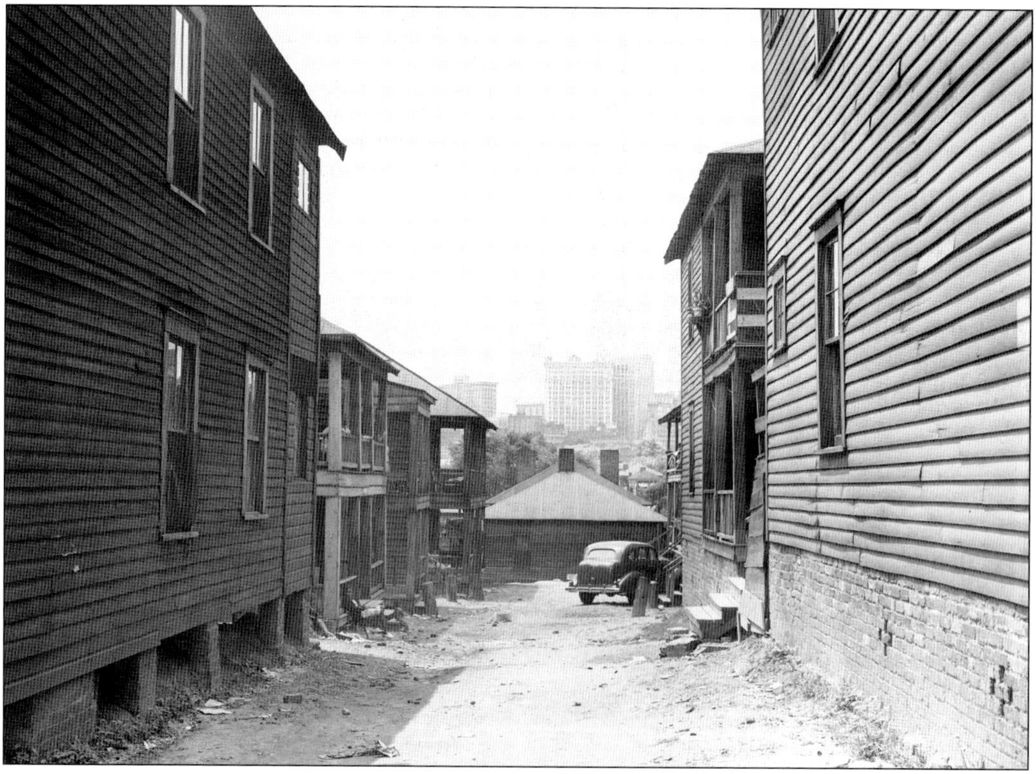

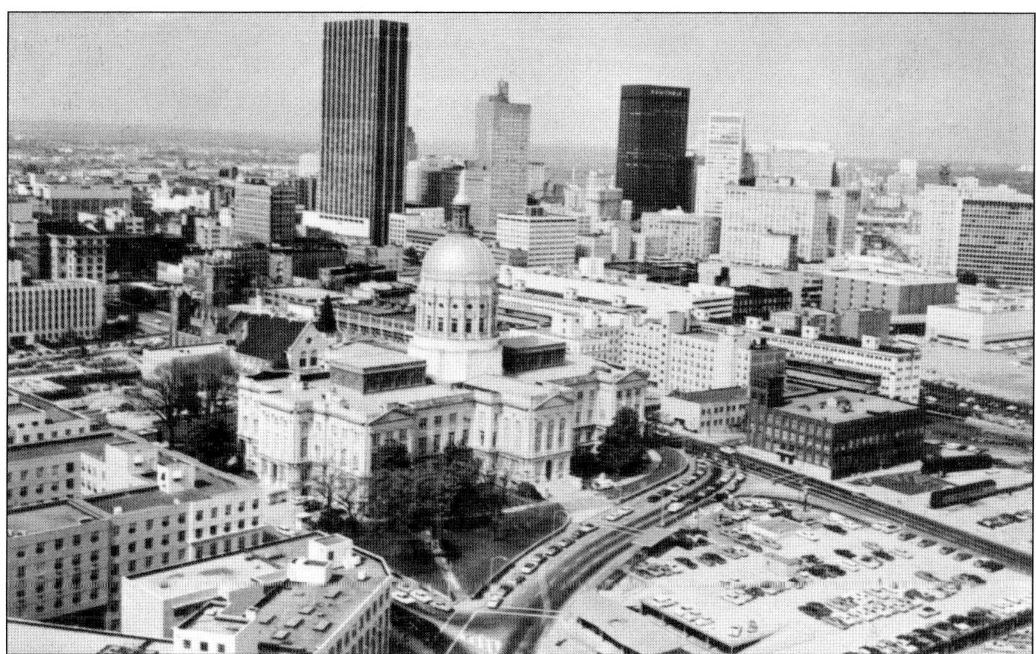

In the early 1950s, a garage and some old buildings neighboring the Georgia State Capitol on the east side were cleared to make way for a new parking structure. Costing $314,000, the two-level deck had room for 5,550 cars. The *Atlanta Constitution* reported that builder J.J. Black and Company fortified it so that it would be able to support a six-story structure should the need arise in the future. (Janice McDonald.)

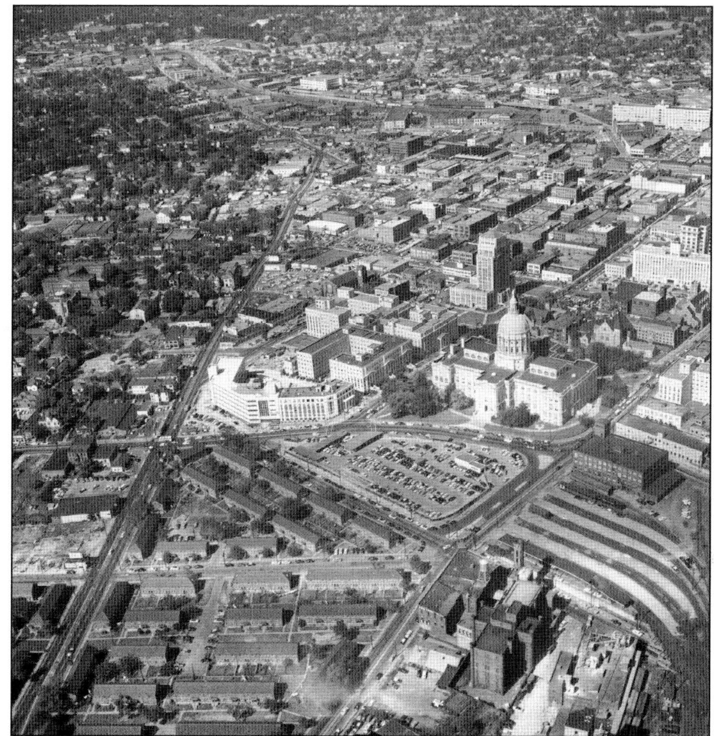

Looking east a decade later in this mid-1950s aerial photograph, Capitol Homes are in the foreground, with Swift Specific to the right (north) along with the rail yards. Within a few years, much of what is in the lower portion of this image would be gone, including 12 buildings from Capitol Homes that were relocated to make way for the construction of Interstate 75. The new highway was built through the heart of Atlanta in the 1960s. (Georgia Department of Transportation.)

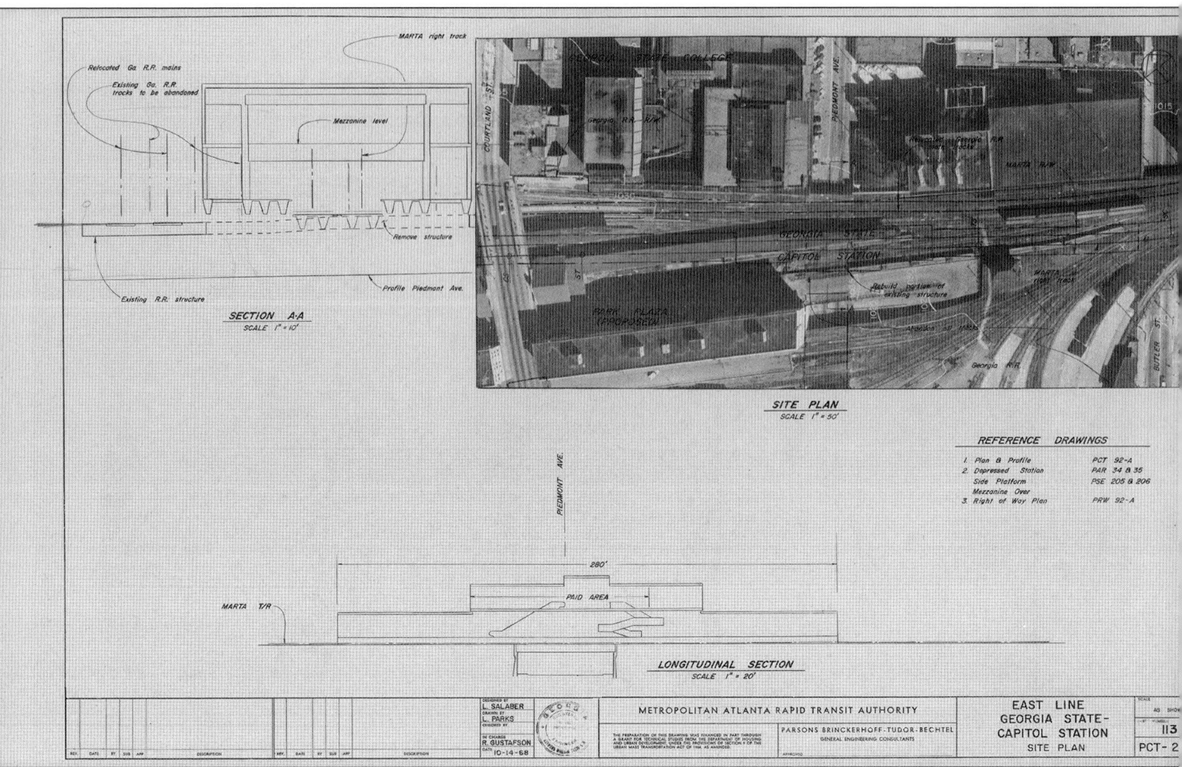

With Atlanta in need of modern public transportation, the Metropolitan Atlanta Transit Study Commission released recommendations in the early 1960s for the development of a five-county bus and rail system. In 1965, Atlanta passed the Metropolitan Atlanta Rapid Transit Authority Act, creating MARTA. These plans for the Georgia State–Capitol Station are dated 1968, but ground breaking for the east-west line of the rapid rail system did not take place until 1975. The first rail service began on June 30, 1979, between this station east to Avondale Estates, just east of Decatur. (GSU.)

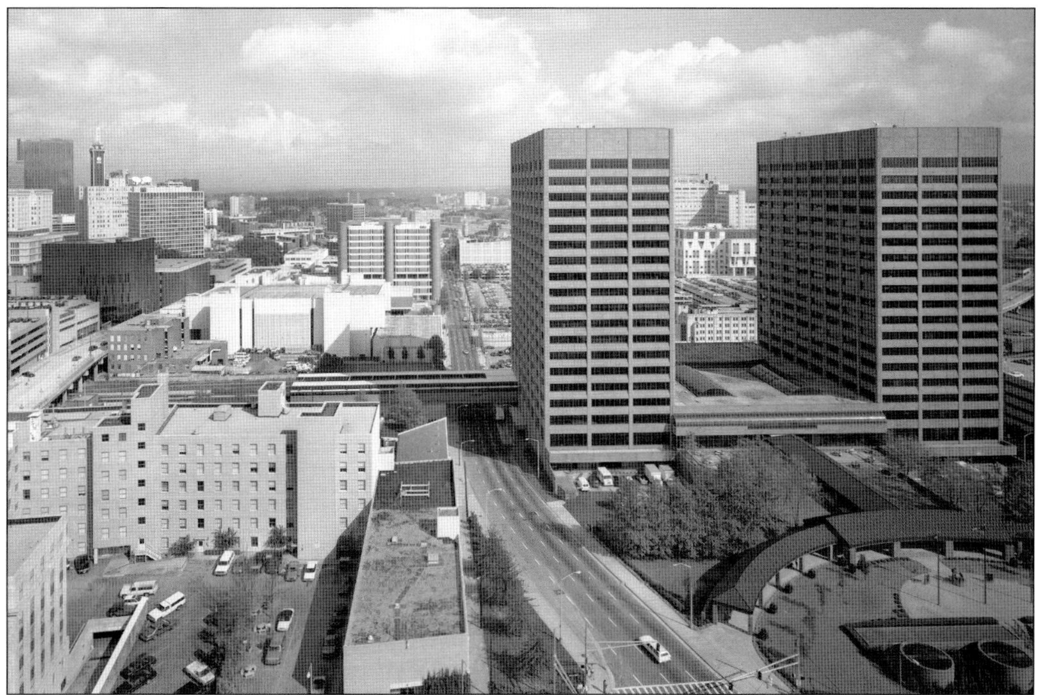

The area around the capitol that houses government buildings is known as the Capitol Complex and has constantly evolved. In the early 1980s, the 20-story Twin Towers Office Building, officially designated the James H. "Sloppy" Floyd Veterans Memorial Building, was constructed next to MARTA. The Towers is the first office building in the Capitol Complex to be higher than the capitol itself. Its high-rise style was part of a 1974 master plan for future state office buildings in the complex. (LOC.)

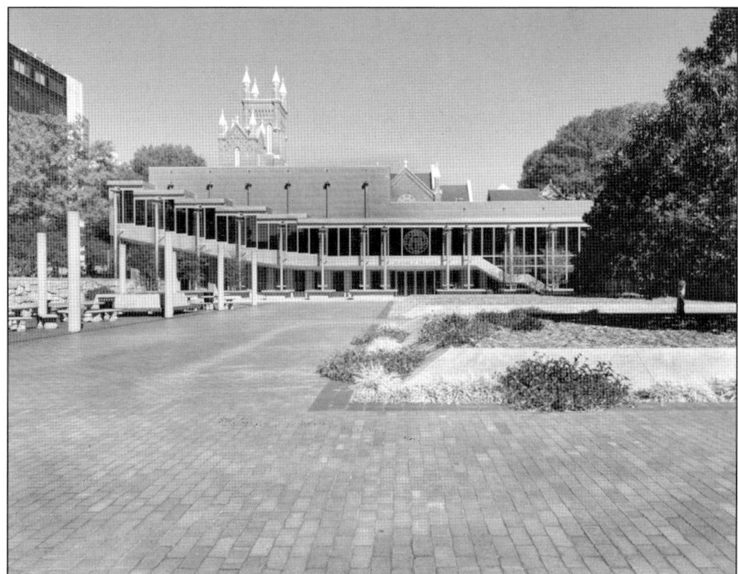

The concept of a plaza first began in the early 1900s. Its size, shape, and features have undergone numerous changes, as has its name. Located where Second Baptist Church once stood, it was called Talmadge Plaza after Gov. and US senator Herman Talmadge in the 1970s. A marker with that name remains. Today's Georgia Plaza Park runs along Mitchell Street between Washington and Pryor Streets. (LOC.)

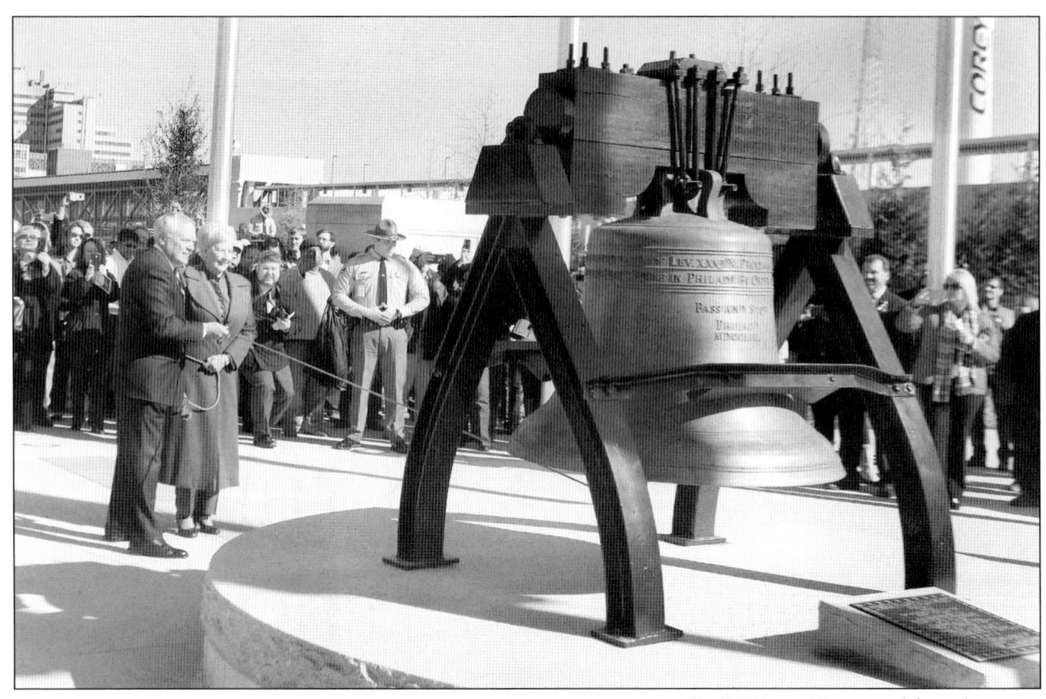

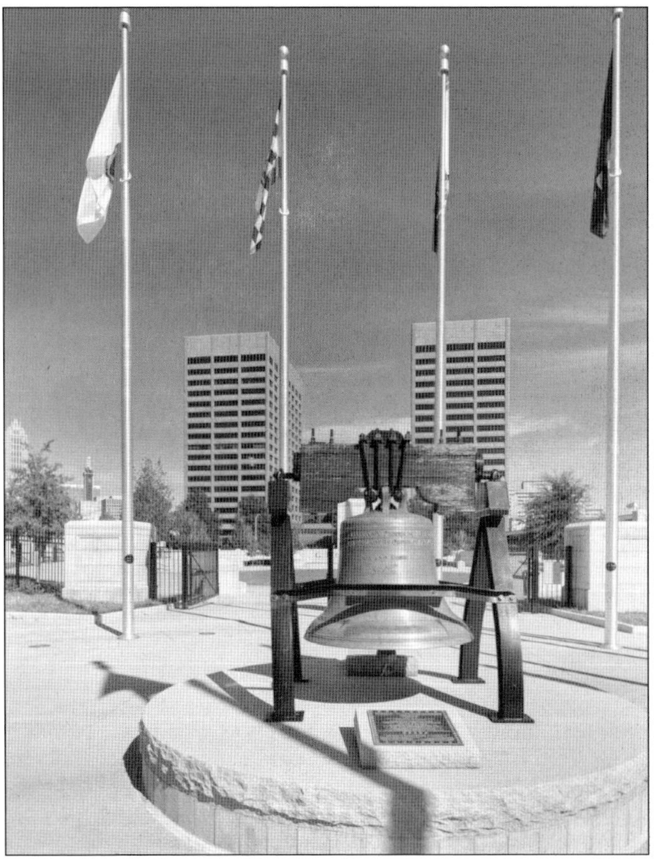

In 2014, a 60-year-old parking deck east of the capitol was demolished to make way for a new public space called Liberty Plaza. It was dedicated on January 16, 2015, by Gov. Nathan Deal and his wife, Sandra. The replicas of the Liberty Bell and the Statue of Liberty that had sat on the capitol grounds since the 1950s were moved to the new plaza. Designed by Stevens & Wilkinson architectural firm, the 2.2-acre plaza was created as a park and gathering place for demonstrations and celebrations. The plaza is large enough to handle crowds of over 3,000 and began hosting events immediately. (Above, Georgia Building Authority; left, LOC.)

Five

People and the Georgia Statehouse

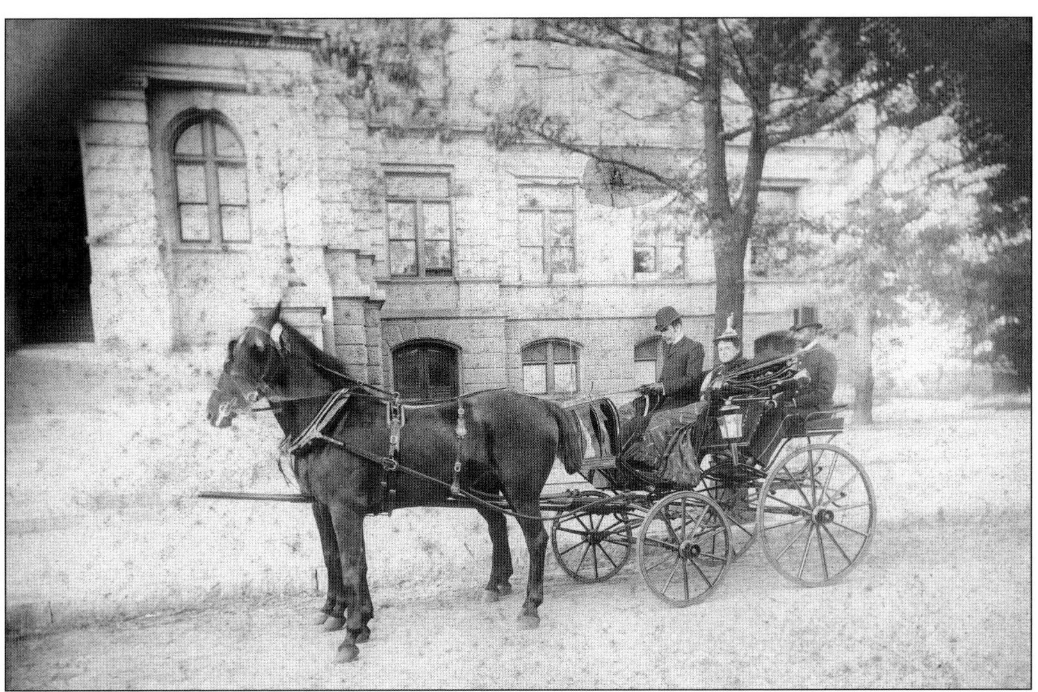

Georgians were immensely proud of their new capitol, often using it as a backdrop for photographs. On their first drive in their Spider carriage, Wilmer L. Moore and his wife, Cornelia, pose at the south entrance with an unidentified footman. Wilmer Moore was a partner in a wholesale dry goods business before becoming president of the Southern States Life Insurance Company. He also served as president of the Atlanta Chamber of Commerce. (AHC.)

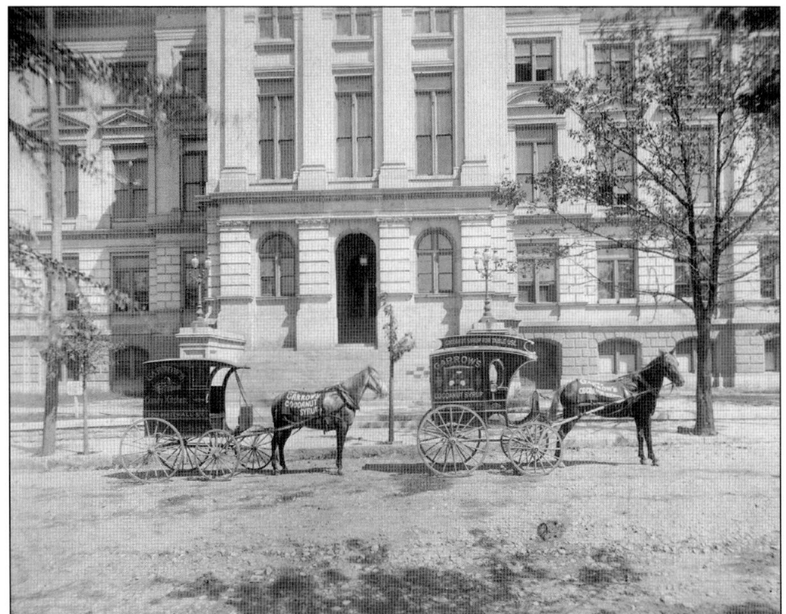

Garrow's Candy Kitchen was a popular store on Whitehall Street owned by George Frederick "Fred" Garrow. Garrow had been raised in Pennsylvania where his father ran several candy stores, but moved to Atlanta to start his own business. The store was known for its delivery service, using buggy teams, delivery wagons, and bicycles to fulfill orders. (AHC.)

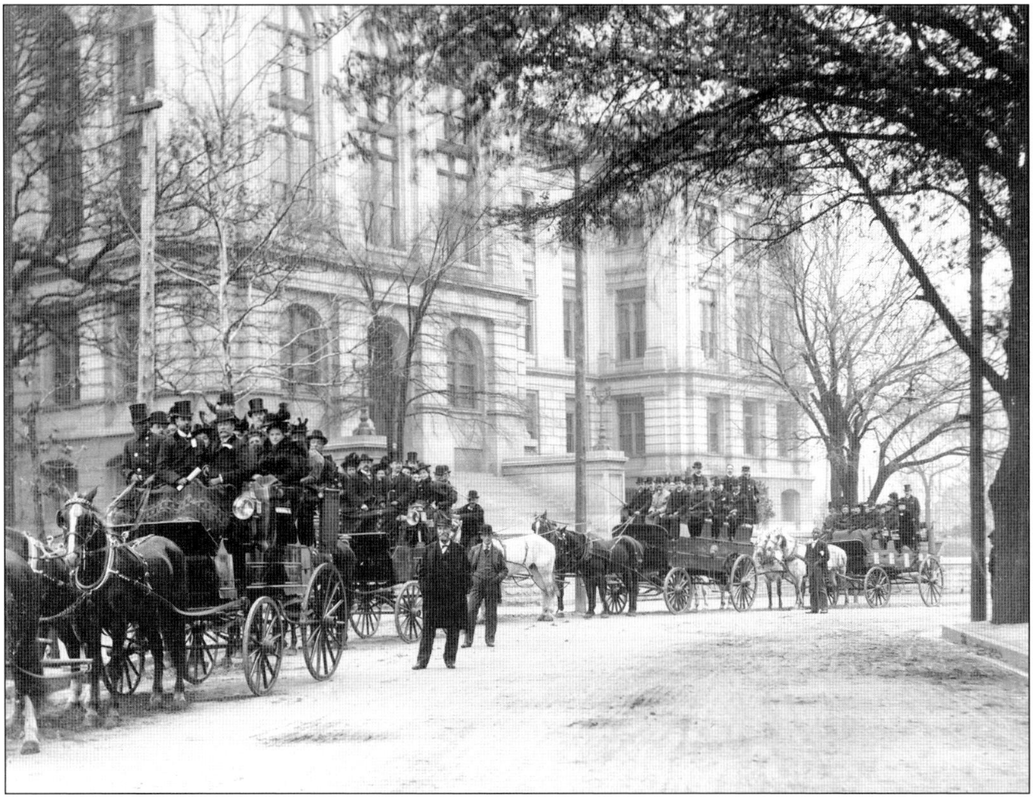

New York's Press Club paid a visit to the Georgia State Capitol in 1895 while in the city to cover Pres. Grover Cleveland's visit to the Cotton States and International Exposition. Nearly 800,000 visitors from the United States and 13 countries came to Atlanta for the exposition, which lasted for 100 days, beginning on September 18, 1895, and ending on December 31, 1895. (AHC.)

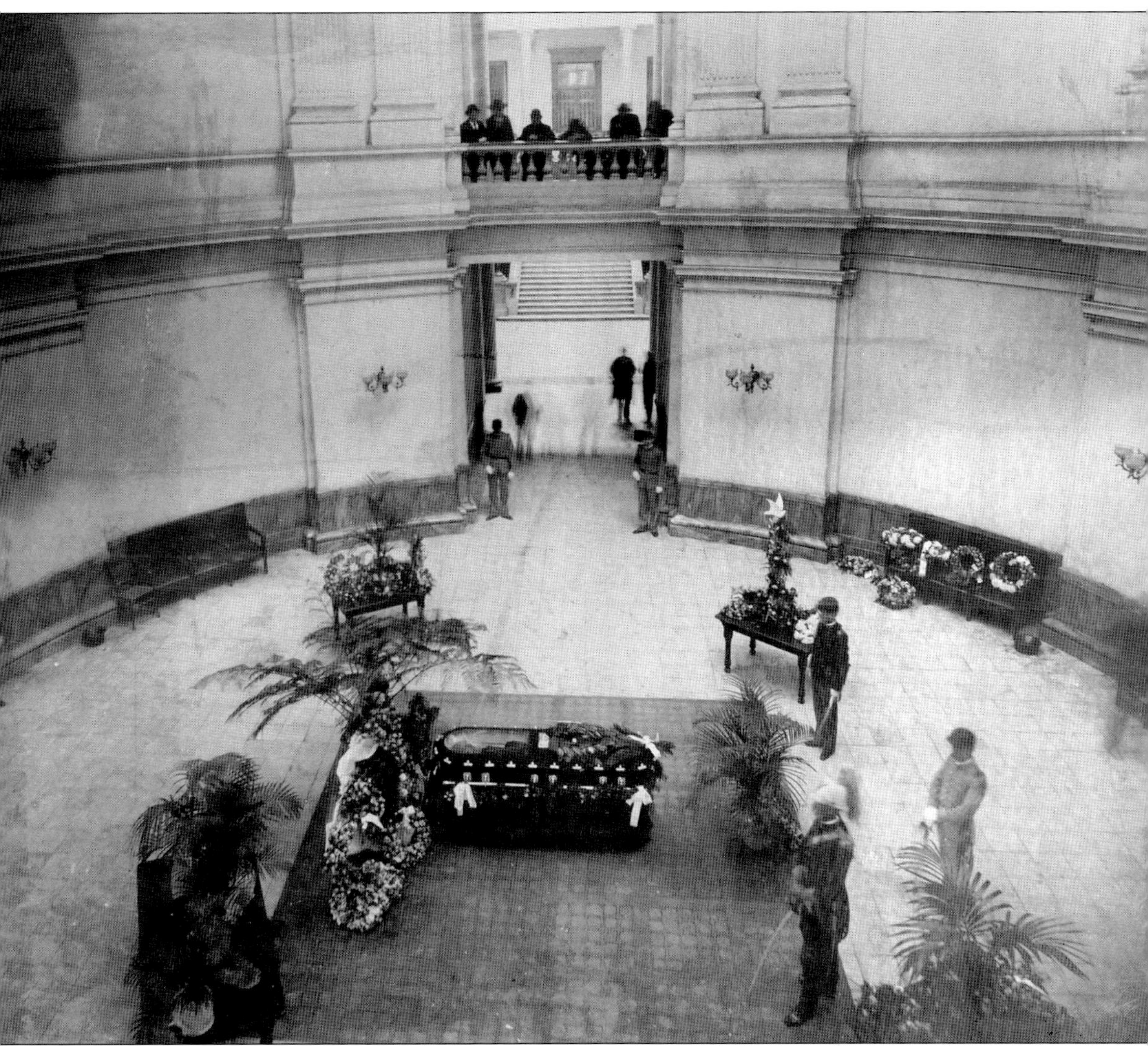

Joseph E. Brown was known as Georgia's Civil War governor, serving two terms. He was the first governor to lie in state in the Georgia State Capitol building. For two days, mourners came to the rotunda to pay their respects. On December 3, 1894, his body was transferred to the hall of the Georgia House of Representatives, where memorial exercises took place in the morning of December 4 to honor the late statesman. That afternoon, Governor Brown's body was taken by procession across the street to Second Baptist Church, the Brown family's church. In 1927, a statue in honor of Brown and his wife, Elizabeth (Grisham), was placed on the corner of the capitol grounds to have the best view of his beloved church. (Judith Vanderver Photography.)

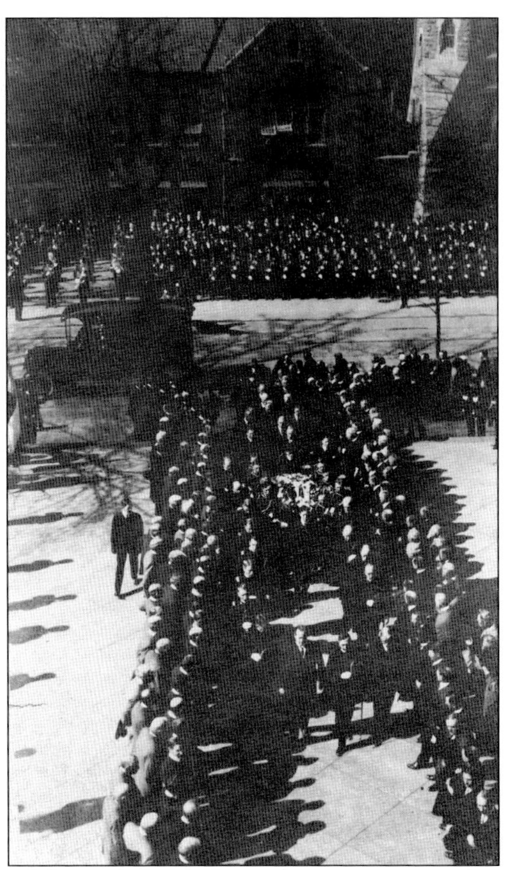

When governor and later US senator John B. Gordon died in 1904, an estimated 75,000 people took part in the services that surrounded his funeral. Having served as a general for the Confederacy, Gordon was the first commander in chief of the United Confederate Veterans when the group was organized in 1890 and held this position until his death. (AHC.)

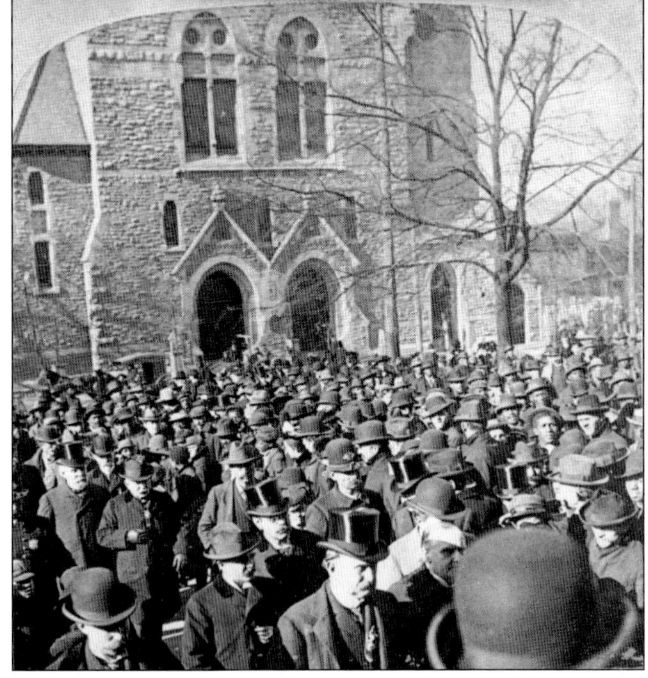

Massive crowds surrounded the capitol on December 14, 1899, when Pres. William McKinley came to Atlanta celebrating the end of the Spanish-American War. He also used his Peace Jubilee tour to seek endorsement of a treaty signed four days earlier freeing Cuba and giving the United States the Spanish possessions of Puerto Rico, Guam, and the Philippines. McKinley entered the capitol with Georgia governor Andrew Candler and delivered a short speech. (LOC.)

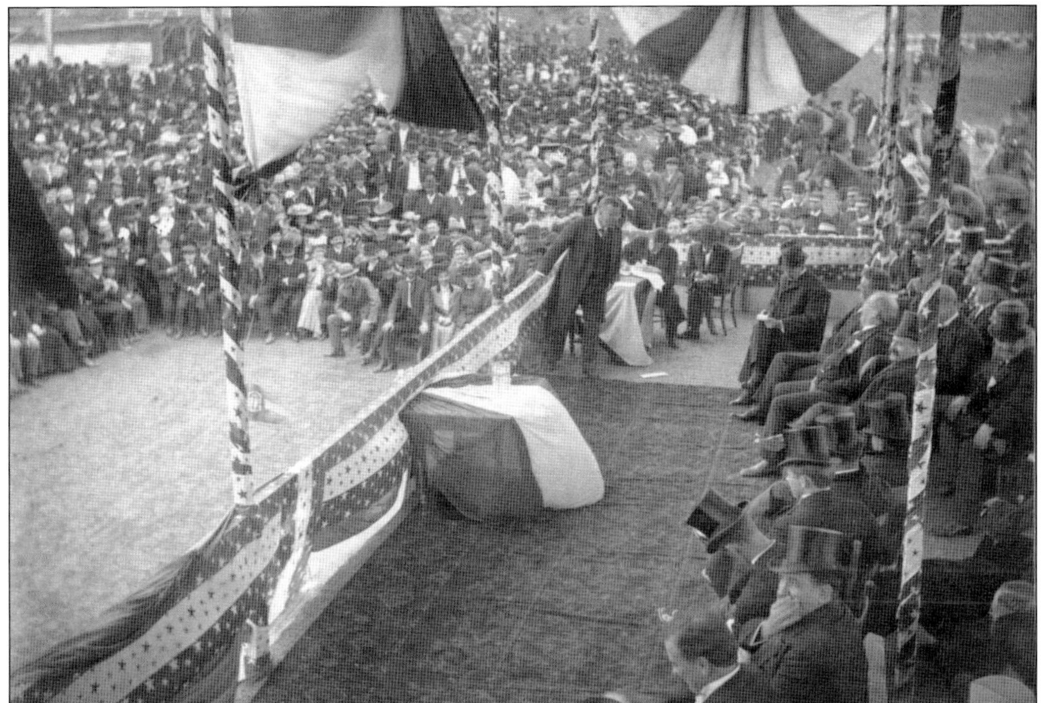

Atlanta was one of Pres. Theodore Roosevelt's key stops as he toured the South in 1905 during his second term in office. Proud of his Southern roots, he sometimes called himself "half a Southerner." Roosevelt had become president after the 1901 assassination of President McKinley. With the Civil War still a recent memory, he often lauded the courage of what he called "Southern heroes" and believed in racial hierarchy. (LOC.)

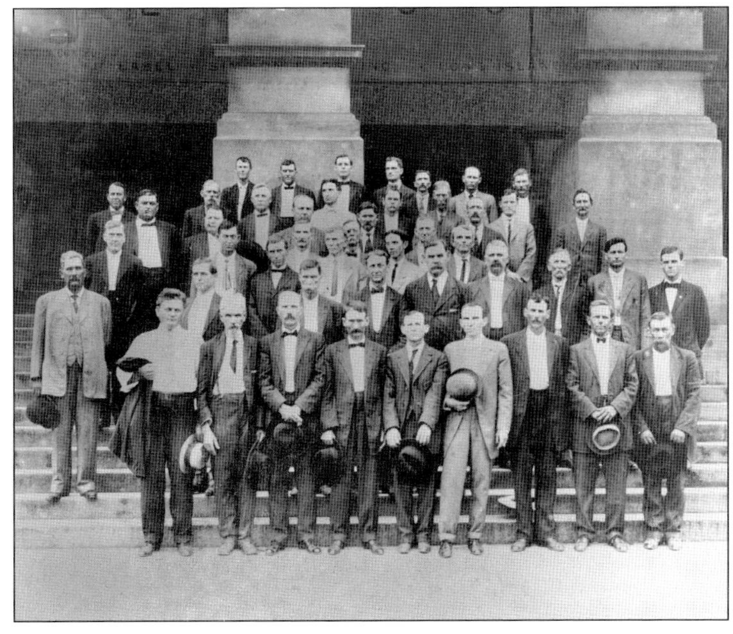

The capitol steps were a common backdrop for photographs of groups visiting the legislature. In 1911, this group of businessmen from the Donalsonville area came to Atlanta to lobby the General Assembly for the formation of Seminole County. Their efforts were successful, and on July 8, 1920, parts of Decatur and Early Counties were used to create the new county. (GSA.)

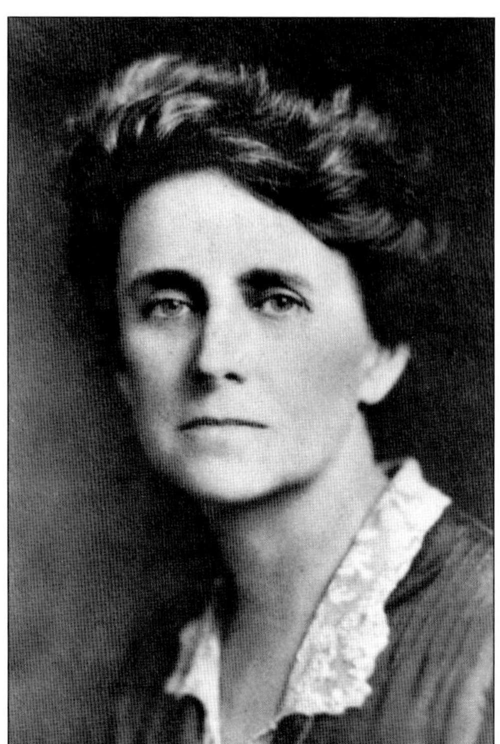

When women won the right to vote in 1920, Viola Ross Napier of Macon got on the ballot, and in 1922, she and Bessie Kempton became the first women elected to the Georgia House of Representatives. Napier had become an attorney after the death of her husband and ran because she found it difficult to practice law. (Middle Georgia Archives, Washington Memorial Library.)

Georgia governor Eugene Talmadge made his reputation as a supporter of small farmers and preached what he said were the true values of rural America. This rally for Talmadge, held at the western entrance of the state capitol, shows the statue of another Georgia politician, Thomas Watson. Watson served as both a member of the US House of Representatives and the US Senate but was controversial because of his racist views. Erected in 1934, his statue was moved to a nearby park in 2013. (GSU.)

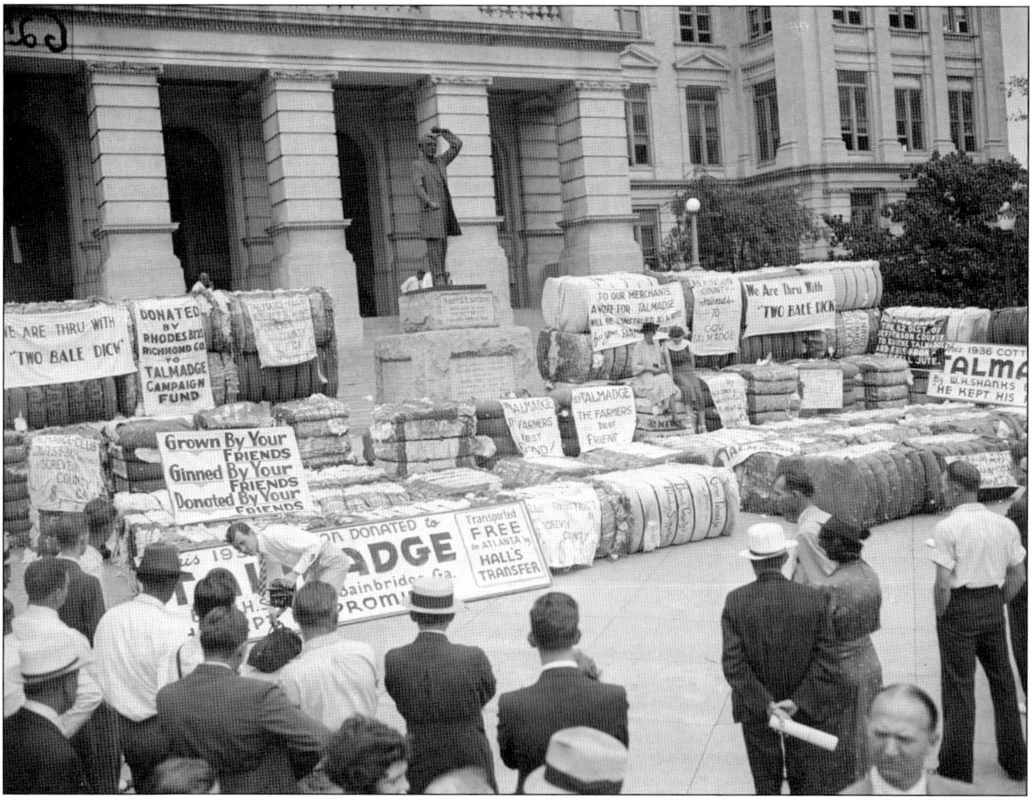

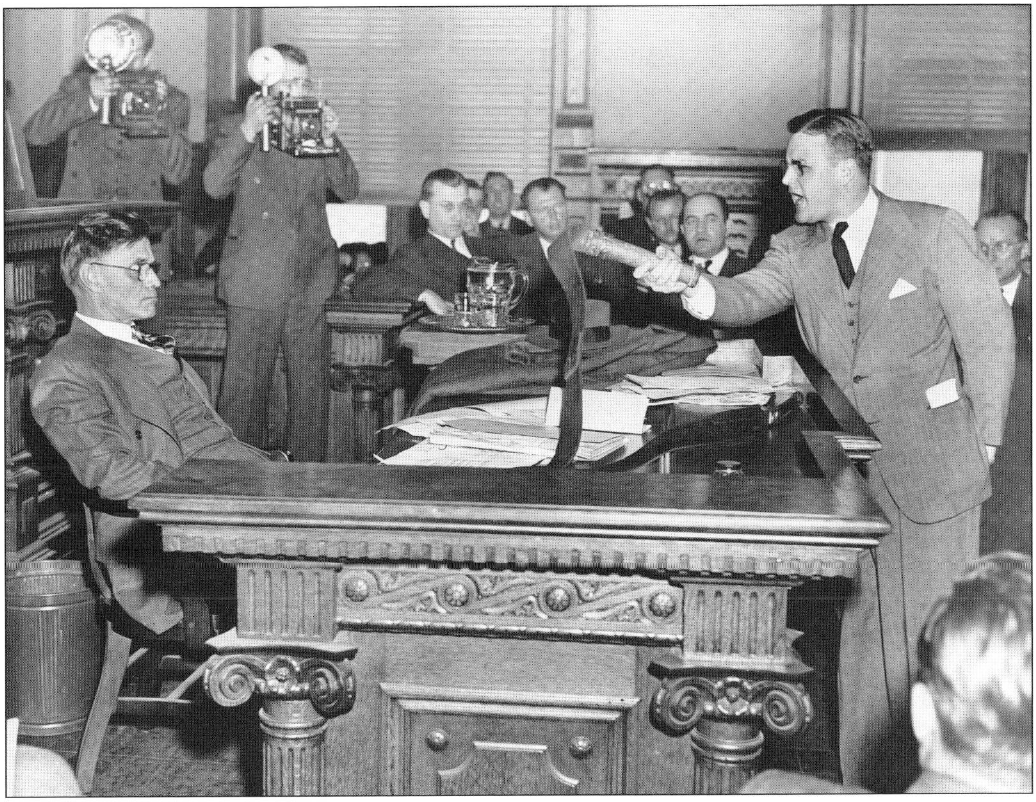

Governor Talmadge had his fair share of confrontations in office, including this one with assistant solicitor Daniel Duke during a 1941 clemency hearing for six Ku Klux Klansmen. Brandishing the bullwhip that the men had used to flog several African American men, Duke declared, "A man could kill a bull elephant with one of these." Although Talmadge denied clemency, he expressed sympathy for the men and said he had once participated in a flogging himself. (AHC.)

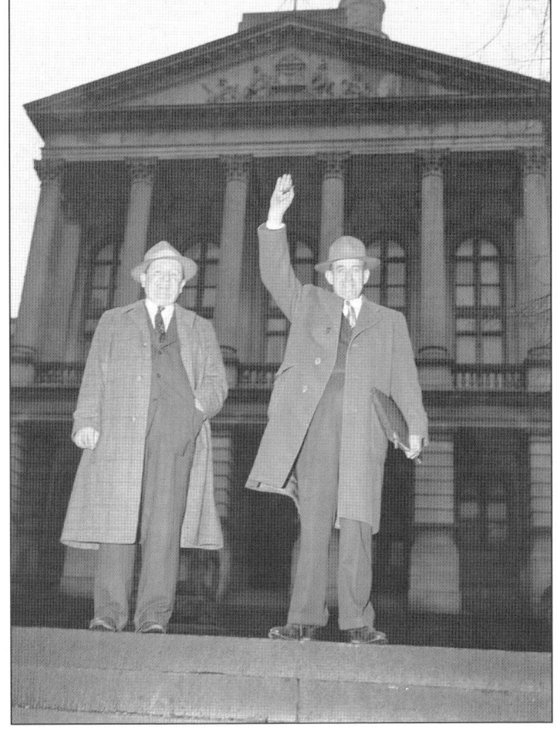

Melvin E. Thompson celebrates on the steps of the capitol in March 1947, ending what was called the "Three Governors Controversy." Eugene Talmadge died in December 1946 after again being elected governor but before his inauguration. Outgoing governor Ellis Arnell sought to remain in office, and Talmadge's son Herman Talmadge also laid claim to the seat, as did Thompson, who was lieutenant governor. The Supreme Court of Georgia declared Thompson governor. (GSU.)

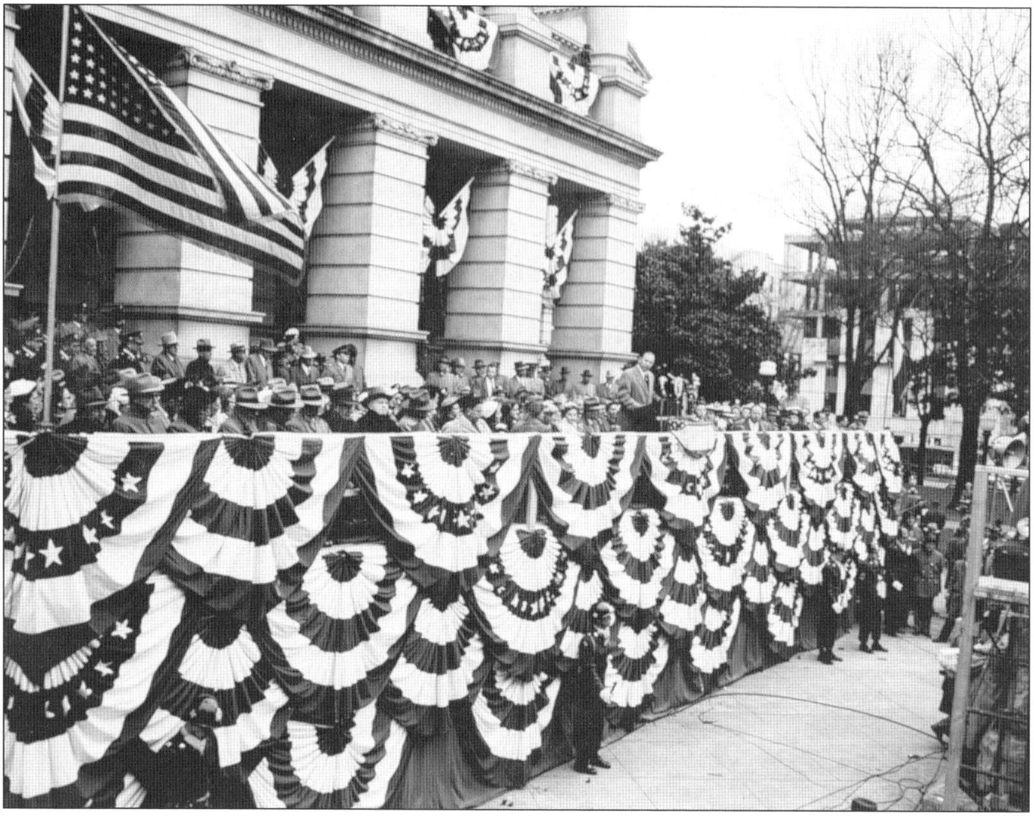

On January 11, 1955, the steps of the capitol were decked with a stage festooned with flags and bunting for the inauguration of Gov. Samuel Marvin Griffin. Griffin had served as lieutenant governor from 1946 to 1955 and was long seen as a successor for Governor Talmadge. A staunch segregationist, he served just one term. (GSU.)

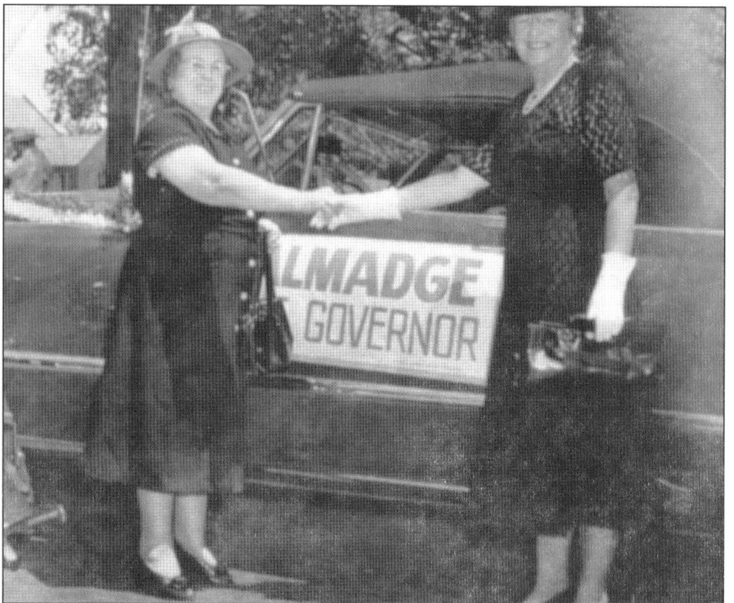

Mary (Clyde) Lee took over operations of the capitol's cafeteria in the 1950s. Amid civil rights protests in the early 1960s, she and her 14 employees, most of them black, lost their jobs after Gov. Ernest Vandiver closed the cafeteria rather than serve black patrons. Lee supported the move and was among those named in the resulting NAACP lawsuit. She is shown here on the left with Governor Talmadge's wife, Betty. (Family of Mary [Clyde] Lee.)

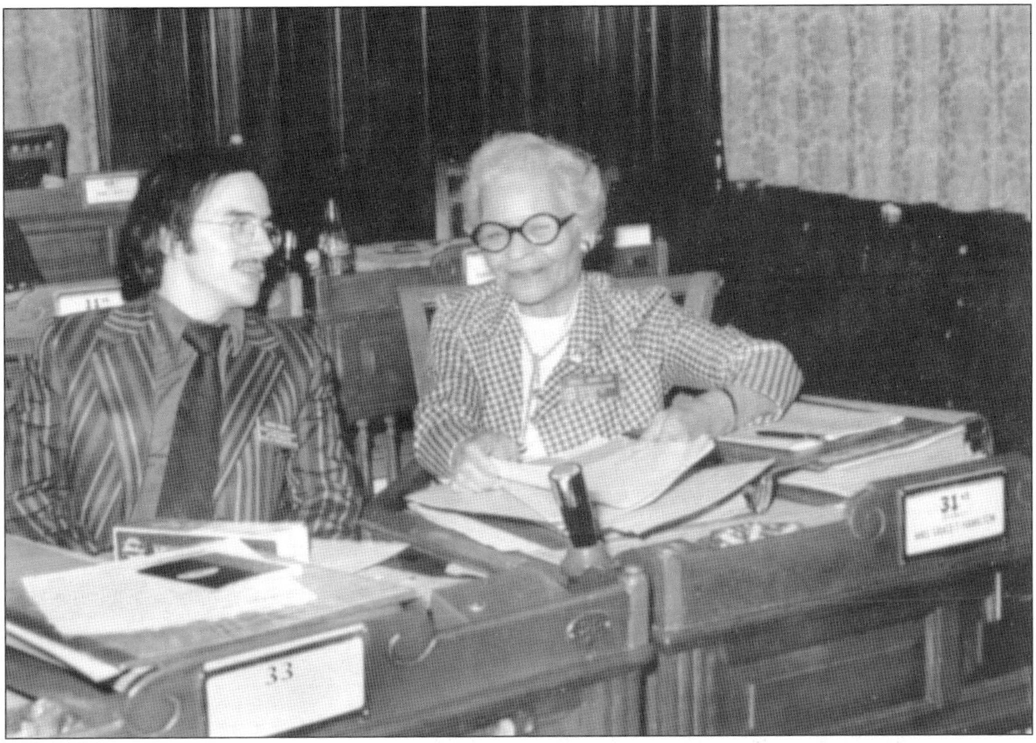

In 1965, Grace (Townes) Hamilton became the first African American woman elected to the Georgia House of Representatives. She had served as the executive director of the Atlanta Urban League from 1943 to 1960. When she left office in 1984, her fellow lawmakers referred to her as "the most effective woman legislator the state has ever had." She is pictured here with fellow legislator Quinn Hudson. (Atlanta University Center Robert W. Woodruff Library.)

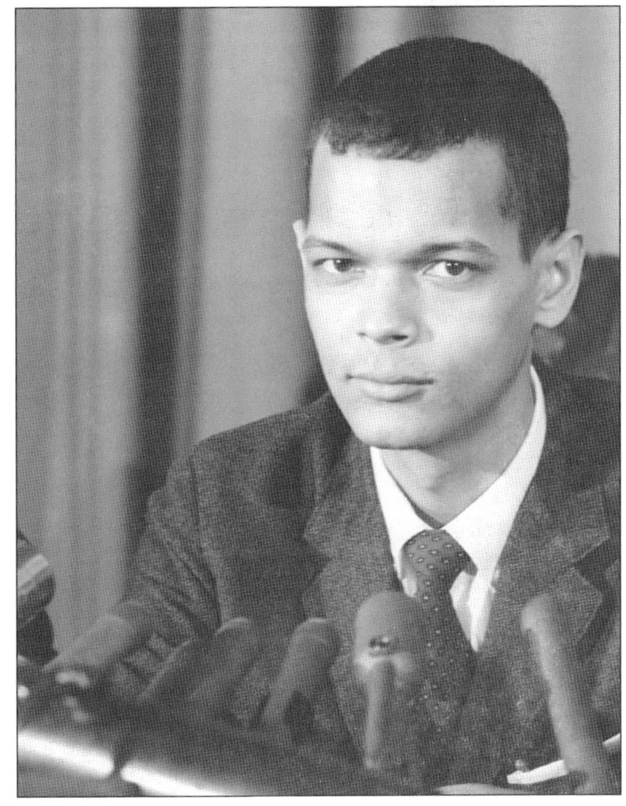

Julian Bond joined Grace Hamilton as one of eight blacks elected to the Georgia General Assembly that year. Also elected to the Georgia House of Representatives were William Alexander, Benjamin Brown, J.C. Daugherty, J.D. Grier, and John Hood, all from Atlanta; Albert Thompson from Columbus; and Richard Dent from Augusta. Elected to the state senate was Horace T. Ward. (LOC.)

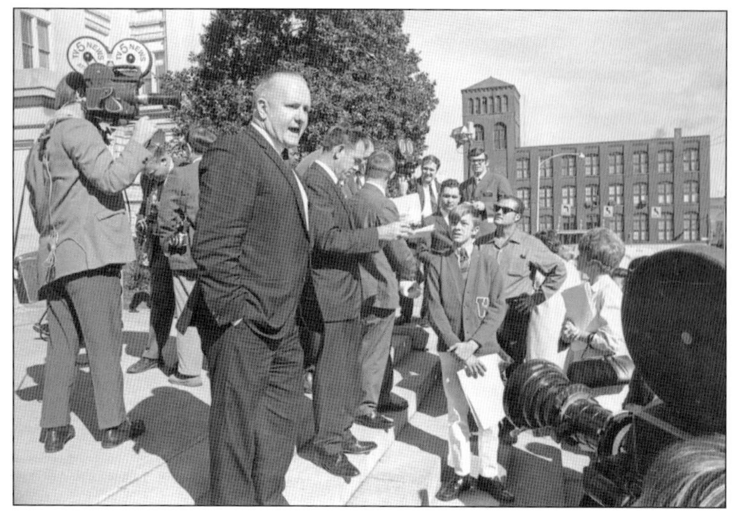

Lester Maddox was Georgia's 75th governor, elected in 1966 on a campaign of states' rights and segregation. He had made a reputation refusing to serve blacks at his restaurant and denying a request to have Dr. Martin Luther King Jr. lie in state at the capitol following his assassination in 1968. Despite that, while in office, Maddox helped integrate the Georgia State Patrol. He served just one term. (GSU.)

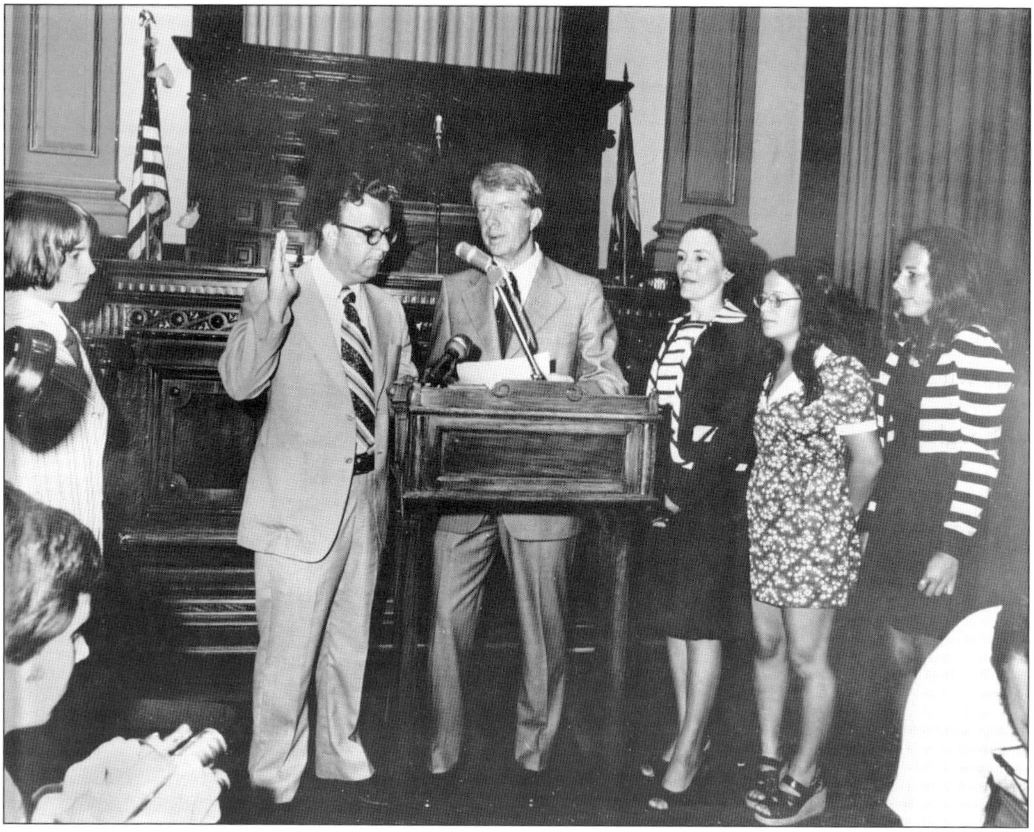

Georgia governor Jimmy Carter is the only Georgian ever elected president of the United States. He is shown here in 1973 in the Georgia Senate chamber at the state capitol swearing in G. Conley Ingram of Marietta as associate justice of the Supreme Court of Georgia. From left to right at right are Ingram's wife, Sylvia; and their daughters Nancy and Lark. (GSA.)

Six

Restoring Splendor

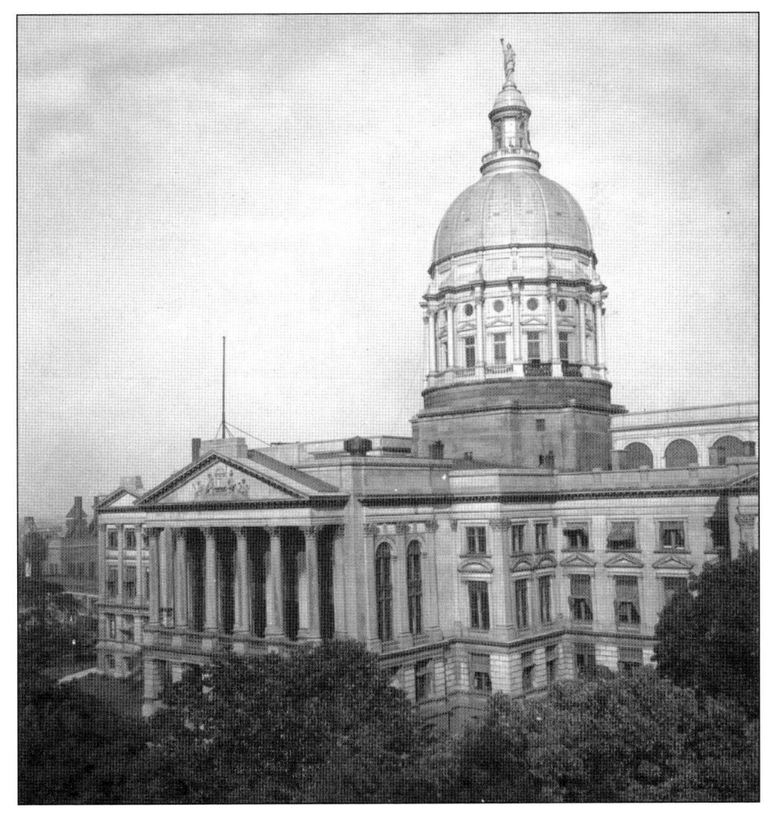

The Georgia State Capitol was designed to accommodate a growing state government, and although it was less than half occupied upon completion, it did not take long for it to be overcrowded and start showing wear and tear from use. In July 1905, the Georgia House Committee on Public Property reported problems with plaster becoming discolored and falling off, especially on the third floor, and that the exterior woodwork needed to be repainted. (LOC.)

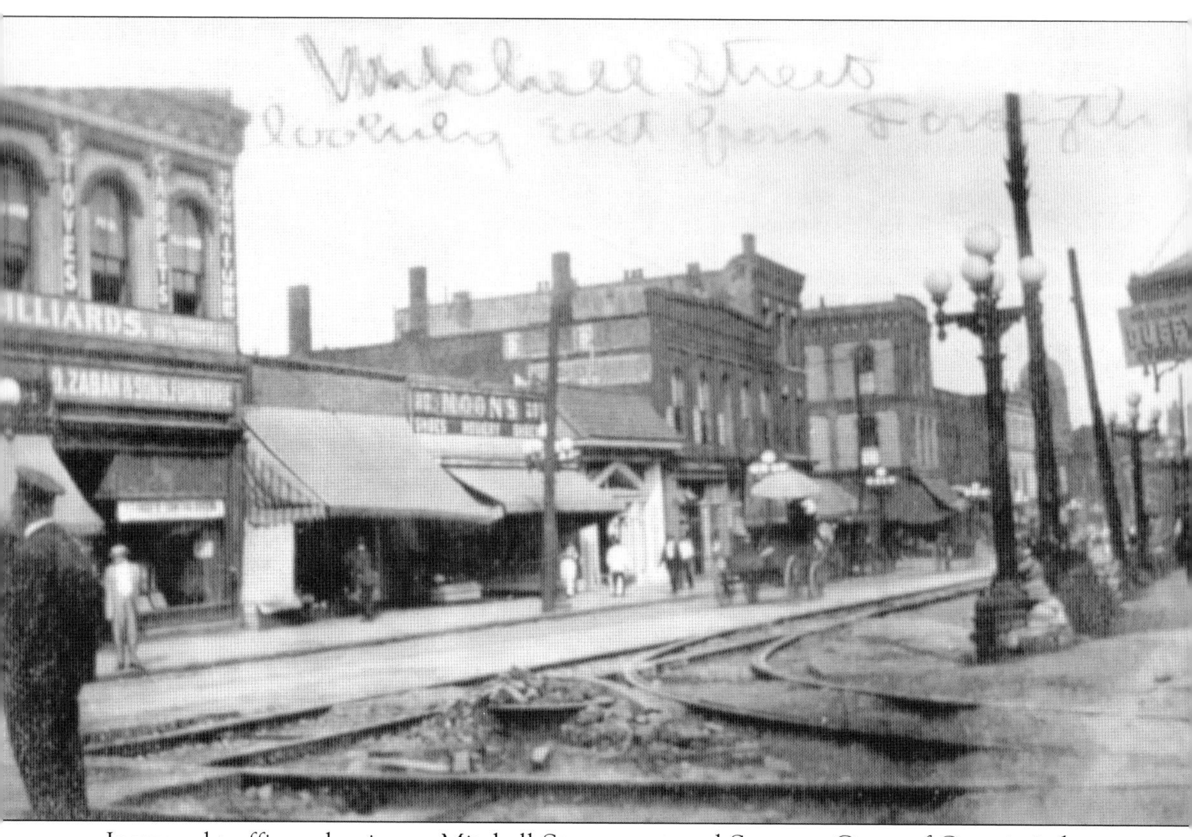

Increased traffic and noise on Mitchell Street prompted Supreme Court of Georgia judges to complain that their sessions were being disrupted, and they demanded the street be paved. In 1923, a windowpane fell out of one of the north clerestory windows, and the need for renovations became more obvious. In 1929, some major repairs and updating took place at a price of $250,000, a quarter of what it cost to build the entire capitol 50 years earlier. The renovations included updating the wiring, installing new pipes, and replacing the old elevator with two new and faster ones. To expand the state government footprint, $50,000 was set aside to buy property along Capitol Square. The capitol went from three floors to four, and the dome underwent some minor repairs and was repainted. (AHC.)

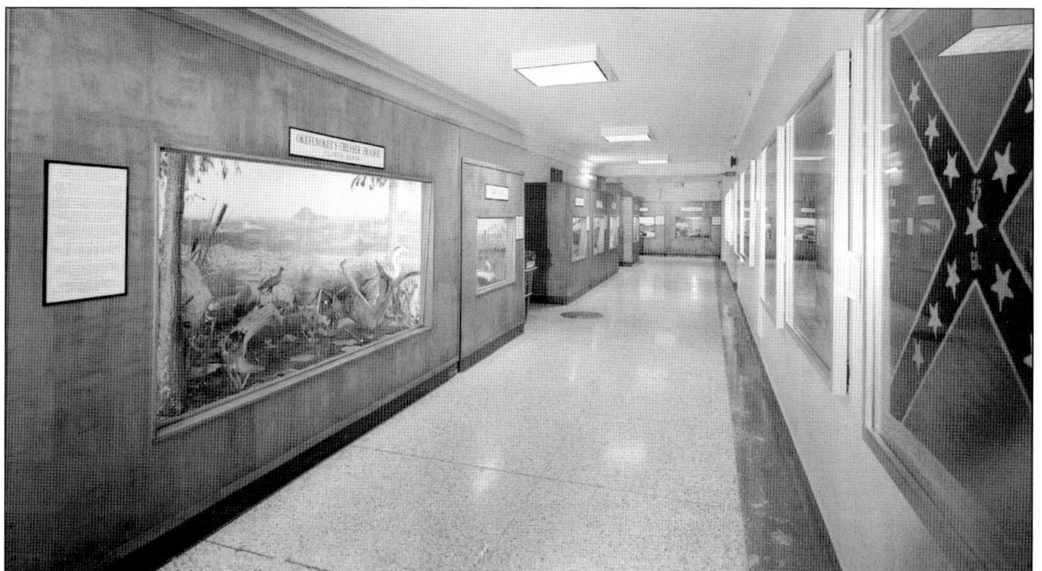

During the 1929 renovations, the mostly unfinished basement was refurbished to make it usable for office and meeting spaces. It had previously been used for storage and for large equipment such as boilers. Early legislators even reportedly stabled their horses there. The 1905 Georgia House Committee on Public Property called the floor "cheap asphalt," saying it was "in extensive need of repair." (LOC.)

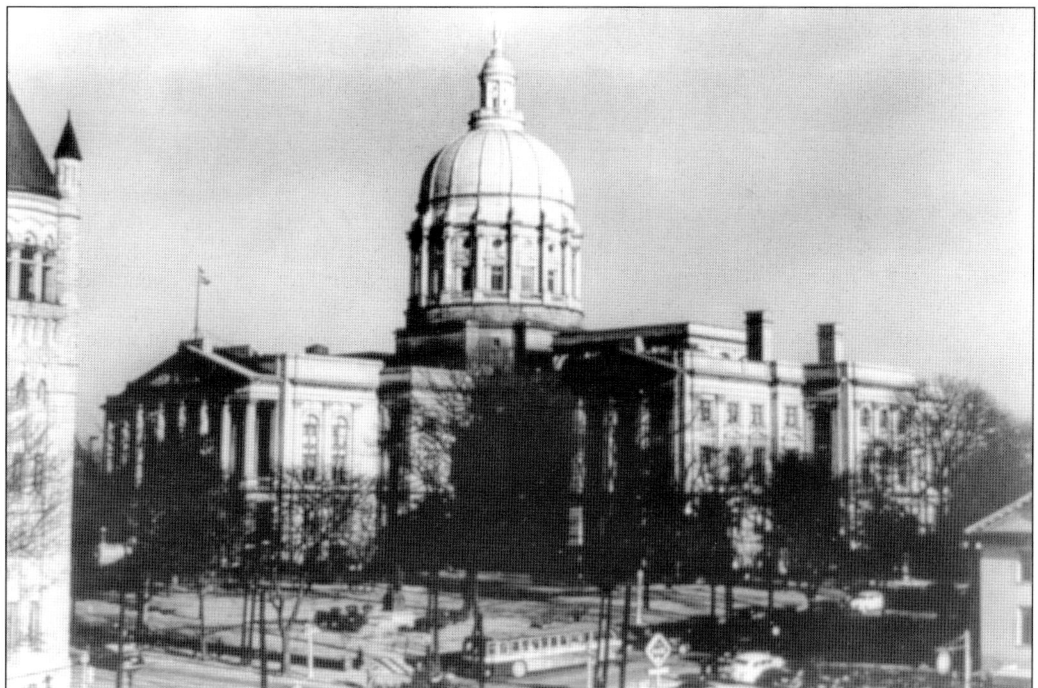

Minor periods of so-called renovations became more necessary. About $40,000 in state and federal funds were appropriated in 1935 and 1938 for repairs, with more work in 1947. A major overhaul was undertaken from 1956 to 1958 at a cost of $1.25 million. Both legislative chambers were completely refurbished, adding lobbies for each. The State Library was moved to the new judicial building and its large space carved into three floors and multiple offices. (LOC.)

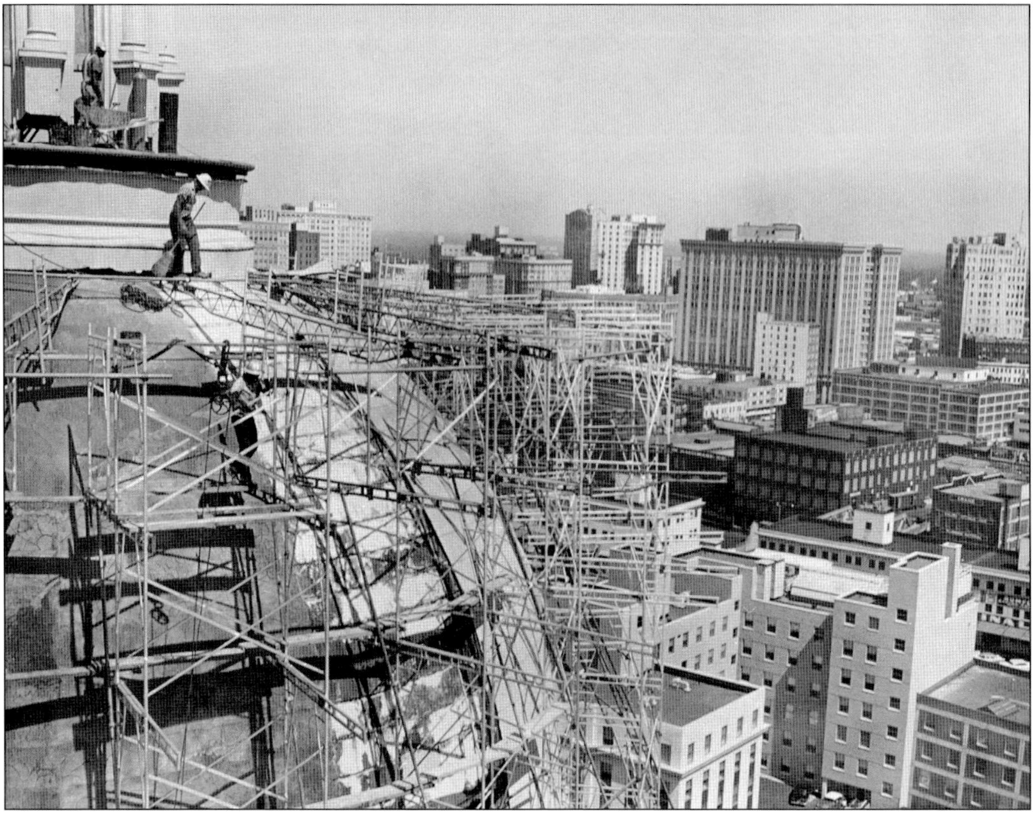

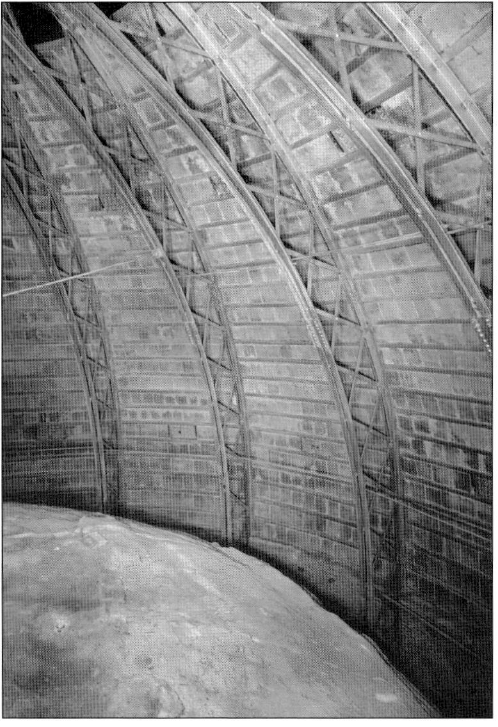

The 1950s renovations finally tackled the ongoing problems with the capitol dome. In a cost-cutting measure during the original construction, cheaper materials were used instead of the planned stone roof. Metal-clad wooden columns and metal-clad bricks had been used to shape the structure, which was then covered in a tin-like metal. Of the $971,095 appropriated for new renovations, at least $640,000 was for the dome alone. Final estimates put the total closer to $729,000. Work included using limestone to replace the tin covering, the balustrades, and the ornamental work. The old metal surface was replaced with the more durable Monel, an alloy including nickel and copper with small amounts of iron, manganese, carbon, and silicon. Highly resistant to corrosion, Monel is stronger and more durable than steel. (Both, GSU.)

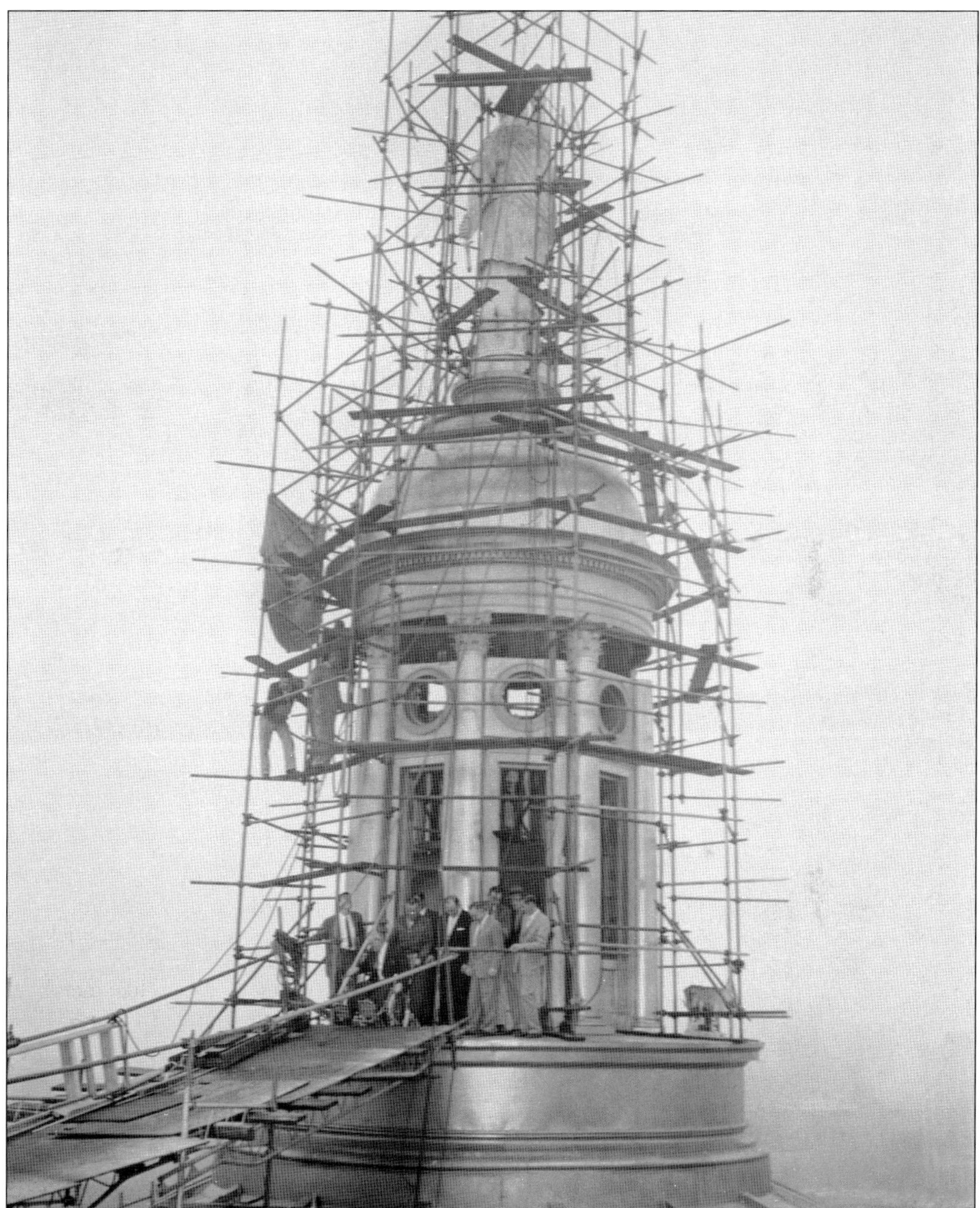

Secretary of State Ben Fortson oversaw the 1950s renovations. Paralyzed from the waist down, he still insisted on inspecting work on the dome personally, including finding a way to reach the top of the cupola on more than one occasion. He is seen here with a group of state officials, including Gov. Marvin Griffin, who is to his right in a dark suit and white shirt. After rolling onto the platform, Fortson agreed the cupola and platform needed to be rebuilt as well. When Fortson took office in 1946, he had expanded his office's duties to include maintenance of the capitol and grounds, the governor's mansion, and Confederate cemeteries. He was later in charge of construction of the Georgia Archives Building, which was finished in 1965 and named for him in 1982. (GSA.)

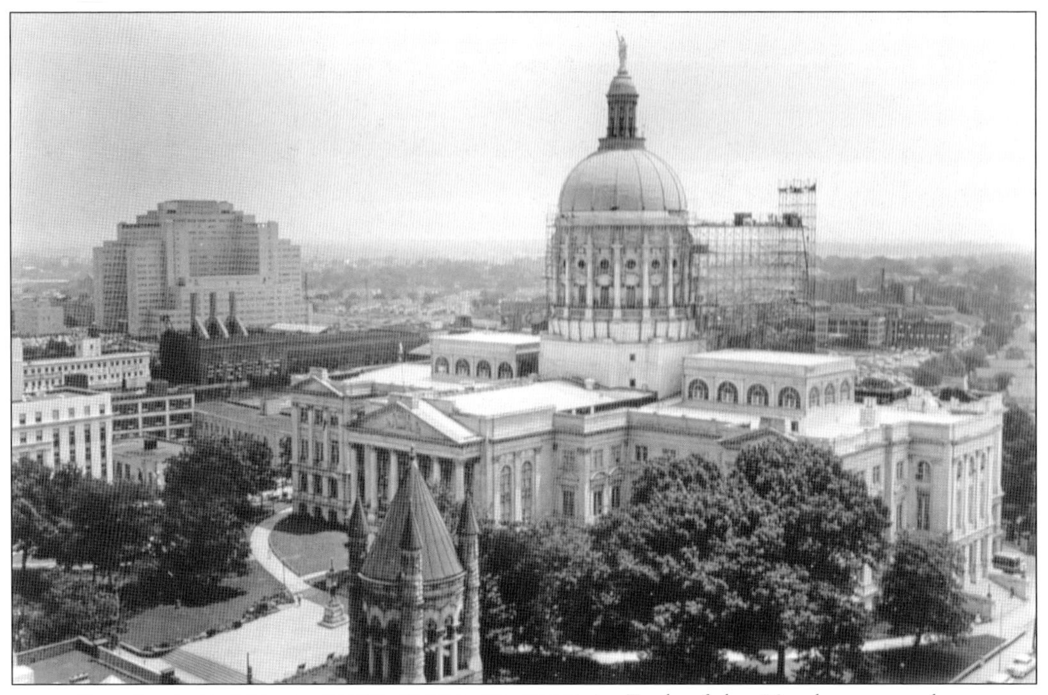

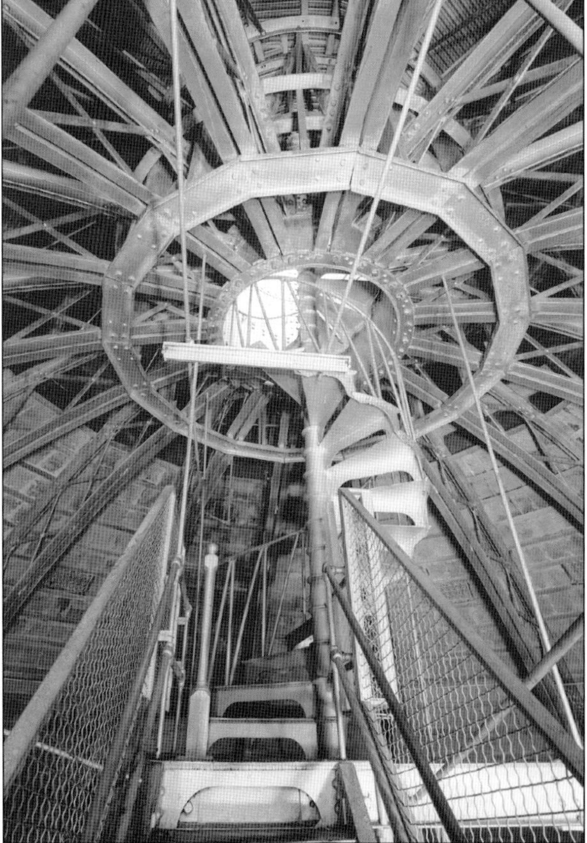

Each of the 16 columns on the exterior of the dome was replaced, and Indiana limestone was again used. The 53-foot-tall columns weighed two tons each and were brought up in sections. A construction elevator was installed on the building's exterior to deliver more than two tons of limestone for the dome repairs. (GSU.)

The iron steps inside the dome, including the spiral staircase to the top of the cupola, were still strong and intact. But after so many years of traffic, they needed to be reinforced. Safety screens were added in the areas that overlooked the rotunda to keep items from falling to the marble floor below. (LOC.)

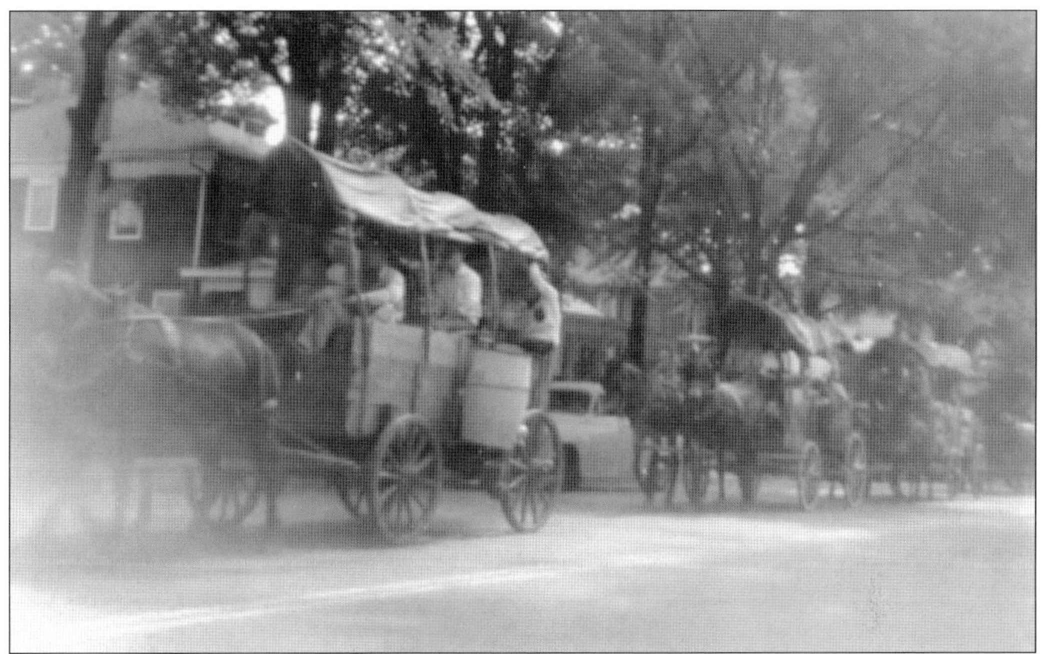

Architect A. Thomas Bradbury had proposed the rebuilt dome be covered in gold. Since America's first gold rush had taken place in 1828 in Lumpkin County, local architect Gordon Price convinced the Dahlonega Chamber of Commerce to organize a day of panning in local streams, and 43 ounces of gold were quickly collected. In August 1958, a parade described in newspaper accounts as "33 adults, 18 children, 15 mules, six horses, one dog, and two State Patrol cars" started making its way to Atlanta. The journey took three days, with the procession spending the last night in Piedmont Park before delivering the gold to Gov. Marvin Griffin at the capitol on August 7. (Above, AHC; below, Chestatee Regional Library System.)

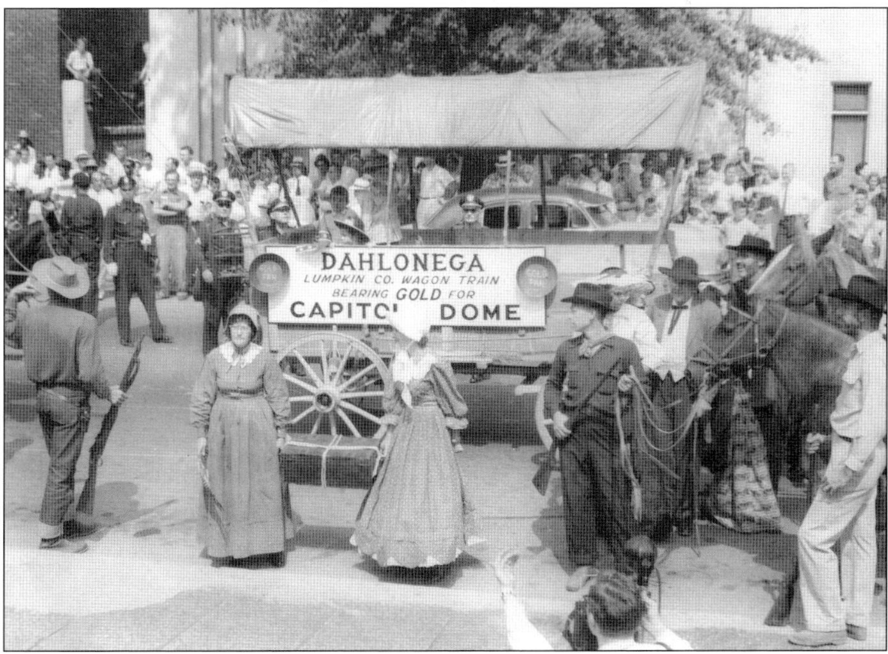

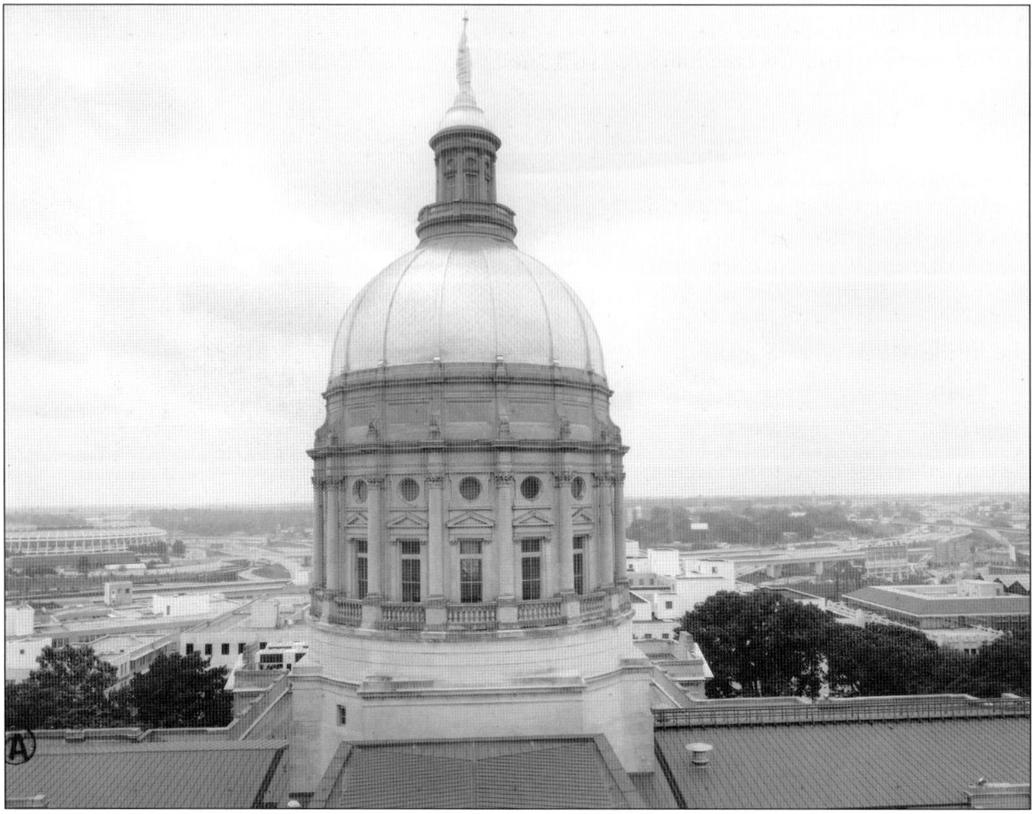

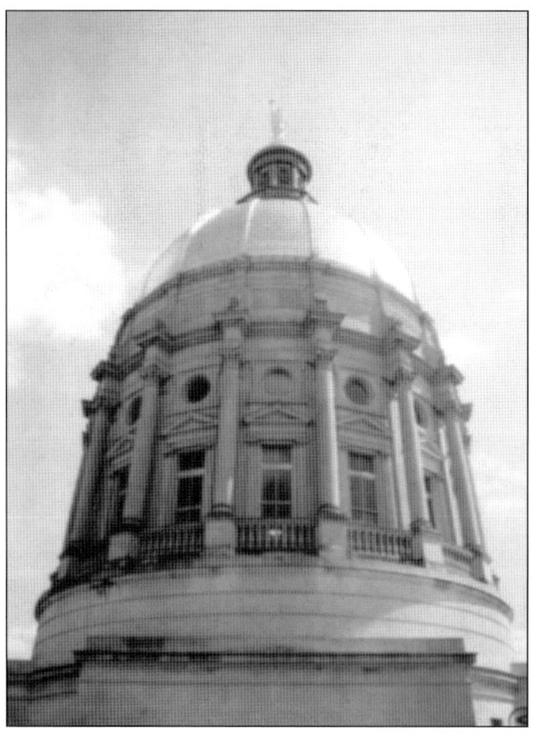

The Dahlonega gold was sent to Philadelphia, where it was milled to an almost impossibly thin gold leaf measuring one 5,000th of an inch thick. Steeplejacks from the small family-owned firm Skyline Engineers of Fitchburg, Massachusetts, were contracted for the specialized work of applying the leaf. A painstaking job of preparing the surface by cleaning it with tetrachloride, priming it, and applying a resin made worse by winter weather, it took months for the company to prep the metal and apply the gilt. The thinness of the gold made it susceptible to the weather, and by the mid-1970s, most of it was gone. Lumpkin County again organized a fundraising wagon train that visited all the former state capitols in a six-week journey. Regilding was completed in 1981, and the process of repairing the gold is now done as needed. (Both, LOC.)

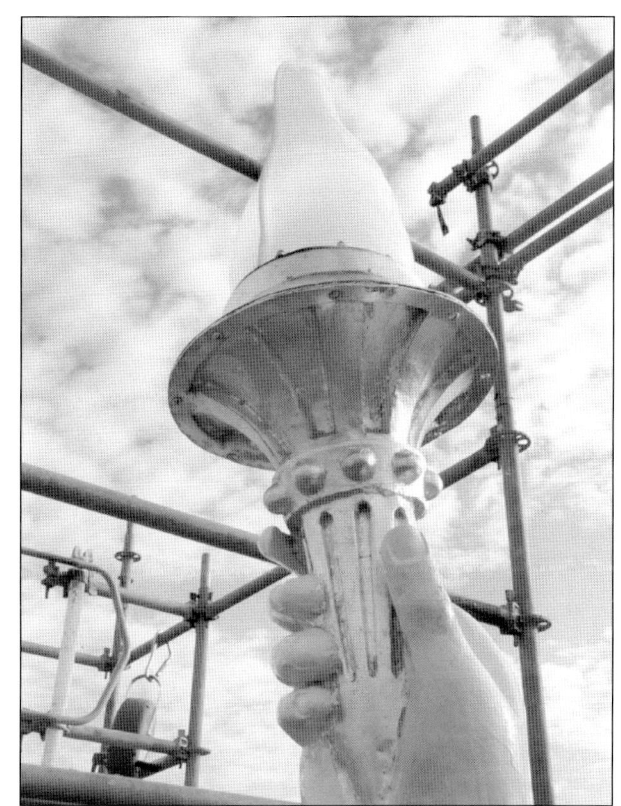

In addition to gilding the dome, the base of the torch in Miss Freedom's hand also got a coat of gleaming yellow metal. Original plans from the 1880s had envisioned that a light would be placed within her torch. It was not until 1959 that this was achieved. A five-inch tube was placed inside her arm and attached to a retractable trolley so that the light bulb can be changed from the inside. (Lord Aeck Sargent.)

The wood in the clerestory windows on the roof of both wings of the capitol was almost completely rotted. Architects said it was incredible that there had only been the singular incident in the 1920s with a pane falling out to the floors below. The window frames were replaced with treated wood covered in Monel to give them more durability. They also received reinforced windowpanes. (LOC.)

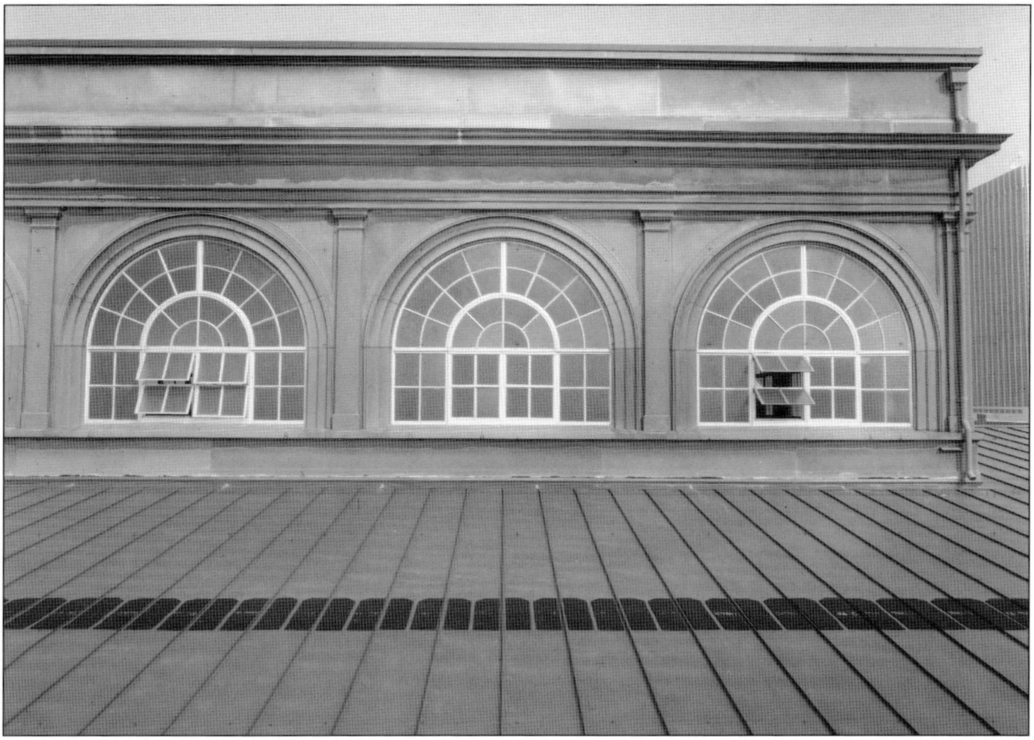

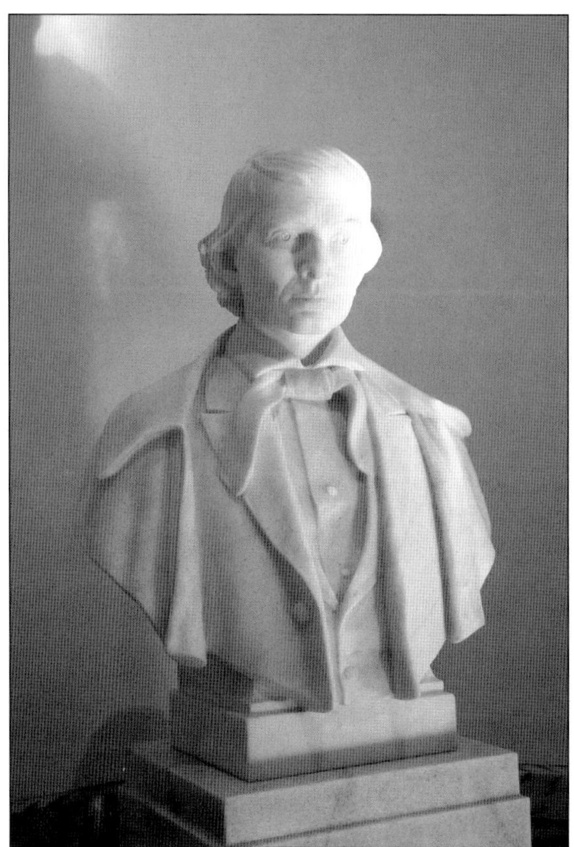

The Georgia Hall of Fame was created in the capitol rotunda following Secretary of State Fortson's push in the 1950s to restore the paintings of the capitol. Lead by the Legislative Committee of the Georgia Division of the United Daughters of the Confederacy, 13 busts of notable Georgians were placed throughout the hall. The first installation was a marble bust of Gov. Alexander H. Stephens in 1954. (Janice McDonald.)

The rotunda officially became the Georgia Hall of Fame on February 7, 1955. Within three months, the Georgia Society of the Dames of the Court of Honor sponsored the addition of Georgia's three signers of the Declaration of Independence, Button Gwinnett, Lyman Hall, and George Walton. The Georgia Hall of Fame now extends to other floors in the capitol and includes *Gone with the Wind* author Margaret Mitchell and Girl Scout founder Juliette Gordon Lowe. (Janice McDonald.)

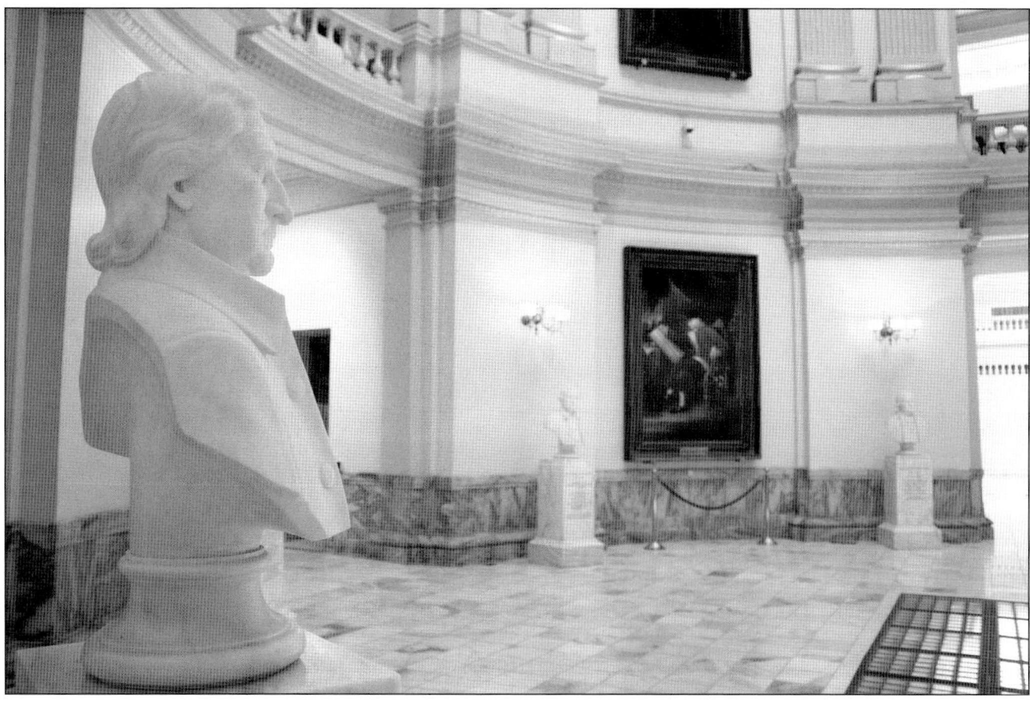

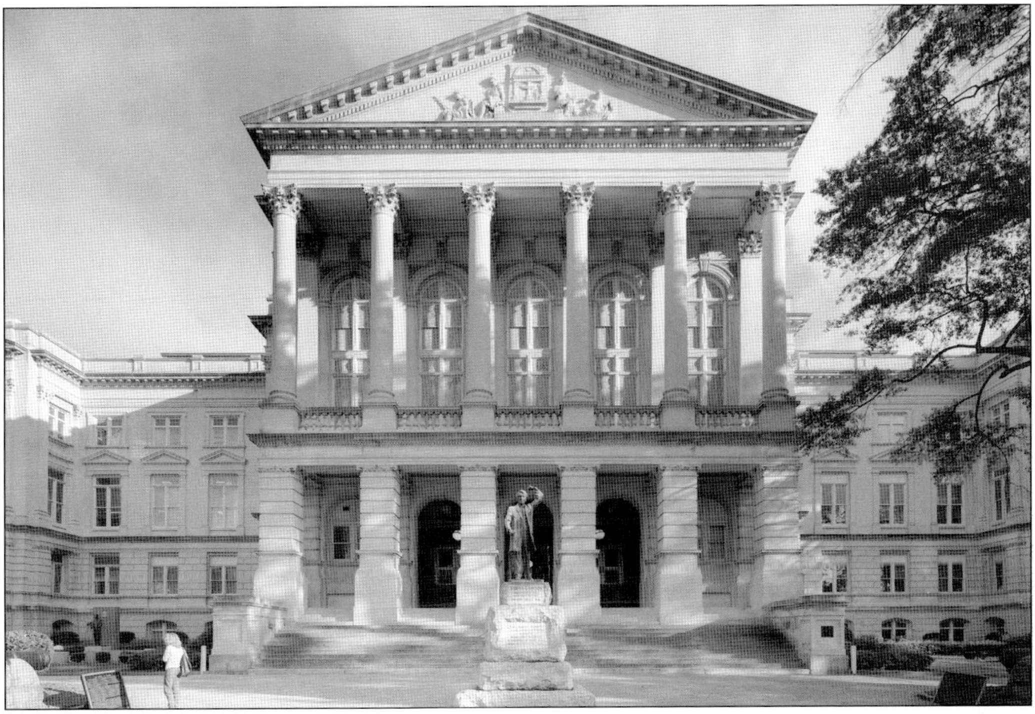

The early 1990s brought concern for the overall condition of the capitol. The General Assembly formed the Commission for the Preservation of the Georgia State Capitol in 1993 to initiate a complete restoration of the more than 100-year-old building. The architectural firm of Lord Aeck Sargent was hired to direct what would be a more than two-decade project. The initial phase's budget was $6.1 million. (LOC.)

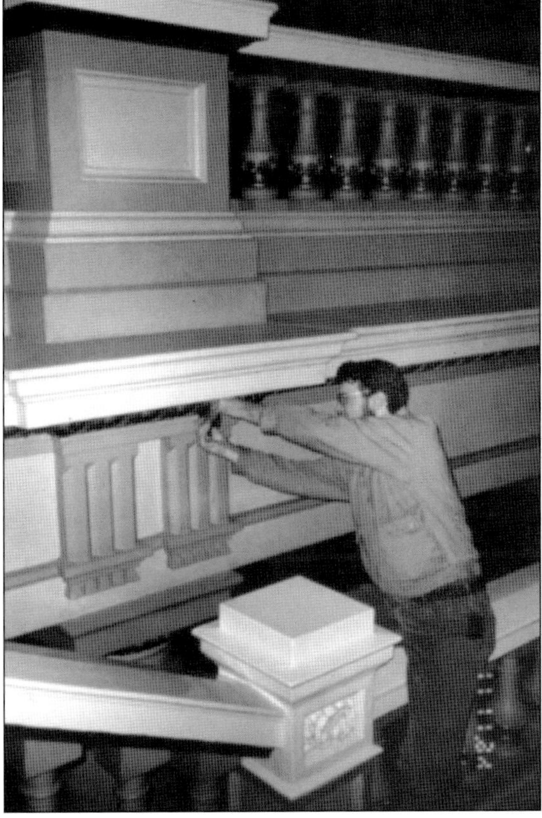

Over the decades, rooms and areas of the capitol had undergone changes in appearance due to so-called modernization efforts as well as evolving functionality. One of the goals of the long-term project was to return as many areas as possible to their original appearance while still updating the infrastructure of the building. (Lord Aeck Sargent.)

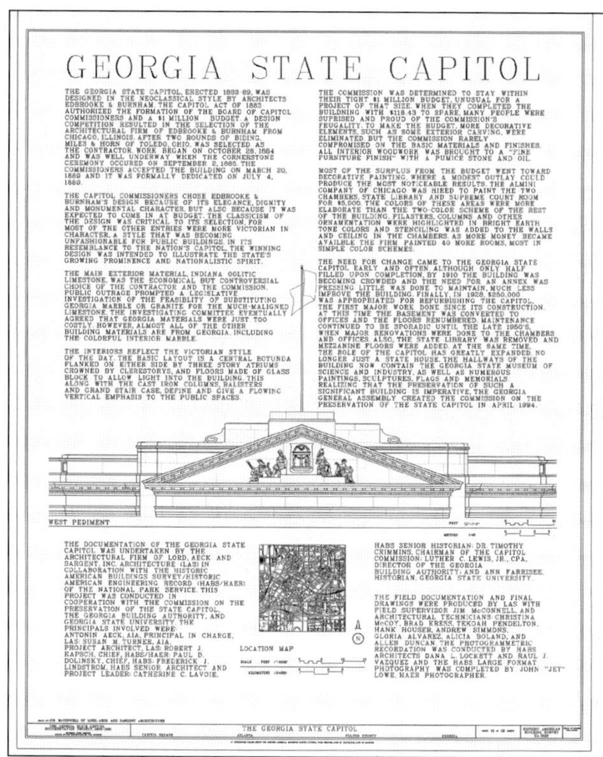

Before any work could begin, the building had to undergo a comprehensive examination to determine exactly what needed to be done. Its history was thoroughly researched and documented in a federal program called the Historic American Building Survey. This cost $200,000 and was funded through the National Park Service, the Georgia Building Authority, the Georgia General Assembly, and the Governor's Discretionary Fund. The documentation made the need for repairs more evident. (LOC.)

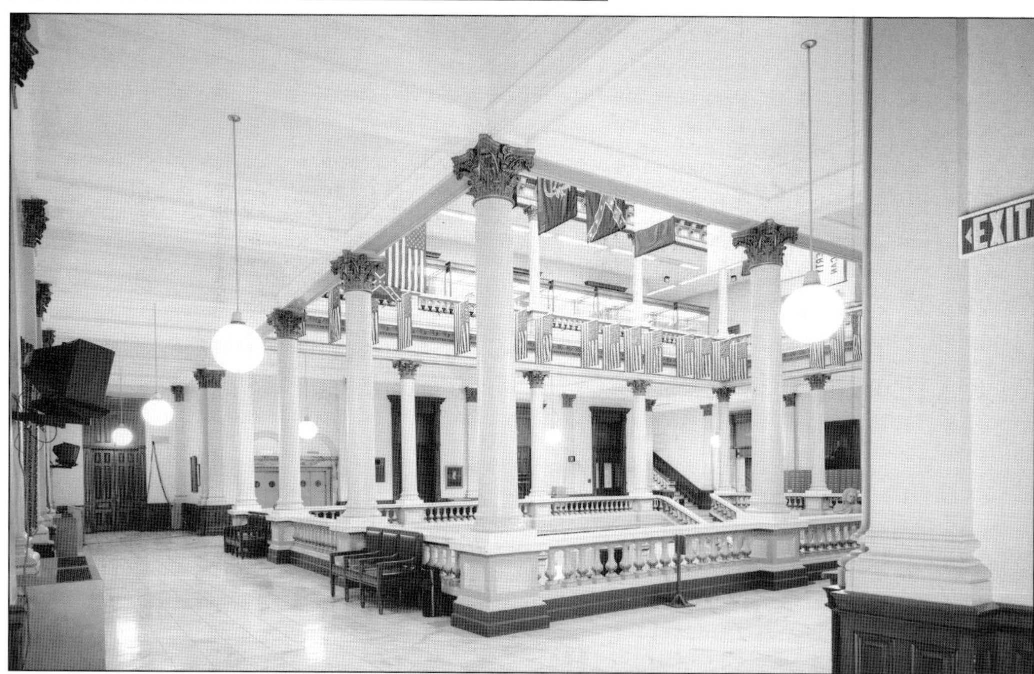

Issues were not just aesthetic, but a matter of safety in some cases. After a chunk of plaster fell from the third-floor ceiling in 1995, it was determined the second- and third-floor ceilings had substantial plaster failure. As the Conference Committee was voting to fund the restoration, rain was dripping through the roof and into buckets on their table. (LOC.)

Paint conservationist and analyst Frank S. Welsh (not pictured) helped determine the original colors and finishes in the capitol's public spaces. Creating exposure windows to see what was beneath the layers of accumulated paint, he found the color scheme had originally consisted of a four-color palette of a pale orange yellow, a light green, a dark gray accent on the column bases, and an orange shellac on all the naturally finished oak wood trim. (Lord Aeck Sargent.)

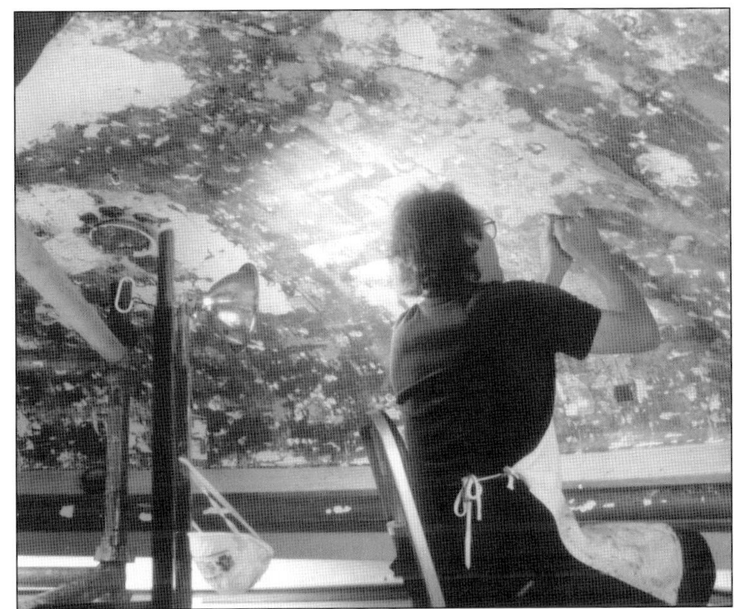

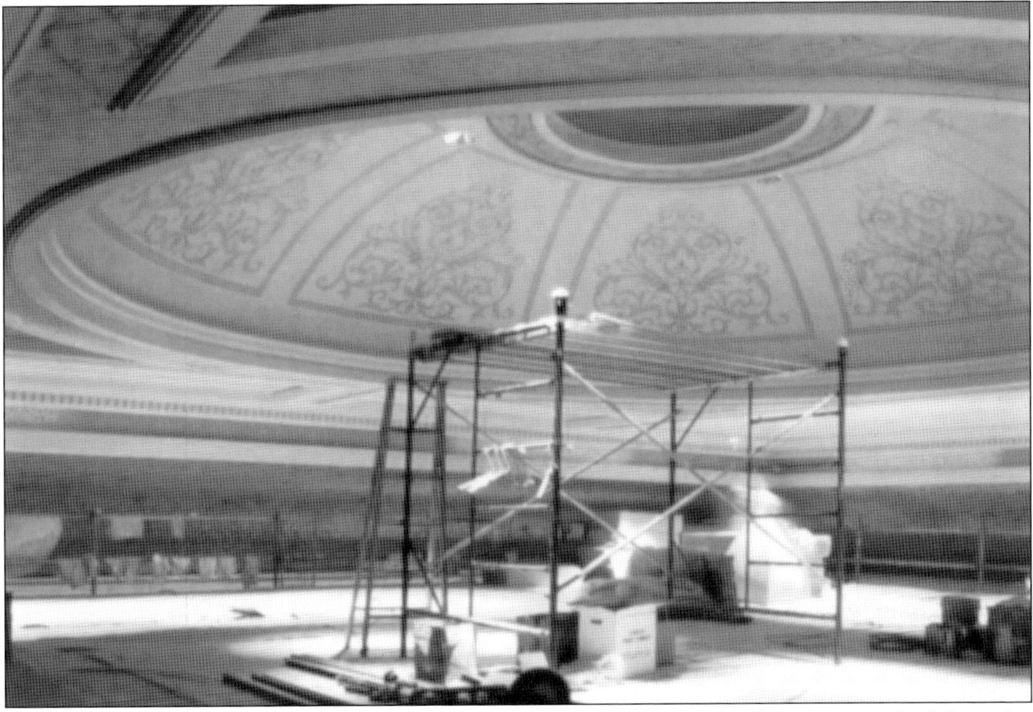

Designs were photographed and traced so they could be re-created and sent to a color lab so the colors could be matched as closely as possible. Scaffolding was erected to allow workers to remove a century of paint and reapply the intricate stenciling patterns that had been discovered. As in the original plans, the restored coloring in the atria and rotunda helped complement the gray and white marble floor, pink marble wainscot, and the natural warm finish of the oak woodwork. (Lord Aeck Sargent.)

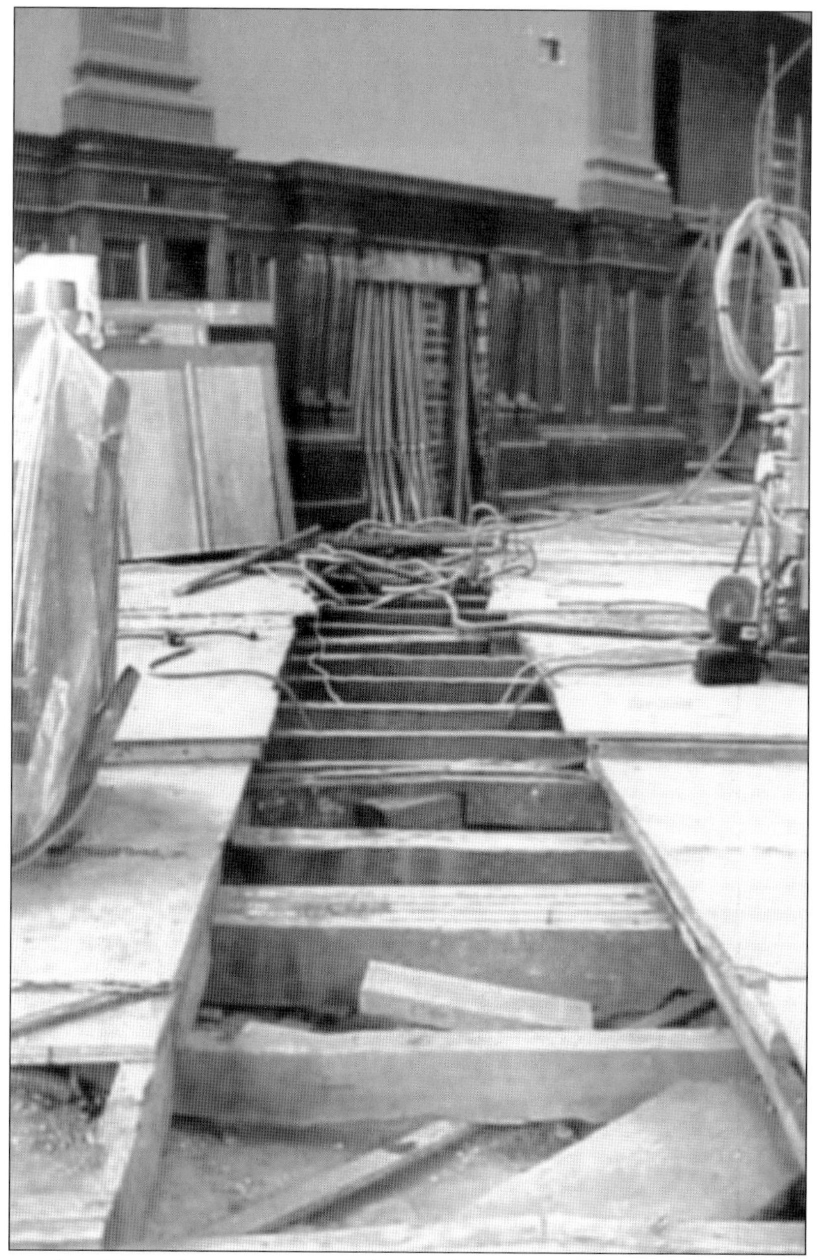

Among the undertakings, the entire capitol electrical system needed an overhaul. The renovators were able to take advantage of the many old heating flues that ran through the solid masonry walls of the capitol to help hide the coils as well as cables needed for new technology. The main switchgear was relocated to an underground vault constructed on the Martin Luther King Jr. Boulevard side of the building. A problem typical in many restorations is how to accommodate changes in technology since the original structure was built, and how to plan for future advances. This meant miles and miles of cable needed to be strung and somehow hidden. The old floors in both legislative chambers had been replaced in the past, which provided a good opportunity to accommodate not just electrical systems but internet for the entire room, including individual desks. (Lord Aeck Sargent.)

Restoration of the legislative chambers was timed to take place during the nine months that lawmakers were not in session. It began immediately after the last lawmaker walked out the door in March 1998 with the removal of desks and chairs, which were also set for refurbishing. Crews worked around the clock. Temporary desks were put in place when the legislature returned in January 1999, with work starting anew after their departure in March. (Lord Aeck Sargent.)

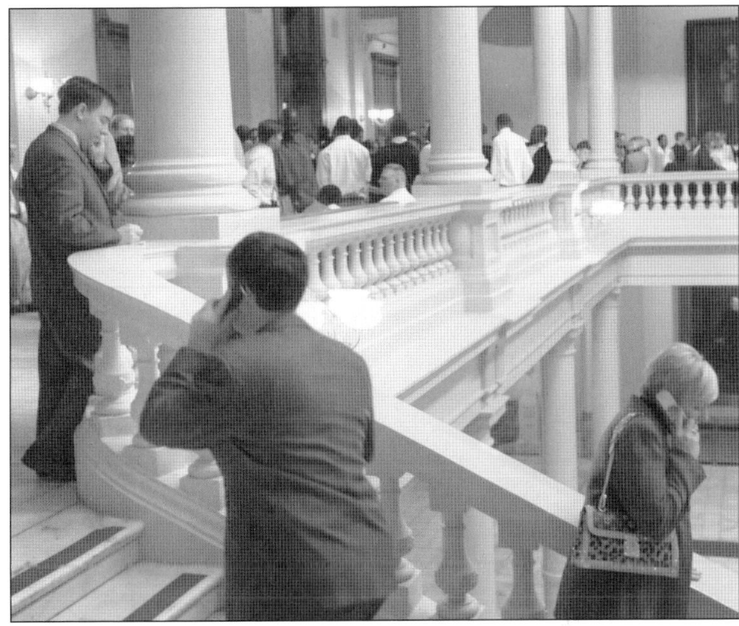

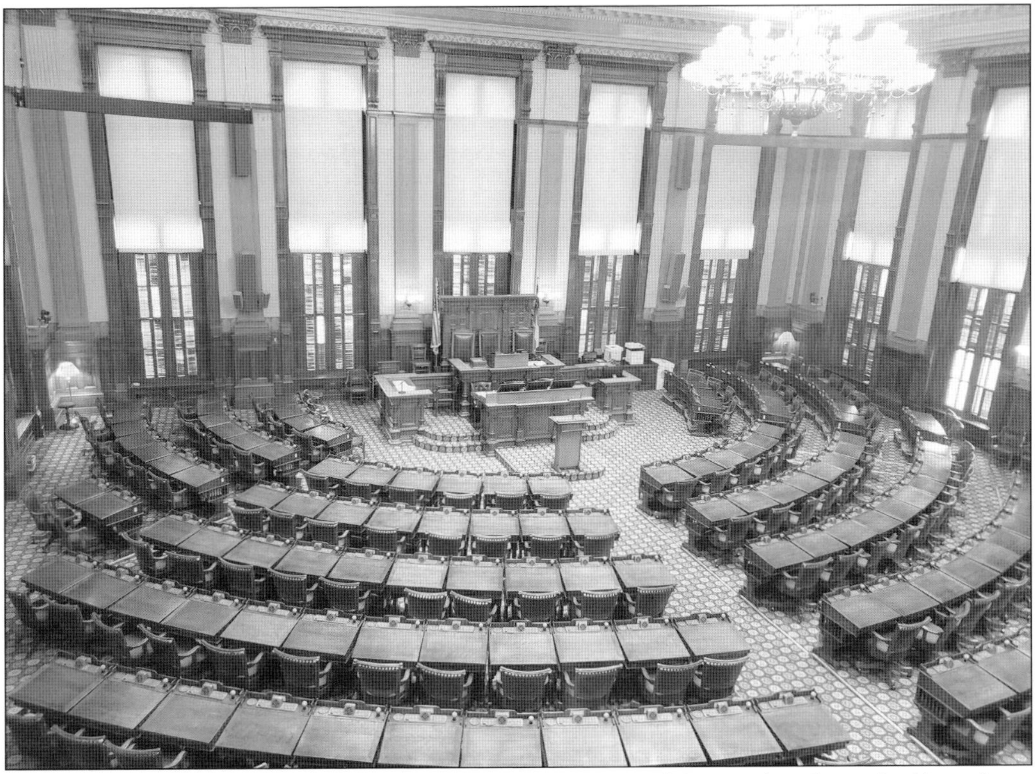

The original lighting plan for the House of Representatives and Senate chambers relied heavily on natural light from the massive two-story windows. Over the years, heavy drapes and thick Styrofoam had been used to cover the windows for insulation. All of that was removed. External window frames throughout the entire building were refinished and repaired using double-insulated glass and new glazing. Once again, the chambers could utilize natural light. (Janice McDonald.)

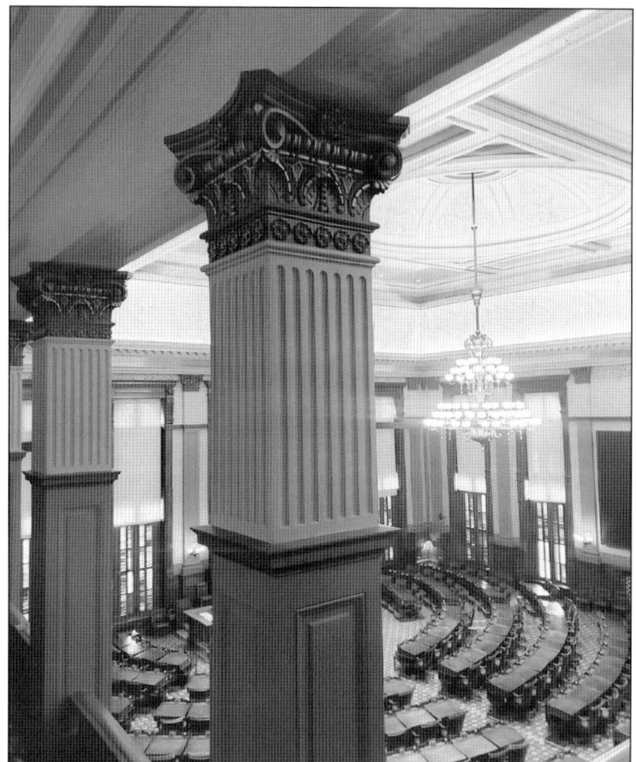

A focal point in each of the legislative chambers was the massive chandeliers. All the original light fixtures were removed in the 1960s. Historic lighting specialists worked two and a half years to re-create the multitiered original chandeliers. They were installed as one of the last bits of workmanship before the General Assembly returned to session and their completely refinished chambers on January 10, 2000. (Janice McDonald.)

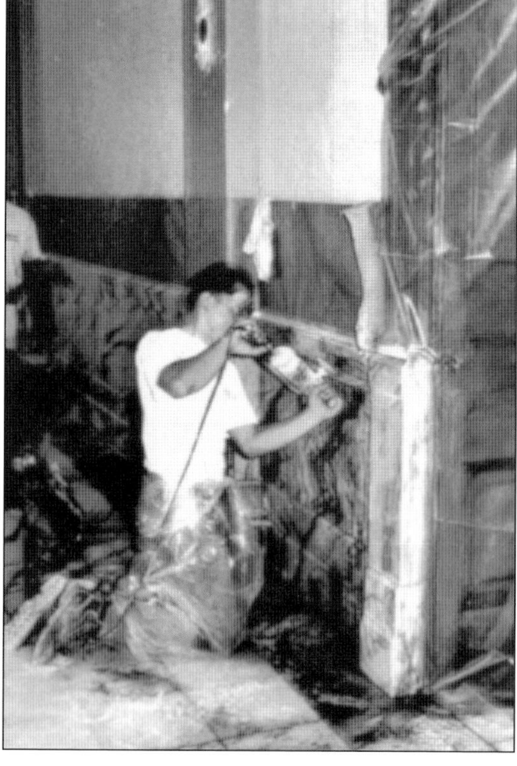

The interior of the capitol contains over one and a half acres of marble on various surfaces. The pink Etowah floris used in the wainscotting had to be polished and the tiles in the floors repaired. Most of the tiles had been improperly bonded, so not only did they need to be cleaned and repaired, but they also had to be removed and reinstalled. (Lord Aeck Sargent.)

The ornate caps on all the pilasters and columns throughout the building also demanded attention. The scope of the project included cleaning, repairing, and refinishing each. That required a great deal of skill as well as a great deal of time. Teams of plasterers and painters worked in stages as the work progressed in sections so that the whole building was not under renovation at one time. Finishes depended on the location. The pilasters in the legislature chambers contained a great deal more detail and flourish than those in the public areas so they would match the more involved stenciling and paint work there. (Right, Lord Aeck Sargent; below, Janice McDonald.)

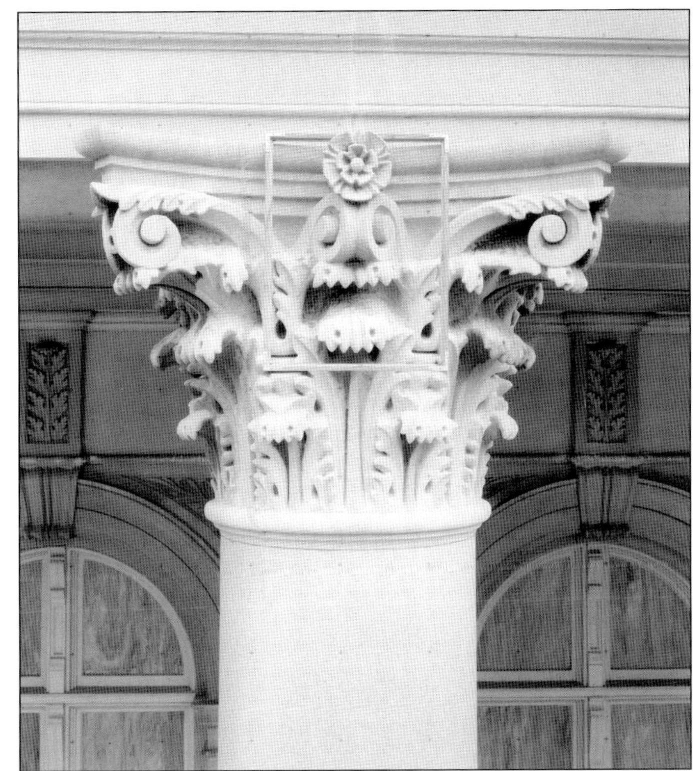

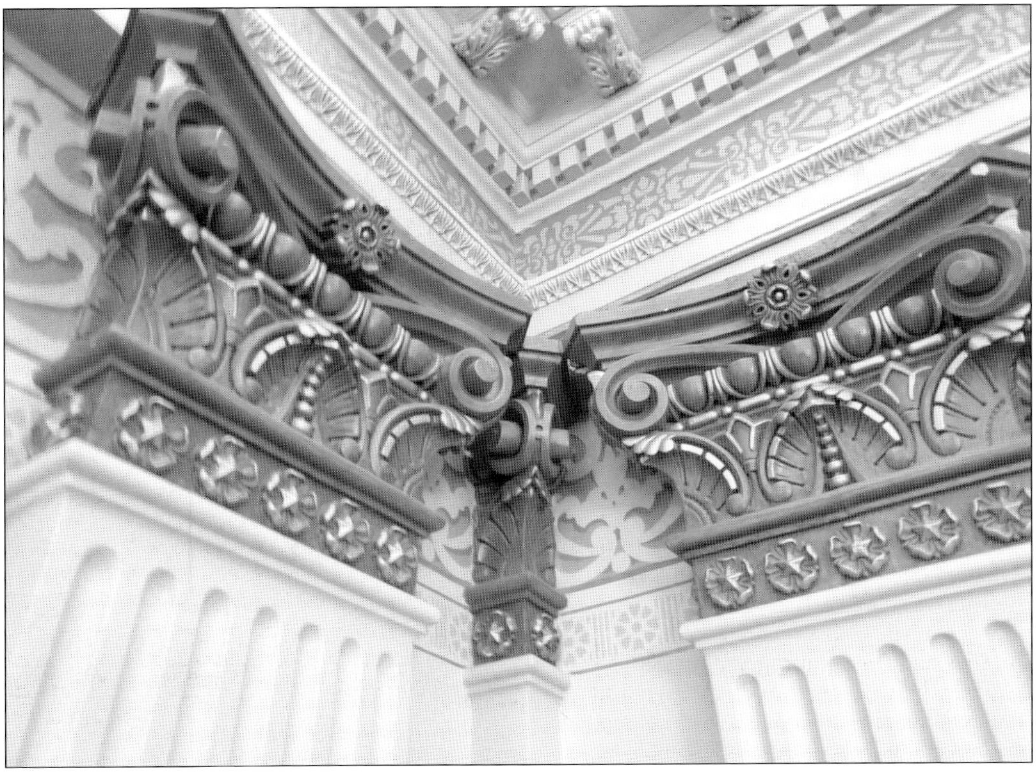

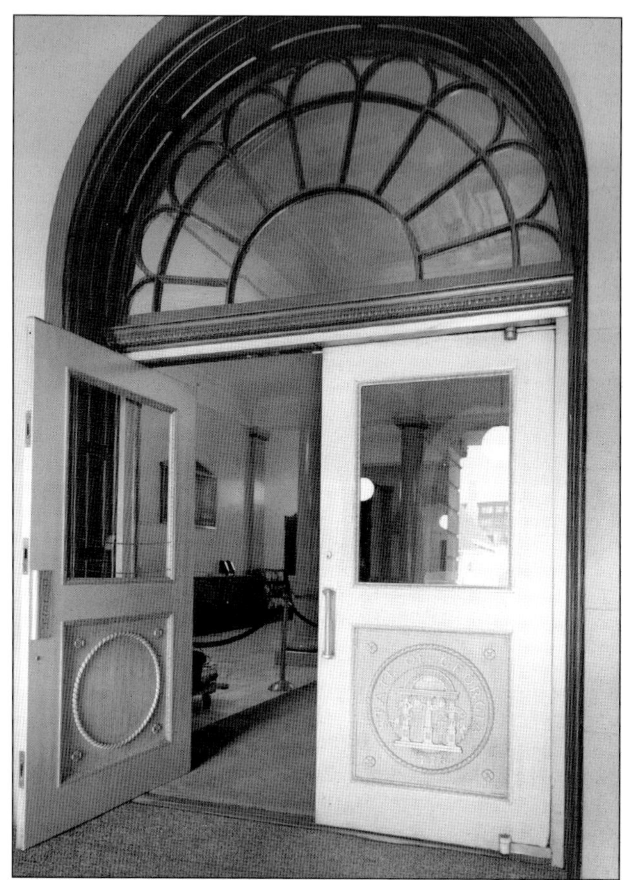

During the 1950s renovation, the capitol's original exterior oak doors were removed and replaced with high-quality aluminum doors with the state seal on them. Although modern for the time, they did not match the building's character. New doors were created to match those found in an old photograph. Constructed with a solid stave core, the exterior was laminated wood blocks of oak veneer. (LOC.)

Early photographs of the capitol proved invaluable as guidelines and to fill holes left in original documentation when it came to restoration. Winter Construction worked to renovate the exterior, cleaning the building skin, repairing masonry, and restoring windows. In addition, the roof, which had leaked almost from the earliest days, needed to be replaced. In 2006, a five-layer built-up modified bitumen membrane roofing system was completed. (GSU.)

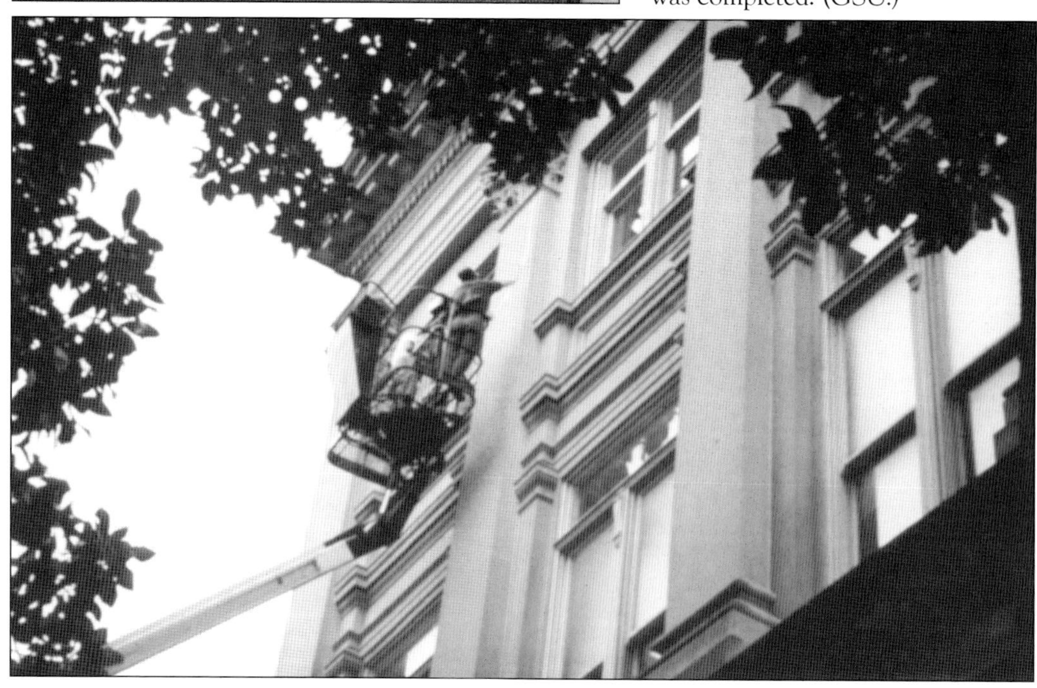

An evaluation of Miss Freedom showed she was swaying and needed major repairs. There was evidence someone had used her for target practice with rifle shots. But removing her from her post to fix her was not an easy undertaking. Standing 23 feet tall, the statue weighs nearly 1,250 pounds. It required days of strategizing to determine how to airlift her using a helicopter. More than one engineer questioned what methods were used in 1888 to put her in place originally. (Lord Aeck Sargent.)

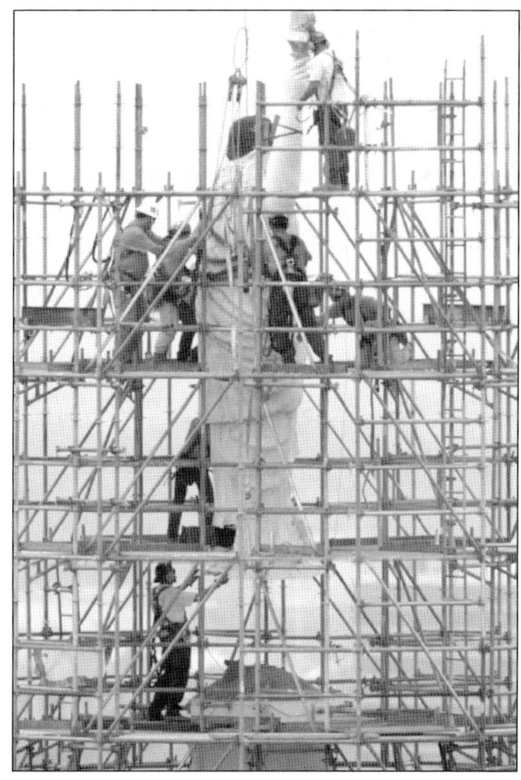

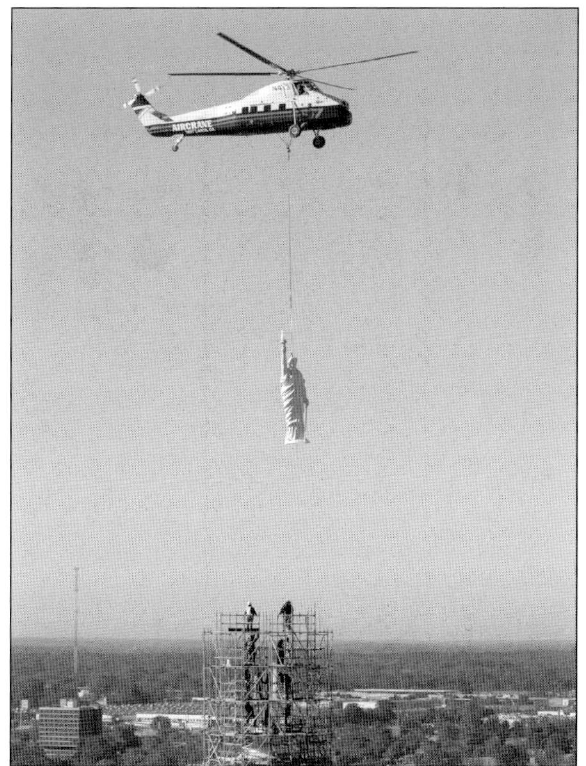

Early on a Saturday morning in July 2004, the entire capitol building was evacuated and surrounding streets were closed while a construction helicopter moved into position. With careful maneuvering, a team of workers helped guide the massive statue safely through the scaffolding that had been holding her in place, and Miss Freedom took flight. (Kelly Holtz Photography.)

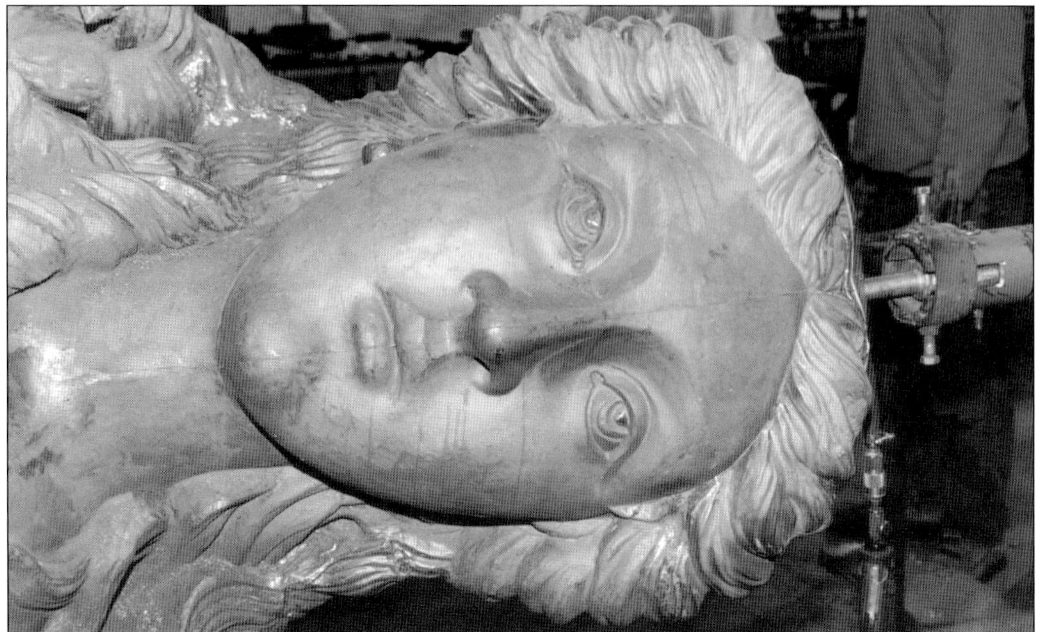

The Canadian firm of Heather and Little was tasked with making Miss Freedom like new again. That required completely stripping the paint from her copper form and virtually rebuilding her. Her Phrygian cap, or pileus, adorned with a star was removed, and a new internal support beam was inserted to stabilize her frame. To reproduce damaged and missing parts, 20- and 24-ounce copper sheets were used. (Heather and Little Limited.)

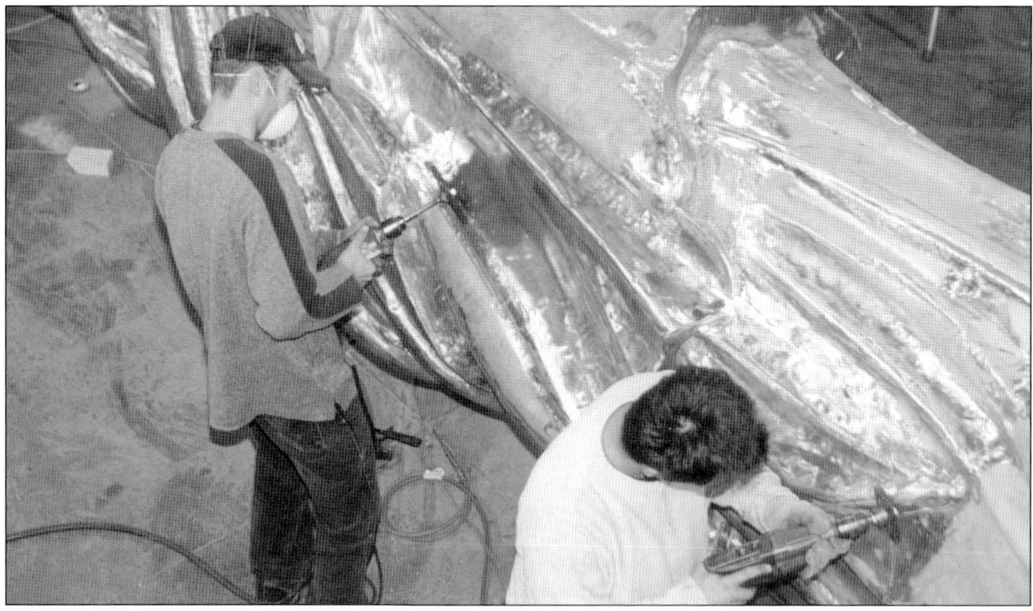

All the statue's seams had to be resoldered and mechanical fasteners put in place to strengthen her. Then the solder joints were ground smooth and cleaned. Galvanized steel was incorporated into her arm to help maintain its structural support as it stands high over her head, ensuring she could withstand at least another 100 years on top of the capitol. Workmen Dave Spear (left) and John Schneider are seen here making finishing repairs. (Heather and Little Limited.)

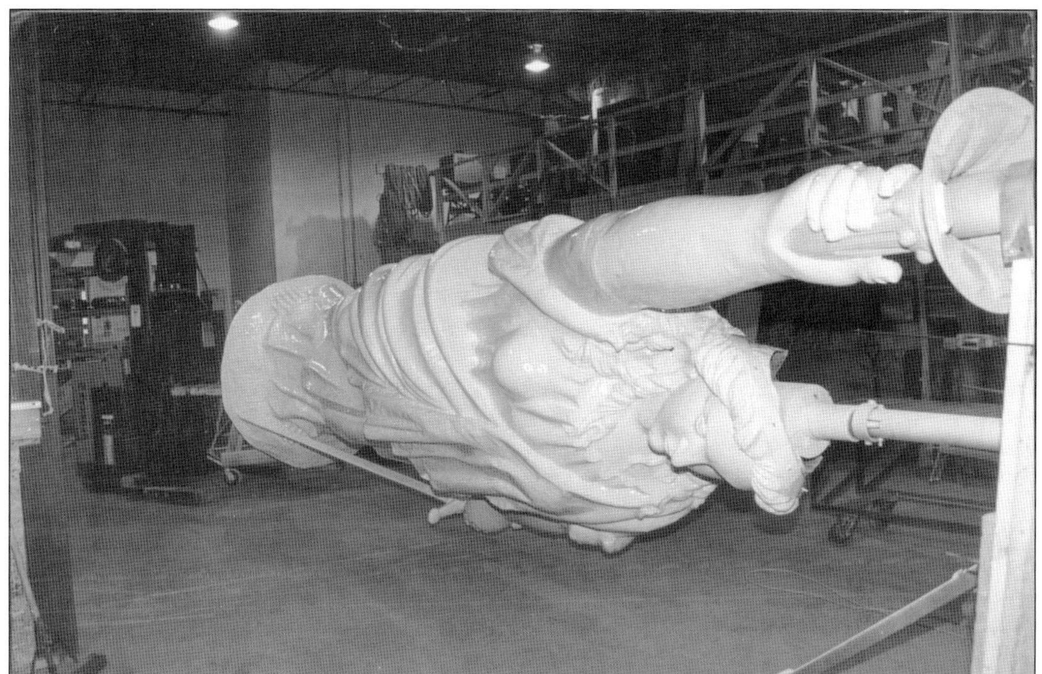

Repairs to Miss Freedom took a little over two months to complete. Once her copper frame was restored and reenforced, she was painted in a thick, durable, protective white coating. The paint is designed to help protect her from the elements as well as help her stand out on top of the capitol cupola. (Heather and Little Limited.)

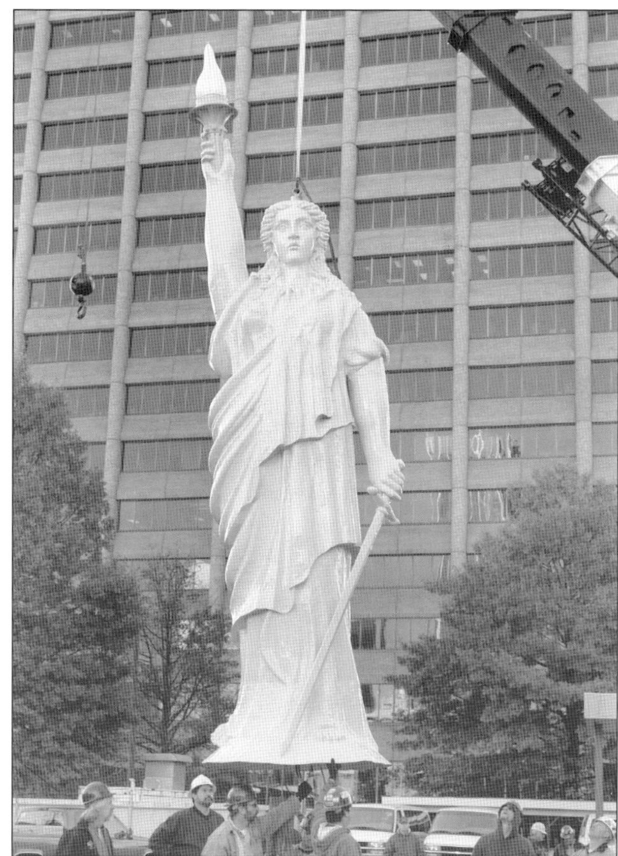

On November 6, 2004, Miss Freedom was ready to resume her spot atop the capitol dome. Photographer Kelly Holtz, who had documented her departure, was there for her return. She was now more than 115 years old but looking new as she was uncrated and prepared to return to her rightful spot. (Kelly Holtz Photography.)

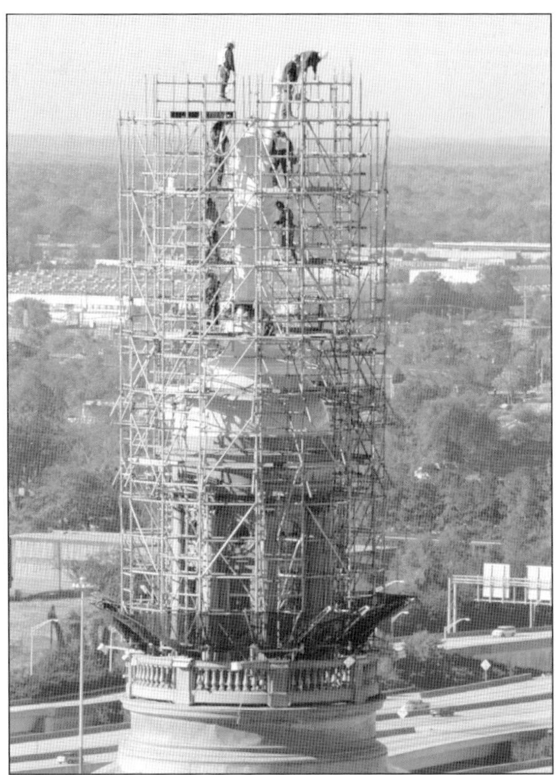

As Miss Freedom was hoisted using a helicopter, a large group of dignitaries, including Gov. Sonny Perdue, got an eye-level view of the undertaking. Perched on the roof of the 20-story James H. "Sloppy" Floyd Veterans Memorial Building across from the capitol, the group watched as Miss Freedom was carefully lowered into the scaffolding where workers could again safely secure her. (Kelly Holtz Photography.)

Once Miss Freedom was secured, the business of regilding the capitol cupola needed to be addressed. The thin gold leaf can only withstand so much assault from weather. R. Alden Marshall & Associates of Galveston, Texas, took on the job. This time, the leaf was reapplied over previous layers using 23.75 karat leaf processed in Germany. Ruth Marshall is shown working on the cupola. (R. Alden Marshall & Associates.)

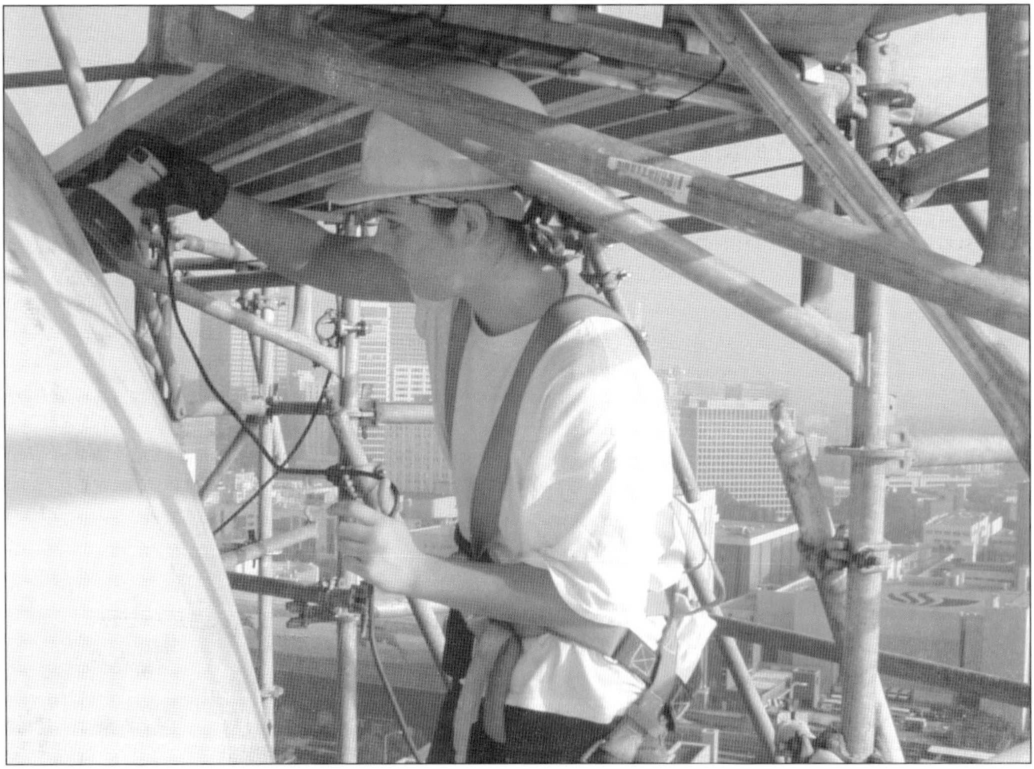

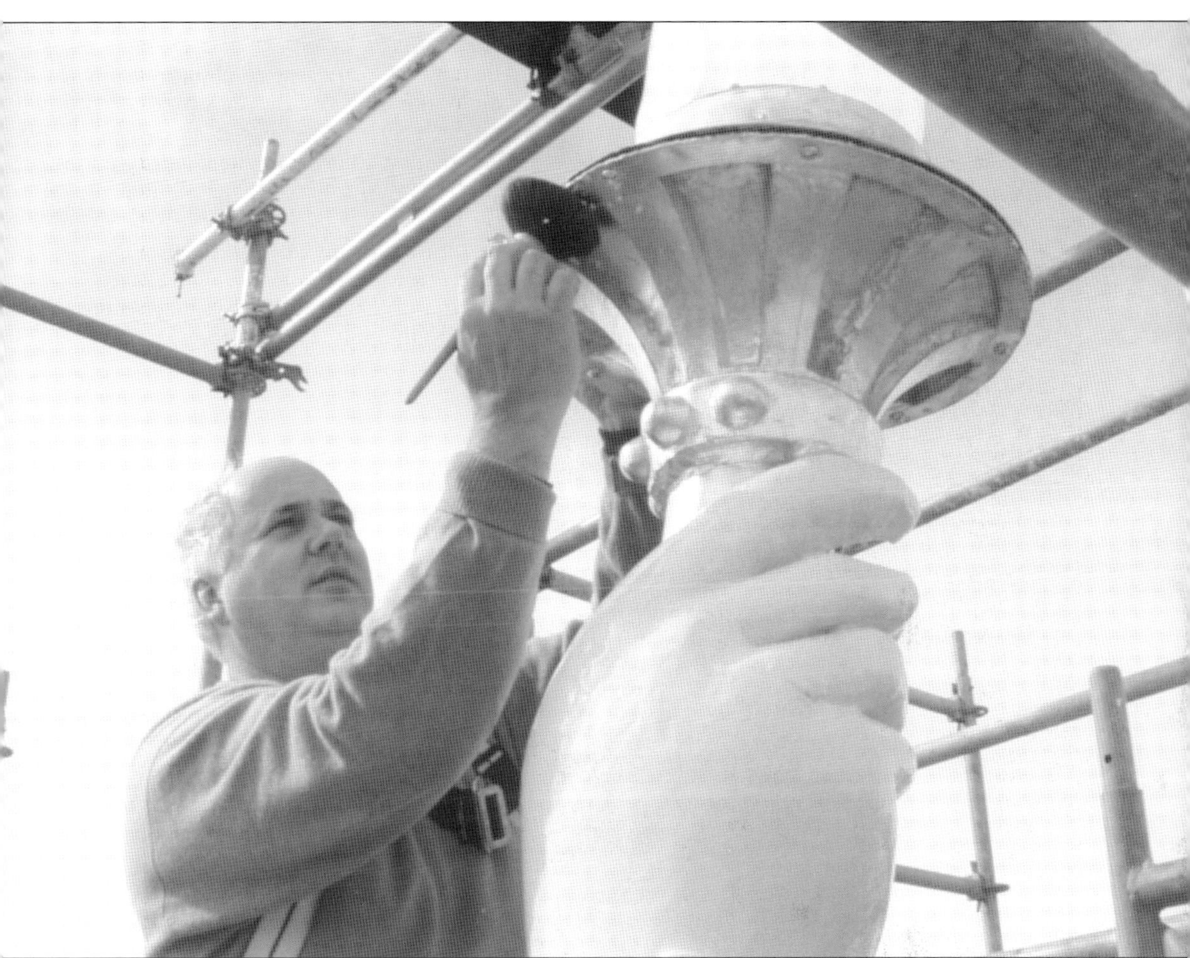

R. Alden Marshall & Associates of Texas not only gilded the cupola but also applied gold leaf to the torch on Miss Freedom. The torch had been gilded during the 1950s restoration, but it had been stripped during the statue's refurbishing. Robert Marshall is applying the finishing touches to the torch. (R. Alden Marshall & Associates.)

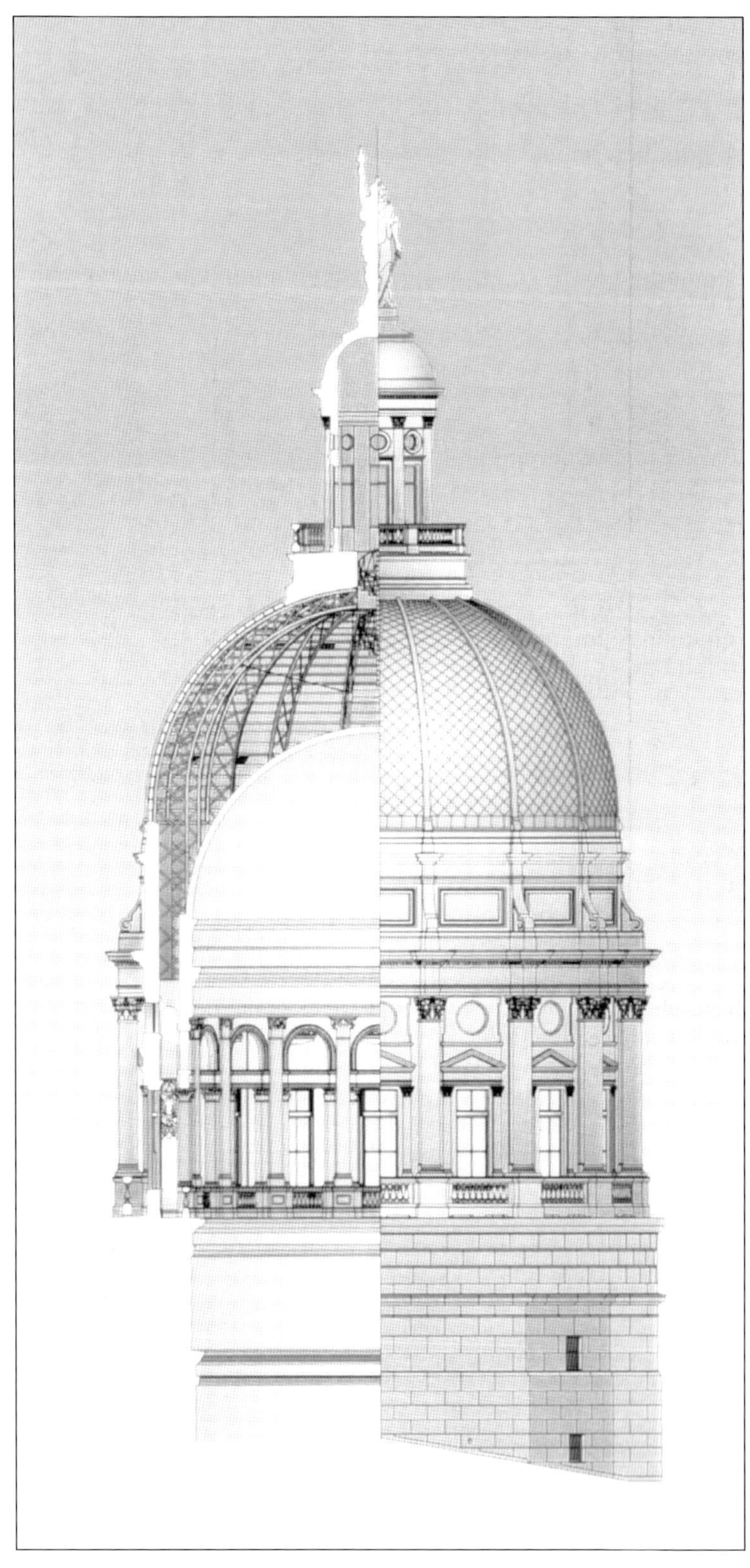

This cross section shows how the dome on the Georgia State Capitol building is structured since its rebuild. The left portion of the image shows the interior with the drum and columns visible inside the rotunda. The supports above it have been reinforced to handle the weight of the stone, the Monel exterior, its gilding, and the cupola. (Lord Aeck Sargent.)

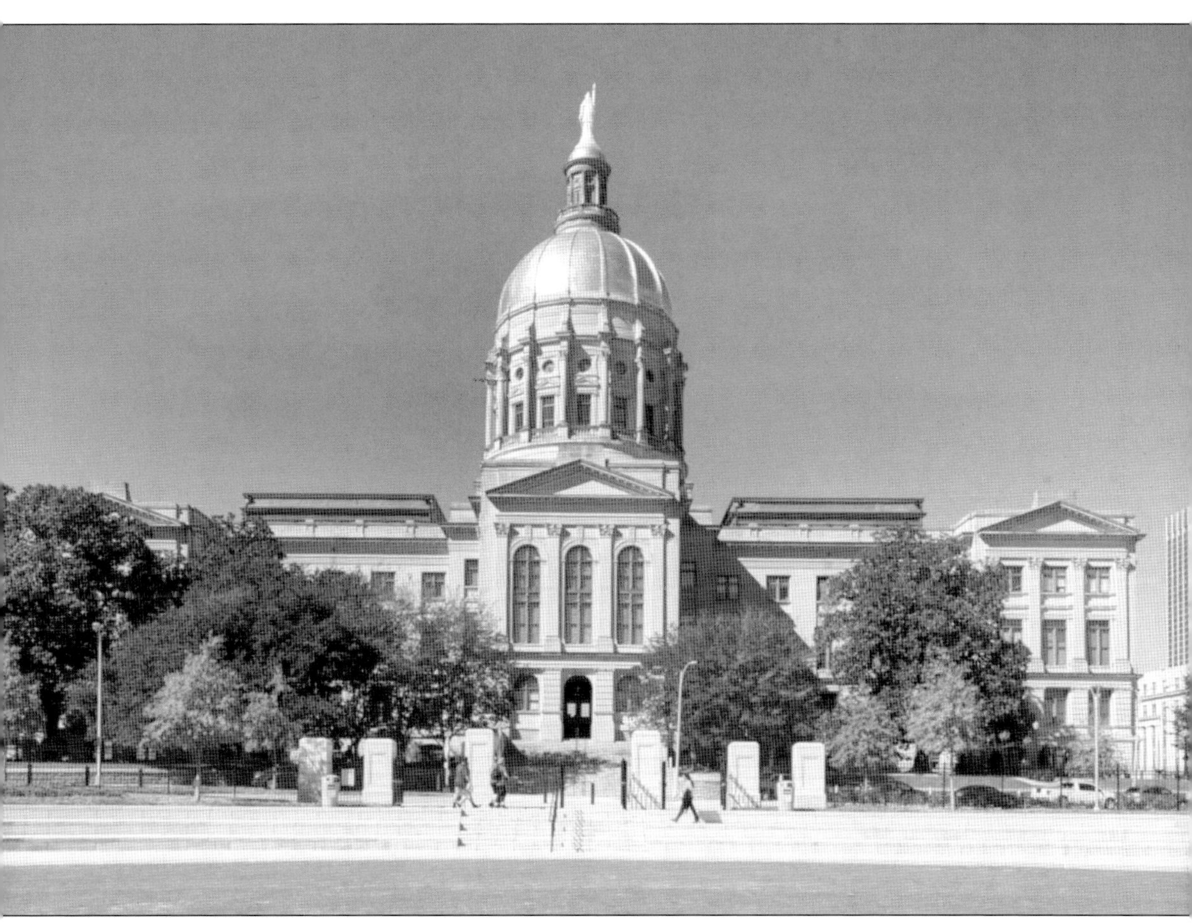

The Georgia State Capitol building stands today as one of the oldest major structures of the Atlanta skyline. Its shining gold dome immediately attracts the eye, whether viewed at 70 miles per hour while passing on I-75/85 or driving through downtown. Restoring it and maintaining it requires the dedication of those who work there for the people of Georgia. Legislation dictates that the governor controls the first and second floors, while the General Assembly controls the third and fourth floors where their chambers, committee rooms, and the legislative budget office are located. The office of the secretary of state oversees that space, which is currently Room 101. Restoring the capitol brought the building's history and significance into focus for many, and it has helped ensure that this monument will continue to stand the test of time. (LOC.)